INCOMES POLICIES, INFLATION
AND RELATIVE PAY

To Susan

Incomes Policies, Inflation and Relative Pay

Edited by
J. L. FALLICK
Lecturer in Economics, University of Manchester

and

R. F. ELLIOTT
Lecturer in Political Economy, University of Aberdeen
Visiting Associate Professor, New York University

London
GEORGE ALLEN & UNWIN
Boston   Sydney

First published in 1981

GEORGE ALLEN & UNWIN LTD
40 Museum Street, London WC1A 1LU

British Library Cataloguing in Publication Data

Incomes policies, inflation and relative pay.
  1. Wage-price policy – History
  I. Fallick, J L   II. Elliott, R F
  339.5   HC79.W24   80–41217

ISBN 0–04–331077–X
ISBN 0–04–331078–8 Pbk

Set in 10 on 11 point Times by Typesetters (Birmingham) Limited and printed in Great Britain by Lowe & Brydone Limited, Thetford, Norfolk

Contents

List of Tables and Figures

TABLES

FIGURES

Acknowledgements

The principal debt which the editors wish to acknowledge is to the individual contributors to this volume. In each case they undertook a considerable amount of new work in order to meet our demands. Almost invariably this came on top of existing heavy commitments, and moreover we imposed an extremely exacting time schedule. Without the enormous effort and enthusiasm of the contributors, the editorial work would have been at once more onerous and less fruitful. We would also like to acknowledge the invaluable assistance of Mr Mike Ingham of Manchester University in compiling the historical Appendix on postwar UK incomes policies. In this context we would also like to thank Mr C. J. Simson, formerly of the Incomes Division of the Department of Employment, and Mr J. Gilbert of Aberdeen University for supplying us with data which was used to check the accuracy and completeness of the historical Appendix. In a multi-authored volume in which each paper went through a number of drafts it would be impossible to acknowledge individually all the people who provided typing and secretarial assistance. However, special thanks are due to Miss Julie Owen at Manchester for her considerable efforts throughout the project. To Julie and the many unnamed but indispensable secretaries we give thanks. Last, but certainly not least, the editors would like to acknowledge the invaluable help of Mr Nicholas Brealey of George Allen & Unwin, without whose considerable talents and energy it would be fair to say the project would have been far more difficult. As usual, we accept final responsibility for the 'product', although as indicated in the Introduction each author speaks for himself in the individual chapters and must therefore accept responsibility.

JLF, RFE
April 1980

The Contributors

DR JOHN T. ADDISON, Associate Professor of Economics at the University of South Carolina

PROFESSOR M. J. ARTIS, Professor of Economics at the University of Manchester

MR ANDREW DEAN, Research Economist at the Economic Prospects Division of the OECD in Paris

MR R. F. ELLIOTT, Lecturer in Political Economy at the University of Aberdeen and a Visiting Associate Professor at New York University

MR J. L. FALLICK, Lecturer in Economics at the University of Manchester

DR S. G. B. HENRY, Director of Research at the National Institute for Economic and Social Research

DR KEN MAYHEW, Fellow of Pembroke College, Oxford and Research Officer at the Institute of Economics and Statistics

PROFESSOR JOHN H. PENCAVEL, Professor of Economics of the Institute for Mathematical Studies in the Social Sciences at Stanford University

MR R. STEELE, Research Fellow of the Health Economics Research Unit at the University of Aberdeen

Introduction

It would be too neat to say that progress in economics occurs fastest in those areas which are furthest removed from reality, but there is sufficient in the charge to cause discomfort. G. D. N. Worswick

quoted in T. W. Hutchinson, *Knowledge and Ignorance in Economics* (Blackwell, 1977)

The economist, in common with other social scientists, does not have a laboratory in which he or she can conduct controlled experiments designed to test hypotheses. On the other hand, economists do have at their disposal considerable amounts of historical data on real world events and these data can frequently be used to generate partial non-controlled hypothesis tests. Because of the requirement that we use data which in general are not specifically designed for the hypothesis tests being undertaken, and because economists from time to time develop new statistical and econometric techniques, which offer improved tests of existing hypotheses or which allow previously untestable hypotheses to be tested, only a very rash applied economist would claim that incomes policies have been 'proved' to be worthless as a tool for macroeconomic management. Moreover, leaving the purely technical (statistical and econometric) aspects of empirical testing on one side, it is important to remember that currently most branches of economic analysis are characterised by a range of theories and theoretical stances, such that one can frequently find wholly contradictory interpretations of most, if not all, empirical results. For these two reasons, the development of techniques and the continuation of theoretical heterodoxy, if for no others, one might justify a further look at incomes policies at this point in time.

However, the case for a reassessment of the conventional wisdom on incomes policies rests on more than the availability of new ideas, data and techniques. Incomes policies are an important example of the once widely held belief that it is possible to intervene in the operation of an advanced mixed economy, and by selective controls and stimuli produce a result which is superior, in terms of employment and on other economic and social welfare criteria, to that which would arise were the economic system to be left to its own devices. At the time of writing, we are in the first year of a major economic experiment in the UK. The Conservative government which was elected in May 1979 has made a firm commitment to reduce the extent of government intervention in the operation of the economy, based partly at least on the notion that past state intervention has not been successful. The present volume does not attempt to attack or support the contentions on which this non-interventionist policy is based. However, a significant part of the case against state intervention in the form of incomes policies is based on the belief that on purely 'technical' economic criteria (those supposedly devoid of any political, social or moral overtones) past incomes policies have failed. The present volume reassesses the crucial elements in this rejection of incomes policies, and presents a comprehensive set of wholly new papers which examine the major issues in this area of theory and policy.

They draw heavily on the UK historical evidence, but they significantly extend the debate to include European and North American data, to ensure that the conclusions reached on the usefulness or otherwise of incomes policies as a tool of economic management are not unduly clouded by the specific political, social and economic events of the historical era from which the test data are drawn. Of course, the assessment of incomes policies cannot wholly be divorced from the economic and political system to which they are to be applied. Nor should it be; it would be of very little practical use to a British Chancellor of the Exchequer to know that a particular economic policy would be effective in the economy of Mars, or in a two-person economy with perfect information, zero transactions costs and perfectly malleable capital. But between these two extremes, of assessment which is unduly influenced by specific historical facts and assessment based on the properties of an irrelevant model, we believe that the present set of papers presents a reasoned reassessment of what economists know of the usefulness or otherwise of incomes policies as a tool of macroeconomic management.

The volume begins with an explicitly theoretical exercise, in which we attempt to show that incomes policies in general, and some specific aspects of past policies, can be seen to be derived from a theoretical picture or model of how the economy operates. Acceptance or rejection of the idea of an incomes policy then depends on the acceptance or rejection of the underlying view of the operation of the economic system in which the policy is to be applied. By beginning at this relatively abstract level we not only gain the advantage of basing our whole assessment on reasoned economic argument but we also see some of the historical background which led to suggestions of an incomes policy type. This chapter provides a sympathetic treatment of the main arguments of theorists and schools of thought opposed to incomes policies, which are used to highlight the distinctive characteristics of those theories which lead one to favour some form of incomes policy.

Chapter 2 presents an assessment of the degree to which incomes policies can be said to have been successful in the UK, in the past. In line with the established procedures in this area, aggregate data are used. Much of the debate to date on incomes policies has revolved around a core of empirical tests of their effectiveness, using a small number of econometric techniques. It has long been recognised that there are severe data and methodological problems inherent in this approach to the question of the efficacy of incomes policies and chapter 2 explicitly recognises and discusses these. The reader is presented with a reassessment of the most important work to date, which is shown to be inadequate in certain respects; finally an approach is suggested which is shown to be superior to the existing techniques and which moreover casts doubt on some 'established' results.

One problem with the aggregate approach to the assessment of incomes policies is that it tends to focus on a single feature of the policies, namely their impact on the rate of change of wages (either wage rates or earnings – the distinction and its significance are discussed in more detail below). However, the actual impact of incomes policies on the operation of the labour market is in general more complex and more varied; and although $\dot{W}_t$ (the rate of change of money wages) is an extremely important variable, and as such commands a great deal of attention, many other aspects of the impact of incomes policies require careful analysis. Accordingly, the next three chapters look in detail at the impact of successive policies on the private and public sector labour markets, beginning with a study of how the relationship between the two has been influenced by the various policies and moving on to describe and analyse the distinctive features of incomes policies in the private sector and the public sector in turn. The analysis of these three chapters is augmented by that of chapter 6, which provides the first comprehensive attempt to show how incomes policies have affected the low-paid. Throughout the preceding chapters on the public and private sector labour markets, the question of the impact of incomes policies on pay differentials and relativities was of central concern. The low-paid are an integral part of this discussion and moreover certain policies have been designed to accord them special preferential treatment. By looking at the impact of the policies on this important group in the labour force, chapter 6 provides valuable additional factual material on how policies work in practice and enhances our general analysis of the extent to which policies can actually achieve their stated aims.

Incomes policies, as the quotation at the beginning of chapter 7 indicates, have been around in one form or another for a very long time. It is not possible for us to say whether or not Diocletian managed to control the Roman economy by means of his edict, but, as chapters 7 and 8 comprehensively document, in both North America and Europe postwar governments of differing political complexion have resorted to incomes policies in their attempts to manage the economy. These policies have taken a very large number of forms, and have met with varying success. These two chapters analyse the nature of the policies in question, discuss why they took the forms which they did and provide an assessment of the gains and losses associated with the various experiments. Although the emphasis is heavily on analysis and the description of policies is kept to a minimum, chapter 8 includes an extensive catalogue of European incomes policies, in the form of an appendix. We have also provided, at the end of the book, the first complete listing of UK incomes policies since 1949, along with precise details of the relevant government documents and publications in which the policy statement was set out and a full description of the principal features of each policy, such as its target, the number and nature of any exception clauses and the precise chronology.

In compiling this historical appendix, we encountered the thorny problem of whether a policy applied to wage and salary *rates* or to *earnings*. In many of the early policies, and indeed in some of the more recent ones such as the so-called 'N−1' policy, the official documentation did not explicitly indicate whether it was rates or earnings that were to be controlled. Clearly this point is of considerable significance both in terms of the eventual consequences of the policies and also, from our point of view, in terms of the way in which one assesses the policies. As will become apparant in the individual chapters, the use of a rates series as opposed to an earnings series on the dependent variable side of the various equations can significantly alter the eventual conclusions. This problem has been resolved by stating explicitly in the historical appendix which of the two the policy was designed to influence *as far as this is possible*. Where the rates/earnings problem impinges on the description and/or analysis of the individual chapters, it has again been discussed explicitly and where necessary a stance has been adopted, and supported by reference to the relevant arguments and documentary evidence.

In chapter 9, the editors provide a summary of the main points which are raised in the previous chapters, and draw together the insights of the individual contributors, in an attempt to form some conclusions on the usefulness or otherwise of incomes policies as a tool for macroeconomic management. While we have benefited greatly from the comments of the individual contributors, the final chapter is the responsibility of the editors and it represents our opinion of what we consider we have learned from this detailed reassessment of incomes policies and their effects. The individual contributors would not necessarily agree with these conclusions and they should not be held responsible for the editorial interpretation of the individual chapters, although each author does bear final responsibility for the contents of his own piece. Although we do not consider that this represents the 'final word' on incomes policies we firmly believe that it constitutes a comprehensive and up-to-date contribution to the research in this important area of applied economics.

Chapter 1

Incomes Policies: Some Rationales

M. J. ARTIS

Introduction

There already exist a number of surveys of incomes policies – for a recent UK survey, see Blackaby (1978) – and there seems little point in adding to the list. Rather, the primary purpose of this chapter is to locate the underlying rationale for incomes policies in an analytical-cum-historical perspective. Thus, a series of rationales is suggested, each of which describes, in part at least, the views of identifiable groups of economists at certain points in time.

The emphasis is on rationales suggested by economic analysis. This implies some restriction on the scope of the treatment in so far as it excludes a detailed account of the political calculus leading to the adoption and termination of incomes policies.[1] This chapter is restricted in another way also; it is mainly concerned with the case in favour of incomes policies and does not attempt to present a full cost-benefit analysis of such policies.

Naturally enough, views among economists about the role for, and rationale of, incomes policies have evolved in conjunction with views about the determination of wages in a market environment, so that in the period with which we are concerned (from the earliest post-Second World War years to the present) there have been oscillations connected with the rise and fall of the Phillips curve, the expectations-augmented Phillips curve, and the real wage resistance views of money wage determination.

The natural starting-point is, however, with the legacy of the Keynesian revolution in macroeconomic thinking, which it is convenient to label, borrowing a phrase from Hicks (1974), the 'wage theorem' view.

1.　The wage theorem view

The macroeconomic habit of analysis promoted by the Keynesian revolution, and instilled by Keynes himself, involves, as Hicks (1974) has pointed out, the 'wage theorem'. Everything in the General Theory is done in terms of variables measured in 'wage units' which, it seems clear, Keynes intended to be taken, most of the time, as the same thing as working in 'real terms'.[2] As the determination of the money wage itself is omitted from the model, the implication of an orthogonality between money wage determination and the economy described by the model seems clear. This is obscured by the habit adopted by Keynesian expositors of working in terms of fixed wages and prices which elides the rather awkward implication of the 'wage theorem' that a rise in money wages is accompanied by an equal proportionate rise in prices and in the money supply, and leads (as described by Hicks) to the misleading impression that the economy recognises only two states: one of less than full employment in which money wages do not rise, and another of full employment in which they do. To complete the Keynesian view, it then seems that one (perhaps both) of two routes can be pursued. First, if wage determination is orthogonal to the economy, it must be determined 'somewhere else' and the task is to describe this. This leads directly to the view that the determination of money wages is a political question. The second alternative is to recognise that the sharp dichotomy between 'under-full' and 'full' employment is too sharp: this route leads to the Phillips curve.

The former view is identified here as the 'wage theorem'-related case for incomes policy. How close it is to what Keynes would have said is impossible to know; but it is now clear that Keynes was well aware of the problem posed by the 'wage-raising' powers of trade unions, and in replying to a comment he received whilst acting as Editor of the *Economic Journal* on a paper of his own, Keynes characterized the issue as 'a political rather than an economic problem' (Keynes, 1980, p. 38). It was, however, a view elaborated upon by Keynesian economists such as Kalecki (1944), Robinson (1937) and Worswick (1944). The argument is that the maintenance of full employment removes the restraint upon trade unions to press for higher wages, that there is a limit to the degree of inflationless redistribution towards labour which can accommodate these increases, and that inter-union rivalry makes it impossible for the lesson that higher wages means higher prices to be learnt; rather, it encourages an inflationary spiral. Individual (group) money wage rates depend heavily on relativities, with the result that the absolute (average) level of money wages (and prices) is essentially indeterminate, for the maintenance of full employment will require monetary accommodation of the money wage-price outcome. The result is that a wage policy is required; and that its successful formulation requires a degree of centralisation of union bargaining. 'Wage bargaining in full employment is, in fact, a political problem, and will be settled on the political plane' (Worswick, 1944).

The starting-point of this approach is very clear. As full employment is to be guaranteed, a discipline of money wage increases by way of reduced employment is not available.[3] Clearly, such a view would be undermined, if it could be shown that the necessary discipline could be enforced at only a marginal sacrifice of full employment. To stand by the 'wage theorem' case for incomes policy if this were true would seem to be sheer stubbornness. In fact, of course, the view denies that a marginal sacrifice of output and employment is all that is required for the maintenance of an acceptable rate of inflation, and suggests — to employ Phillips curve language — that not only is the slope of the Phillips curve shallow, but that it is also unstable.[4]

The earliest formulations of the 'wage problem', and the associated rationale for an incomes policy seem in essence to capture most of the significant elements in subsequent debate. In particular, they point to the significance of the issue of relativities, the significance of the stability and the slope of the short-run Phillips curve, and so on. And, whilst they do not employ the conceptual elaborations afforded by later theoretical and applied work, these formulations stand up well to subsequent experience. We shall therefore return to an elaboration of this view in the concluding section of the paper.

2 The Phillips curve

The 'discovery'[5] of the Phillips curve (Phillips, 1958) was, it seemed at the time (and for some while after) a severe blow to the wage theorem view. It suggested that there was a relationship between the rate of wage change and the level of unemployment, and early versions of the relationship stressed the relative steepness of the curve. Although closer inspection revealed that the stability of the Phillips curve was far from guaranteed, and Phillips's fitting procedure was criticised,[6] the construct was accepted with considerable enthusiasm by the economics profession and empirically replicated by economists for other countries and times. One reason for its ready acceptance is no doubt that it seemed to fill in a missing box in the Keynesian system: it endogenised the money wage to the economy modelled by the system, an intellectually more satisfying achievement (and more appealing to the intellectual imperialism of economics!) than the orthogonality implicit in the wage theorem. Perhaps for this reason Johnson described the Phillips curve as 'the only significant contribution to emerge from post-Keynesian theorizing' (Johnson, 1970). A stable, steeply sloped Phillips curve dispenses with the premium on incomes policy; for it leaves open the use of demand management policy to achieve an acceptable trade-off of inflation and unemployment. Thus Paish (1962) argued that demand management policies could bring about an acceptable level of inflation with unemployment at 2¼ per cent or more.[7] Nevertheless, incomes policies were widely pursued in practice and their success diagnosed by reference to the Phillips curve. Thus, an incomes policy could be viewed as shifting the intercept term and/or the slope of the Phillips curve and its efficacy accordingly estimated by measuring the size and significance of such shifts. One of the better-known investigations of this type is that by Lipsey and Parkin (1970). Their results led them to suggest that the effect of incomes policy was to shift and swivel the Phillips curve in such a manner as, historically, to have achieved a kind of optimum-pessimum result. The argument is illustrated in Figure 1.1. In that figure, PC1 is the Phillips curve without incomes policy and PC2 the curve with incomes policy imposed. The incomes policy effect clearly allows for 'social welfare' improvement, as indicated by the

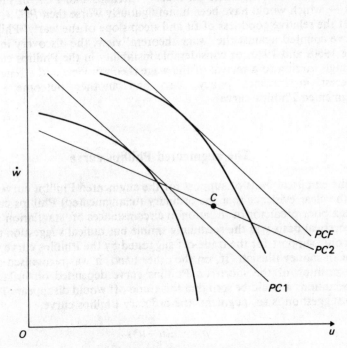

Figure 1.1 The Lipsey–Parkin analysis of incomes policy

preference schedules (drawn concave to the origin, since both inflation and unemployment are 'bads'). However, Lipsey and Parkin indicated that the authorities had actually chosen a position like *C* on *PC2*, clearly a grievous error. Whilst the analysis suggested by the investigation was interesting, it was nevertheless flawed in two respects: first, the data scatter was too concentrated to support the projections suggested. Secondly, and more fundamental (being a criticism of a large number of other studies of incomes policies effects), the test for the effectiveness of incomes policies involves the counterfactual 'what would inflation have been (given employment) had no incomes policy been in operation?' The use of the Phillips curve to supply the answer to the counterfactual implies that the period in question, in all respects except the imposition of the incomes policy, was homogeneous with the sample from which the Phillips curve was estimated. However, it is possible, if not indeed probable, that the adoption of the incomes policy was itself prompted by reasoning that the inflation experience of the period would not have been a random drawing from the sample, but would, rather, have been significantly worse. If so, the appropriate counterfactual is represented by some other schedule – perhaps like *PCF* in Figure 1.1 – which would have been unambiguously worse then *PC2*.[8]

If the relative goodness of fit and steep slope of the 'early' Phillips curve counted against the 'wage theorem' view, the discovery in the late 1960s and 1970s of considerable instability in the Phillips curve, though leading to a revival of the wage theorem view and a renewed interest in incomes policy, also had another outcome – the augmented Phillips curve.

3   The augmented Phillips curve

If the empirical basis of support for the augmented Phillips curve lay in the clear evidence that the ordinary (unaugmented) Phillips curve was a poor predictor of inflation in circumstances of 'stagflation', its theoretical basis was the seemingly simple but radical suggestion that the only support for the trade-off suggested by the Phillips curve was that of money illusion. If, on the other hand, it was recognised that the position of the short-run Phillips curve depended on inflation expectations it could be seen that this trade-off would disappear. Thus the suggestion is to 'augment' the ordinary Phillips curve,

$$\dot{p} = -\alpha(u - u^*)$$

where u and u^* are respectively the actual and non-inflationary rates of unemployment and $\dot{p}$ the rate of inflation, by a term in inflation expectations ($\dot{p}^e$) as:

$$\dot{p} = -\alpha(u - u^*) + \beta\dot{p}^e$$

Setting $u = u^*$ and $\dot{p} = \dot{p}^e$ here gives a long-run solution of $\dot{p} = 0$ in either case, provided $\beta < 1$. On the other hand, if money illusion is completely absent ($\beta = 1$), the equilibrium solution for $\dot{p}$ is indeterminate. In this case, u^* must be renamed the 'natural rate of unemployment', a rate which is compatible with any steady rate of inflation.

The augmented Phillips curve provides a less attractive unemployment-inflation trade-off in the long run than the unaugmented curve –

$$\frac{\delta u}{\delta \dot{p}} = \frac{\beta - 1}{\alpha}$$

rather than $-\alpha^{-1}$, and zero in the case where 'money illusion' is completely absent (that is, where $\beta = 1$). A steeper trade-off, on previous argument, would make the case for incomes policy less attractive since inflation control can be bought for less sacrifice of employment and, in the limit here, there is no opportunity for the sacrifice of employment. However, this is a long-run result: a case for incomes policies can still be made, provided that the formation of inflation expectations is sensitive to such policies.[9]

This case is that, if an incomes policy can reduce inflation expectations, then the cost of an inflation control programme in terms of lost output and employment can be reduced. What is saved in these terms is directly dependent, for a given expectations-generating process, on the slope ($-\alpha$) of the short-run Phillips curve. A relatively shallow slope, again, raises the cost of a programme of inflation control without incomes policy as against one which incorporates such a policy.

Whilst a case for incomes policy along these lines thus exists and may seem quite a powerful one in conditions in which the short-run Phillips curve is relatively shallow, a condition which seems to be amply fulfilled by recent estimates of the UK Phillips curve,[10] it may be queried whether the relevant expectations-generating processes allow room for an incomes policy effect.

Early modelling of this process was based on the adaptive expectations hypothesis, which led to the identification of the augmented Phillips curve with the accelerationist hypothesis.[11] This implies that a higher-order 'Phillips curve' relating the rate of change of inflation ($\ddot{p}$) to unemployment would be stable, but there is evidence to suggest that such a relationship would also be unstable. This can be viewed as a comment on the restrictive nature of the first-order adaptive expectations hypothesis, and has been viewed as evidence of a transition to higher-order adaptive schemes,[12] if not to 'rational expectations'.[13] The standard interpretation of the latter, as 'Muth-rational expectations' in the context of a 'new macroeconomics' theory of the economy does not seem at all plausible in relation to the labour market, however,[14] and 'rational expectations' less restrictively interpreted might be taken to suggest that a credible incomes policy has a potentially powerful role to play in disciplining expectations. The 'catch' is whether the policy is credible or not; cynics would argue that the past ineffectiveness of incomes policy would rob it of the necessary credibility, but this seems to be too harsh a judgement since there is evidence that incomes policies *are* effective at certain times. In this connection it must be pointed out that an awkwardness arises from anticipations of incomes policy; anticipated effective policies will lead to attempts by individual bargaining groups to 'beat the gun' on the inauguration of the policy, possibly forcing governments to an earlier adoption of the policy than planned or even to the adoption of such a policy when none is planned. In order to avoid such a contingency, a government which is sceptical of the value of incomes policy will be inclined to declare its scepticism in stronger terms than its own convictions imply, in order to defuse the expectation that it will itself introduce such a policy. This in turn is liable to weaken the credibility of the policy when it *is* adopted.

A further reason for supposing that incomes policy may have helpful effects on anticipations comes, by indirection, from the reason given for publicly announcing monetary growth targets. The public announcement of such targets, as opposed to their unpublicised pursuit, may be argued to be justifiable by reference to their expectations impact. It seems a small step from here to the position that such targets have a less clear significance for wage-earners than the announcement of targets for money wage or wage bill growth; in this way the argument for an incomes policy is supported, but more strongly, by the same arguments which support the publication of monetary targets.[15]

A specific form of incomes policy suggested by the expectational argument is that of indexation. The rationale is that an offer of indexation can 'buy out' the incubus of unduly high inflation expectations (such as would be generated by adaptive expectations in a period of accelerating inflation), and so reduce the employment and output cost of an inflation control programme. The suggestion is, clearly, that the government has an information advantage over the private sector, enabling it to offer costless insurance in the form of threshold indexing which will reduce the excessive money wage claims otherwise seen as necessary by the private sector to provide cover for its (mistakenly high) inflation expectations. Some such rationale can be seen as underlying the phase of incomes policy employed in the United Kingdom (1972–3)[16] when official anticipations of future commodity price movements were comparatively sanguine and when it must have seemed plausible that private sector inflation expectations were over-influenced by the recent experience of rising commodity prices. Unfortunately, it turned out that official anticipations were wide of the mark and the 'costless insurance' proved most expensive to service.

A second, alternative, rationale for incomes policy entertained by the APC would be one which was directed towards moderating u^*. Whether such a policy makes much sense turns on the interpretation of u^*. Friedman's description of this is that it is

> the level of that would be ground out by the Walrasian system of general equilibrium equations, provided there is embedded in them the actual structural characteristics of the labour commodity markets, including market imperfections.

This is not very helpful. The 'Walrasian' qualification implies a general equilibrium system approach which advocacy of the APC as an inverted 'surprise supply function' illustrates. With rational expectations, this view of u^* identifies it as the unemployment correlate of classical 'full employment' equilibrium.

Thus, setting $\beta = 1$, $\dot{p} = -\alpha(u - u^*) + \beta\dot{p}^e$ can be rewritten as

$$\dot{p} = \gamma(y - y^*) + \dot{p}^e$$

where y^* is the 'full employment' level of output corresponding to u^*, so that

$$y = y^* + \gamma^{-1}(\dot{p}^e - \dot{p})$$
$$\text{or} \qquad y = y^* + \gamma^{-1}(\hat{p} - p)$$

where $\hat{p}$ is the (t_{-1}) expectation of the price level at time t.

This is the form of the APC employed in the rational expectations literature. Its underpinnings are clearly classical and individualistic.

However, it need not be viewed this way. Adherents of a bargaining view would find congenial the interpretation that 'union power' has raised u^*, or reduced the level of employment consistent with no-inflation and could view incomes policy as an instrument for reversing this. The chances of incomes policy being successful in such an endeavour are, however, not obviously large, for what seems to be at stake is a willingness to see incomes policy as a means of reducing the power of unions to raise real wages and so to reduce employment. If unions are to be involved in the implementation of the policy, the employment costs of their actions must be internalised to them, and it is not clear how this is to be achieved.

4   Real wage resistance

An alternative wage determination hypothesis which has commanded limited popularity recently is that provided by the so-called real wage hypothesis (RWH).[17] As against the APC, whose underpinnings, where explicitly provided, have been of an individualistic nature, the real wage hypothesis has the merit of seeming to be more clearly specified as a correlate to labour market 'bargaining'. The central idea of the hypothesis is that nominal wage inflation is the outcome of a process in which unions endeavour to secure a path of real after-tax wages. Thus nominal wage inflation responds positively to a rise in actual and expected inflation and to a fall in the actual or expected 'retention ratio' (complement of the average direct tax rate). Thus, in symbols, a simple form of the real wage resistance hypothesis can be expressed as follows

$$\dot{w} = \alpha \left[\left(\frac{\lambda w}{p} \right)^* - \left(\frac{\lambda w}{p} \right)_{-1} \right]$$

where $\dot{w}$ is the rate of nominal wage increase and

$$\left(\frac{\lambda w}{p} \right)^*, \quad \left(\frac{\lambda w}{p} \right)_{-1}$$

are the 'aspiration' and actual real after-tax wage levels respectively, λ being the retention ratio. A possible addition to the simple form is that the RHS should be scaled up to allow for expected inflation and expected change in the retention ratio. However, the 'no money illusion' property of the RWH is preserved by the lagged real wage term and does not 'require' an additional term in expected inflation,[18] and it is, perhaps, doubtful whether changes in λ are anticipated. More important is the issue of the role of unemployment (u) and incomes policy (F). Two (not exclusive) alternatives are available here: either γ may be specified as a function of u, F or

$$\left(\frac{\lambda w}{p} \right)^*$$

may be so specified. However, in either case, the effects of u, F are only temporary. As soon as incomes policy is removed, or unemployment returns to its former level, the inflationary pressure reasserts itself fully. A permanent reduction in inflationary pressure could only occur if the incomes policy or unemployment experience induced a long-lasting reduction in 'aspiration' real wages or an increase in the capacity of the economy to 'deliver' higher real wages. If the reverse occurs, most plausibly if the incomes policy period *reduces* real wages, then the removal of the policy will produce an explosive 'catch up' effect. RWH models are in general deficient in leaving the determinants of aspiration real wages undefined and there is clearly something wrong with this since an infeasible path of aspiration real wages must produce steady inflation or steady deflation, if the actual wage path falls below or above it, and accelerating inflation or deflation if this condition occurs *and* inflation expectations, based on adaptive behaviour, also adorn the RWH equation.

Setting this point on one side as the (unnecessary) artefact of econometric expressions of the RWH,[19] the scope for incomes policy implied by the approach is wide. Such a policy may be viewed as a useful short-term expedient on the basis already described, and perhaps, but tentatively, as a potential 'educator' of the long-run real wage aspiration. In either case it can be viewed as an alternative to spells of unemployment, in the latter case to permanently higher unemployment.[20]

The RWH approach also offers a purchase on the use of fiscal policy (bearing on λ) as a substitute for, or complement of, incomes policy in inflation control. The rationale is that changes in the retention ratio may be offered to defuse inflationary pressure and to lighten the burden on incomes policy.[21] Such packages were part of incomes policy under the Healey regime.[22]

5 Incomes policy and redistribution

Traditionally, statements of the case for incomes policy are expressed in distributionally neutral terms. The control of 'money things' is seen as compatible with a variety of real outcomes and with the use of tax policy to achieve distributional aims. It is obviously attractive to present the case for the policy in this manner, but it seems naive to suppose that incomes policy practice can ever be distributionally neutral; nor does it seem that modern advocacy of incomes policy is any longer so exclusively based on such simple invariance assumptions.

The first point is that any policy which seeks to lay down norms or limits to wage increases faces the problem whether these should be expressed in flat rate or percentage terms, or in what mixture of the two; moreover, incomes policies cannot be implemented in a political vacuum. The assent of the electorate and of important vested interests is required. As a strong selling point of incomes policies is their 'fairness in adversity', it is perhaps not surprising that they have a bias in intent towards equalisation, a bias which can, for certain historical episodes, also be attributed to the prevailing balance of power in the trade union movement. Whether it is a 'plus point' or 'minus point' of incomes policies, their visibility assuredly draws attention to distributional issues in a way which would not otherwise occur, so it seems inevitable that policy practice will not be distributionally neutral.

Moreover, it seems clear that this visibility constitutes one of the principal difficulties for the successful implementation of incomes policy. Feelings of outrage about changes in differentials are easily focused on incomes policy and become its undoing.

Whereas the wage theorem view implicitly maintains full employment and locates the role of incomes policy as one of ensuring that, however relativities are settled, they are settled within the framework of a 'reasonable' outcome for average money wages; and whereas the expectational case for incomes policies relies on essentially the same argument, the case of those who describe incomes policy as a means of reducing u^* is quite different. For what is implied here is that incomes policy should aim to reduce real wages, thus reducing u^*. The issue is a distributional one between those who are employed and those who are not employed. Unless it is maintained that the employment consequences of wage bargaining are unforeseen and unwanted by the unions involved, this issue cannot be dodged. It clearly makes the task of 'presenting' incomes policy less straightforward and its successful implementation less likely than otherwise.[23]

A final problem is that most evidence seems to suggest that accelerating inflation favours an increase in the share of labour's income as a whole vis-à-vis profits. Whilst most observers would probably argue that such gains are transitory and are necessarily limited by the need to maintain profitability if the capitalist basis of the economy is to be retained, policies to contain inflation will necessarily be suspected of attempting to turn back labour's gains and their appeal will therefore be limited. The short-run experience of incomes policy almost inevitably supports this view for wage restraint generally precedes effective price restraint and incomes policies are usually enforced during periods of crisis and austerity so that identification of incomes policy with restraint of real wages is reinforced by historical experience, whether or not this is the long-run intention of policy.

We have also already remarked on the educative functions of incomes policy in a real wage resistance context, particularly important where a terms of trade deterioration is involved. Here the intention of the policy is to enforce recognition that real wages must fall for given employment objectives, and in that sense the policy seems to exploit the view that employment objectives should be retained at the expense of real wages.[24] But this does involve a distribution issue.

There are, therefore, considerable distributional implications of incomes policy in practice, both as between segments of labour and as between labour and profits. In these circumstances, policy presentation is both difficult and highly important.

6   Some other incomes policy aims

The actual practice of incomes policy, as already noted, compels attitudes to be struck regarding its distributional objectives. In much the same manner, the visibility of the criteria employed for permitting price increases encourages the development of a policy with regard to productivity and efficiency. This may be at a relatively *ad hoc* level as exemplified for example in those episodes of incomes policy where a 'case history' is built up by the way of price references to some such body as the National Board for Prices and Incomes. The reports of such bodies bring to bear on firms' decision-making the resources of a free (but compulsorily purchased!) management consultancy, and historically have produced or helped to produce some significant changes.[25]

There is no way of saying how important these side-effects have been, and we do not propose to comment further on them, except to note that the internal logic of 'fairness' in practical incomes policies invites the development of criteria leading to interventions of this type, and that these aspects of incomes policy both attract and repel support for it in ways which are broadly predictable. It should certainly not be forgotten in this context that the complaint that incomes policy 'distorts' the resource allocation process can be countered by the view that it affords the occasion for constructive intervention by watchdog bodies, which improves it.

7   Conclusions

In the preceding paragraphs, we have attempted to outline the case for incomes policy as it emerges from alternative views of the macro determination of money wages. The 'pure' case of incomes policy, and historically its primary case, identifies a conflict between maintaining a chosen level of employment and inflation, viewing incomes policy as an instrument to govern the outcome of the conflict. This case remains highly significant today.

Nevertheless, the case has evolved somewhat. Early statements of the view assume, in effect, that there would be no dispute about the appropriate level of employment, and that redistributive questions can be left to the tax system. With no dispute about real wages and employment, the case for incomes policy can be viewed as a variation on the theme of 'public goods'. No individual bargaining group feels (correctly) that its wage bargain has much influence on prices; each feels that it must match expected inflation plus its desired real wage gain; none has an incentive to wage restraint, for this would only expose it to real losses. Wage restraint thus has the quality of a public good: if all groups operate within a framework of agreed restraint provided by an incomes policy, then similar real gains can be secured with less inflation.[26] This kind of rationale for an incomes policy can equally be applied to the 'expectational' case for incomes policies. The difference is that in the case of the latter theories, the rate of unemployment (u^*) is not in the choice set of the authorities and not amenable to incomes policy on this rationale.

The evolution of the wage theorem case that seems to have taken place is to add to it a role for incomes policy as employment regulator:[27] that is, incomes policy is looked on as a means of influencing both real wages (and hence employment) and the inflation rate. This raises the question of the feasibility of incomes policy to a new level, for what is at issue is not only the ability of such a policy to ensure the public goods quality of wage restraint against its disintegration by 'free riders' but also the ability of such a policy to secure a different allocation of the workforce between employment and unemployment. The argument that employment figures with small weight in trade union utility functions suggests that this objective may be very difficult to secure since it seems implied that the object of the policy is a violation of the preference-maximising of the very agents whose co-operation the policy seeks.[28]

There are only three ways out: to conceive of incomes policy as a device for bringing pressure to bear on union preference functions; to suppose that unions would in fact be more 'responsible' with regard to employment within an incomes policy framework than outside it, where mistakes are unforeseen and provide misleading evidence of true preferences; or to propose that the benefits of inflation control would in the long run provide a context for the superior functioning of the economy, enabling dominant real wage/employment points to be reached. Advocates of a permanent incomes policy probably must rest their case on the last of these lines of argument.

The absence of a permanent incomes policy shows that such policies have failed to command an enduring consensus. Why? The usual answer is that incomes policy is undermined by a failure of consensus on the distributional issue of 'relativities'. The common picture is that the 'freeze' phase of an incomes policy works, only to be succeeded by a collapse in the subsequent 'thaw' phase, the problem being that the appeal to rough justice which suffices to enforce the freeze is not succeeded by any comparable consensus in the thaw. The difficult irony of this, for 'permanent incomes policy' advocates, is that the non-inflationary management of relativities is precisely the principal object of incomes policy in the first place, so that the problem the policy is designed to solve has, so far, turned out only to be capable of temporary short-circuiting by the policy, rather than of an enduring solution.

It is for this reason, perhaps, that the kinds of institutional reform supported by incomes policy advocates are just those which would seem likely, on their own, to help remedy the problem addressed by the policy in the first place. In particular, in this connection, emphasis is placed on the centralisation of bargaining and internalisation to the trade union side of the relativities problem. Generalised so as to further internalise, in addition, the welfare of the unemployed, such reforms could produce a system of bargaining which was more responsive to begin with to the realities of real income distribution and less prone to produce wage-price spirals.

In an important sense, however, incomes policies *are* with us all the time. There is the point that the government is, directly and indirectly, a very large employer in the United Kingdom, that there must always be an incomes policy in that sense: indeed there have been occasions when incomes policy consisted solely in trying to exploit a leading role for the public sector with hoped for 'follow-on' effects in the private sector. There is also the point that incomes policies have been sufficiently often employed by government of both political colours that their anticipation and previous presence plays, at any time, a more or less important role in governing the going rate of wage settlements. 'Catch up' on the last phase of policy and 'beating the gun' on the next are both important features of wage behaviour, with the incidental side-effect of inhibiting confidence in the ability of econometric analysis to deliver reliable verdicts on the factors determining the rate of wage inflation.

This suggests that incomes policies are part of the 'meta-rule' of policy behaviour attributed under 'rational expectations' by the private sector to the government. The difficulty about this is that a modified form of instrument instability is invited as behaviour conforms to the expectation that incomes policy *will* be imposed, whatever current government statements to the contrary are made. In this light advocacy of a 'permanent incomes policy' has an advantage; for it is properly to be compared *not* with *no* incomes policy but with a regime of 'temporary incomes policies'.

The instability of a regime of 'temporary incomes policies' is thus a factor persuasive of the long-run superiority of a permanent policy. The temporary incomes policy regime also implies that governments have found it very tempting to adopt policies of short run restraint; the reason is not far to seek – short-run Phillips curves are very shallow, inflation expectations mechanisms are *not* geared by rational expectations to money supply targets. Inflation control is a costly business. All this implies in turn that cost-benefit analysis of the incomes policy instrument starts off with some substantial benefit (in opportunity cost terms) to its credit. It would not be surprising to see renewed efforts in the long-drawn-out attempt to develop a satisfactory incomes policy being undertaken in the future. Whether these will be policies which attempt to leave more initiative with the market ('tax-based incomes policies', for example) or policies which take further the interventionist character of such policies as they have been practised in the past remains to be seen. It is perhaps a secondary question.

Notes: Chapter 1

1   The dividing line between 'economic' and 'political' rationales is not, of course, at all well defined in this context, but we pay no attention here to such factors as the prompting provided by the electoral cycle for the adoption or abandonment of incomes policies, or to the alleged addiction of governments to the cosmetic value of incomes policies.

2   Compare Keynes (1936), chapter 4, where the choice of units is discussed.

3   It is also implicit that unemployment is 'different' as between a regime of free market forces and *laissez-faire* in which unemployment is a fact of nature and a regime in which it is 'known', on the basis of the Keynesian revolution, that government is responsible for the control of unemployment. In the latter regime unemployment is 'political': cf. Kalecki (1944).

4   All these points are clearly made in Worswick (1944).

5   A similar construct had in fact already been indicated by A. J. Brown (1955).

6   A paper which severely criticised the original paper by Phillips is that by Routh (1959). It is also worth noting that both Phillips and Lipsey, in a paper widely regarded as 'confirming' Phillips's hypothesis (Lipsey, 1960) entered substantial reservations about the relationship.

7   The formal treatment of the Phillips curve as providing a technically determined 'menu of choice' was set out by Rees (1970).

8   See K. Wallis (1971). It may be objected that this is merely a counsel of nihilism – for how is the investigator of incomes policy effects to 'discover' PCF? This objection, however, is no excuse for the continued pursuit of misleading techniques and, more positively, is simply premature in advance of the more detailed, if admittedly 'subjective', kind of analysis called for.

9   Tobin (1972) provides an alternative account of the wage mechanism, heavily dependent on relativities, which is capable of yielding comparable 'no long-run

trade-off' results to those suggested by the APC, but in which it is not obviously appropriate that β should be interpreted in terms of degrees of 'money illusion'. (Rather $\dot{p}^e$ should be replaced by some moving average process in wage movements.) Here too, it is noted that there is 'an arbitrary, imitative component in wage settlements' which 'maybe...can be influenced by national standards' (i.e. by incomes policies).

10 See Artis and Miller (1979).
11 See Friedman (1968).
12 Flemming (1976).
13 Sargent and Wallace (1976).
14 See, e.g., Shiller's (1978) strictures on the matter.
15 Of course, the announcement of monetary targets has other impacts in mind, e.g. on the financial markets, which may be less impressed by wage targets.
16 See the Appendix, p. 271.
17 See Hicks (1974); Sargan (1971); Henry, Sawyer and Smith (1976).
18 See Artis and Miller (1979).
19 Generally, in econometric work, the aspiration real wage path has been modelled as a simple time trend: see, e.g., Henry, Sawyer and Smith (1976).
20 Artis and Miller (1979) have shown that the APC and RWH differ in this respect for the crucial case of a terms of trade deterioration. While the RWH requires a permanently higher level of unemployment to avoid inflation, the APC requires only a temporary increase.
21 And, *per contra*, increases in the retention ratio have been viewed as the leading factor in the wage explosion of the late 1960s. See Jackson, Turner and Wilkinson (1972).
22 Providing confirmation of Kalecki's (1944) prediction.
23 We are maintaining a classical labour market demand assumption here as a long-run property. In the absence of enforceable 'no redundancy' wage agreements which force employers to employ supra-marginal labour, this seems appropriate.
24 Incomes policy objectives in this context are underlined by Malinvaud's (1977) analysis.
25 The most notable example in the UK is the NBPI's *Report on Bank Charges*, which played some role in stimulating a reappraisal of the nation's banking system and framework of monetary regulation. A less *ad hoc* kind of interventionism is indicated by the price code provisions of more recent incomes policy episodes, based on American experience, which exemplified an attempt to use the framework of restraint to enforce 'best practice' cost management.
26 Von Weizacker (1978) describes this 'public goods' quality of wage restraint.
27 This is the 'assignment' suggested, for example, by Meade (1978).
28 There is, of course, nothing new under the sun. At least as long ago as 1946 Pigou advanced the hypothesis that the generally higher level of unemployment benefits available in the interwar years compared to previous decades reduced the disutility to unions of unemployment, encouraged higher wages and consequently lower employment, although Pigou was careful *not* to attribute the Great Depression to an exacerbation of this cause.

References: Chapter 1

Artis, M. J., and Miller, M. H. (1979), 'Inflation, real wages and the terms of trade', in J. K. Bowers (ed.), *Inflation, Development and Integration* (Leeds University Press)

Blackaby, F. T. (1978), 'Incomes Policy' in Blackaby, F. T. (ed.), *British Economic Policy 1960–1974* (Cambridge University Press)

Brown, A. J. (1955), *The Great Inflation 1939–1951* (Oxford University Press)

Flemming, J. S. (1976), *Inflation* (Oxford University Press)

Friedman, M. (1968), 'The role of monetary policy', *American Economic Review*, March

Henry, S. G. B., Sawyer, M. C., and Smith, P. (1976), 'Models of Inflation in the United Kingdom: an evaluation', *National Institute Economic Review*, No. 77

Hicks, J. R. (1974), *The Crisis on Keynesian Economics* (Oxford: Blackwell)

Jackson, D., Turner, H. A., and Wilkinson, F. (1972), *Do Trade Unions Cause Inflation?* (Department of Economics, Cambridge, Occasional Paper 36)

Johnson, H. G. (1970), 'Recent Developments in Monetary Theory', in Johnson, H. G., and Croome, D. R. (eds), *Money in Britain 1959–1969* (Oxford University Press)

Kalecki, M. (1944), 'Three ways to full employment' in Oxford University Institute of Statistics: *The Economics of Full Employment* (Oxford: Blackwell)

Keynes, J. M. (1936), *The General Theory of Employment, Interest and Money* (Macmillan)

Keynes, J. M. (1980), *Activities 1941–6: shaping the post-war world: Bretton Woods and reparations*, Vol. 26 of Collected Writings (Macmillan)

Lipsey, R. G. (1960), 'The relation between unemployment and the rate of change of money wage rates in the United Kingdom 1801–1957: a further study', *Economica*, 27, pp. 1–31

Lipsey, R. G., and Parkin, J. M. (1970), 'Incomes Policy: a reappraisal', *Economica*, May

Malinvaud, E. (1977), *The Theory of Unemployment Reconsidered* (Oxford: Blackwell)

Meade, James (1978), 'The meaning of "internal balance"', *Economic Journal*, September, pp. 423–5

Paish, F. W. (1962), *Studies in an inflationary economy: the United Kingdom 1948–1961* (Macmillan)

Phillips, A. W. (1958), 'The relation between unemployment and the rate of change of money wage rates in the United Kingdom, 1861–1957', *Economica*, November

Pigou, A. C. (1946), *Income: an introduction to economics* (Macmillan)

Rees, A. (1970), 'The Phillips Curve as a Means for Policy Choice', *Economica*, August

Robinson, Joan (1937), *Essays in the Theory of Employment* (Macmillan)

Routh, G. (1959), 'The relation between unemployment and the rate of change of money wage rates: a comment', *Economica*, 27, pp. 299–315

Sargan, J. D. (1971), 'A Study of Wages and Prices in the United Kingdom 1949–1968' in Johnson, H. G., and Nobay, A. R. (eds), *The Current Inflation* (Macmillan)

Sargent, T. J., and Wallace, N. (1976), 'Rational expectations and the theory of as economic policy', *Journal of Monetary Economics*, 2, pp. 169–83

Shiller, R. J. (1978), 'Rational expectations and the dynamic structure of macro-economic models', *Journal of Monetary Economics*, 4, pp. 1–44

Tobin, J. (1972), 'Inflation and unemployment', *American Economic Review*, March

Wallis, K. F. (1971), 'Wages, prices and incomes policies: some comments', *Economica*, August

Weizacker, C. C. von (1977), 'The employment problem: a systems approach' (mimeo)

Worswick, G. D. N. (1944), 'The Stability and Flexibility of Full Employment' in Oxford University Institute of Statistics, *The Economics of Full Employment* (Oxford: Blackwell)

Chapter 2

Incomes Policy and Aggregate Pay

S. G. B. HENRY *

1 Introduction

In this paper the effects of incomes policy on aggregate pay will be discussed using econometric models of wages (basic wage rates) and earnings. It will partly survey existing models of inflation but, for brevity, will consider only the augmented Phillips curve and target real wage versions. These are taken to span substantially different explanations of the inflationary process, and because empirical results when using these models have indicated widely different effects for incomes policies – Henry and Ormerod (1978), for example, as contrasted with Parkin, Sumner and Ward (1976).

The rest of the paper will be organised as follows. The next section will give a short description of the alternative models. Then the periods of incomes policy used in the empirical estimates will be described. Finally, the alternative models will be estimated on, as far as possible, a common data base, and policy conclusions of the results will be noted.

A study of the effects of incomes policy is largely one of the study of the determinants of changes in aggregate pay. This present paper will be like others in this respect. Unlike a recent paper by Sargan (1980), however, which was directed at deriving an eclectic model for wages, earnings and prices, the present paper will attempt to put some of the more important theoretical, and hence policy, issues in sharper focus. It will also provide tests of these using a common data base.

* I would like to thank Alastair Dawson, members of the joint economics seminars of North Staffordshire Polytechnic and Keele University, and the economics seminar, University of Leeds for comments. Responsibility for remaining error in the paper is, of course, my own.

Lastly, I owe a great deal to the patient research assistance of Julian Treasure and the skilled typing of Carole Bracken and Rita Leach, for which I would like to express my gratitude.

A short survey that adequately deals with the current state of work on inflation is probably a contradiction in terms. So in this introduction it seems desirable to announce those topics which, largely for reasons of space, will not be discussed. Perhaps the most important topic ignored here is the explicit modelling of expectations, particularly of price expectations. A great deal of theoretical discussion had been devoted to specifying non-myopic expectation schemes, and important contributions to the econometrics of estimating 'rational' expectations schemes have been made by Wallis (1980) and Wickens (1979). In mitigation of this omission, however, it might be said that few serious attempts have been made to implement rational expectations models in the UK, hence this topic need not appear even in a partial survey, though an earlier paper (Henry and Ormerod, 1979) suggested that empirically the use of rational expectations schemes yielded no noticeable improvement over alternative 'naive' predictions for price inflation.

Other deliberate omissions in the paper will be the problem of the adequacy of the wage index, alternative pricing models, and any reference to non-UK empirical work. The question of the disaggregation of settlements into size and frequency components has received considerable attention and important initial work has been reported by Elliott and Shelton (1979). Substantial problems remain with this approach, including the identification of joint models of the frequency and size of payment, but these are not discussed further here. Nor will the models be extended to incorporate prices, important though this variable is for implications for real wages. The reason for this omission is one of limited space. From the point of view of system modelling, the equations for wages and earnings may be thought of as part of a larger system involving pricing behaviour also. Since the equations are recursive, the reported results may be expected to give reasonably precise estimates of the parameters of those equations (assuming no serious problem of correlated errors between equations). A fully simultaneous model estimated by appropriate methods would none the less be desirable, though it is beyond the scope of this short study. (See Sargan (1980) for a full information approach to wages, earnings and prices, though his estimation period ends in 1973.)

Finally, this paper will not discuss those attempts at resurrecting Phillips curves based on remeasuring the level of unemployment where, it is asserted, the 'natural' rate of unemployment has increased (Parkin, 1979). It is argued that the natural rate has increased due to changes in supply behaviour produced by changes in social security provisions. In particular, changes in the 'replacement ratio' (the ratio of potential benefits to potential net earnings) are supposed to be largely responsible for the changed supply conditions. Arguing in this way, it is possible to suggest there still exists a negative short-run relationship between wage inflation and (remeasured) unemployment. In order to see why this argument fails, one must turn to evidence from unemployment models. There it is clear that after 1973 there is virtually no relationship between changes in the replacement ratio (properly measured to allow for take-up) and unemployment. Before that date, evidence from cross-section data indicates a small influence from the replacement ratio – see Nickell (1979) for an effective account. Thus these attempts at resurrection are best seen as mere *post hoc* rationalisations, which, however, do not conform with evidence on labour market behaviour from other sources.

2   Some current models of inflation

According to Artis and Miller (1979), 'The real wage hypothesis . . . together with the augmented Phillips curve appear to dominate current empirical work on the subject.' This is the view adopted in the paper and in the rest of this section I will describe some of the problems that have emerged in the development of each of these models.

(i) *The augmented Phillips curve*
The general rule in Phillips curve models is to treat the labour market as determining one dimension of labour input only, that of numbers employed. Problems of refining measures of labour input to allow for variations in average actual hours worked or varying productivity of measured labour input rarely figure in this. This convention will be followed in part in this paper, not because it particularly commends itself, but simply because it is the format commonly used. Indeed, it may be argued that failure to implement this assumption carefully has led to faults in the testing of some models, by ignoring the difference between wage rates and earnings. Because of its importance, this argument is elaborated on next.

The basis of this simple model of the labour market is the production function

$$Q = f_1(L) \tag{1}$$

where the single factor 'labour' (L), is measured as numbers employed. From familiar profit and utility maximising assumptions the demand and supply of labour are respectively

$$W/P = f_2(L) \tag{2}$$

$$L = f_3(W/P) \tag{3}$$

The existence of fiscal influences may be allowed for by expressing the demand function (2) as gross of (the marginal rate of) tax and other stoppages, and the supply factor (3) as net of income tax at the marginal rate. From (1), however, it is clear that the appropriate wage argument in each equation is total earnings (weekly or hourly) per worker, without adjustment for overtime. Equations (2) and (3) then serve as the basis for the augmented Phillips relation by making the assumption of Walrasian adjustment, by approximating excess supply of labour by unemployment (measured again by numbers of workers), that is

$$\Delta(W/P) = \Lambda(D_L - S_L) , \qquad \Lambda > 0 \qquad (4)$$

and

$$(D_L - S_L) = f(U) \qquad (5)$$

give the augmented Phillips relation

$$\dot{W} = \alpha_0 + \alpha_1 U + \alpha_2 \dot{P}^e \qquad (6)$$

after replacing actual with expected rates of price inflation.

An alternative modelling of the labour market distinguishes components of the labour input, separately identifying numbers employed and their utilisation rate (which may be proxied by average hours worked). There has been little research effort devoted to this aspect of wage inflation modelling. Henry (1980) gives some recent examples of labour demand equations based on this, and Hart (1979) discusses some problems of the theory as it relates to inflation. In implementing this disaggregated approach, one obvious problem is in linking measurable quantities such as earnings and basic rates of pay with the theoretical magnitudes such as the price per worker and per hour in the disaggregated model. While average earnings may approximate the price per worker, measured basic rates may only approximate movements in hourly rates per worker on extreme assumptions about the form of the typical payments function, the proportion of time versus piece rates of payment, and so on. A simplification, based loosely on the sort of disaggregation described above, is to allow for matrix adjustment, i.e.

$$\begin{pmatrix} \Delta W \\ \Delta E \end{pmatrix} = \begin{pmatrix} A_{11} A_{12} \\ A_{21} A_{22} \end{pmatrix} \begin{pmatrix} W^* - W \\ E^* - E \end{pmatrix} + \beta \underset{\sim}{Z} ,$$

where $A_{ij} \underset{<}{\overset{>}{=}} 0$, (W^*, E^*) are equilibrium values for wages and earnings and $\underset{\sim}{Z}$ is a set of predetermined variables. Equations of this form are discussed more fully in the results, section 4. For the present we first return to the single factor case.

An earlier paper (Henry *et al.*, 1976) showed there was little empirical support for the augmented Phillips curve. An alternative approach implied by equations (1) to (6) and not covered by the earlier paper is that of Parkin, Sumner and Ward (1976). Their model uses demand and supply of labour as depending explicitly on gross and net real wages respectively. The definition of excess demand which they use is also extended to allow for traded as well as non-traded sectors. Thus, the definition of excess demand is

$$D - S \equiv D_1\left[\frac{W(1 + T_1)}{P_E}\right] + D_2\left[\frac{W(1 + T_2)}{P_F}\right]$$

$$- S\left[\frac{W(1 - T_2)(1 - T_3)}{P_C(1 + T_4)}\right] \qquad (7)$$

where T_1 = employers' social security contribution, T_2 = employees' social security contributions, T_3 = income tax and T_4 indirect tax rates. P_E is the export unit value, P_F the wholesale price and P_C the consumer price index, net of indirect tax.

In section 4 below the model is re-estimated, though, following the earlier discussions, it is used as a model of earnings inflation. Other problems in this model have led to a substantial respecification before it is estimated even for earnings. These are

(i) The paper assumes that demand and supply decisions depend on average rather than the theoretically correct concept of marginal tax rates.

(ii) The assumed dynamics of the equation are inconsistent. Both the level and rate of change of excess demand determine wage inflation in their model. This would suggest an equation of the general form

$$\dot{W} = f(\dot{X}, X)$$

which is not unreasonable. However, Parkin *et al.* do not use this. Instead they assume

$$\dot{X} = - X \qquad (8)$$

which states that excess demand moves to eliminate (the level of) excess demand. From (7) the approximate expression for $\dot{X}$ is

$$\dot{X} = -\alpha_1[\dot{W} + T_1 - \dot{P}_E] - \alpha_2[\dot{W} + T_2 - \dot{P}_F]$$
$$- \beta[\dot{W} + T_2 + T_3 - \dot{P}_C - T_4] \tag{9}$$

where α_1, α_2 and β are dependent on demand and supply functions and all other variables are treated as constants. Next, the Walrasian adjustment

$$\dot{W} = -\lambda(\dot{X}) , \ \lambda = 1 \tag{10}$$

is assumed, which from (8) is equivalent to the familiar Phillips curve version

$$\dot{W} = \lambda(X) , \ \lambda = 1 \tag{11}$$

If (8) holds, it appears that the wage equation may be estimated in the form given by (10) *or* (11), but Parkin *et al.* contrive to adopt both simultaneously, and this leads to problems with their theoretical specification. Thus from (9) and (10) they obtain an equation in the rate of change of excess demand,

$$(1 + \alpha_1 + \alpha_2 + \beta)\dot{W} = \alpha_1\dot{P}_E + \alpha_2\dot{P}_F + \beta\dot{P}_C - (\alpha_1 + \alpha_2)T_1$$
$$- \beta(T_2 + T_3 - T_4) \tag{12}$$

Equation (11) is then used to introduce excess demand in levels form

$$(\alpha_1 + \alpha_2 + \beta)\dot{W} = -\dot{W} + \alpha_1\dot{P}_E + \ldots - \beta(T_2 + T_3 - T_4)$$

which from (8) gives

$$\dot{W} = (\alpha_1 + \alpha_2 + \beta)^{-1}[X + \{\alpha_1\dot{P}_E + \ldots - \beta(T_1 + T_3 - T_4)\}] \tag{13}$$

In their preferred equations $(\alpha_1 + \alpha_2 + \beta) = 1$. Abiding by this constraint means that according to (11), the term in $\{\#\}$ on the RHS of (13) is zero. This indicates that $\dot{X} = 0$, which according to (10) then implies that $\dot{W} = 0$.

Instead of pursuing the model in this form, a generalised dynamic version is estimated in section 4, using the techniques described by Hendry and Von Ungern-Sternburg (1980). In this way it is hoped to employ the essence of the Parkin *et al.* model without incorporating its mistaken dynamics.

(ii) *The real wage hypothesis*
The notion that real wages enter explicitly into the wage equation has

received considerable attention in the empirical literature for the UK. Examples are Sargan (1964), (1980), Johnston and Timbrell (1973), Henry, Sawyer and Smith (1976) and Minford and Brech (1979). However, there are substantial differences between these authors about underlying theory and econometric specification, so that the description 'real wage model' must be treated with caution.

Many proponents of this equation base it on a partial adjustment hypothesis, for example, Sargan (1964), Henry *et al.* (1976). Thus

$$\Delta W = \lambda_1[(W/P)^* - (W/P)]_{-\eta} + \lambda_2\Delta P + \dots \tag{14}$$

where $(W/P)^*$ is the desired or target real wage (Sargan) or desired real net earnings (RNE) as in Henry *et al.* Approximating the desired value by a time trend produces important policy implications, and these will be described later in this section. This feature is, however, shared by more complex formulations of the real wage model. For example, the recent study by Sargan (1980) uses an 'error-correction' formulation – see Hendry and Von Ungern-Sternburg (1980). A representative version of his wage and earnings model is given below (taken from Sargan Table IV, p.105, and, since this will not be discussed further in this paper, the price equation also quoted in the table is ignored).

$$\Delta W_t = \alpha_1(E - W)_{t-1} + \alpha_2(W - P)_{t-1} + \alpha_3(W - P)_{t-3} + \alpha_4\Delta W_{t-1}$$
$$+ \alpha_5\Delta W_{t-2} + \alpha_6 S_{t-1} + \alpha_7 R_t + \alpha_8{}'$$
$$\Delta E_t = \beta_1\Delta W_t + \beta_2(E - W)_{t-1} + \beta_3\Delta P_{t-1} + \beta_4 hr_{t-1}$$
$$+ \beta_5 I_{t-4} + \beta_6\Delta U_{t-1} + \beta_7{}' \tag{15}$$

where in addition to wages, earnings, unemployment and prices, the equations use a three-year moving average of the number of working days lost (S), the average income tax retention ratio (R), the ratio of actual to standard hours in manufacturing (hr), and the ratio of market price to factor cost measures of GNP (I).

On a steady state growth path defined by $\Delta W = \Delta E = \Delta P = g$, where disequilibrium terms $\Delta U = hr = 0$, and where for simplicity S, R and I are assumed to be constant and, without losing generality, are set to zero, then the system above may be collapsed into the single equation

$$(\widetilde{W}/P) = k_1 e - k_2 t \tag{16}$$

Here the tilde $(\sim)$ indicates variables are measured in levels, and the definitions of the ks are

$$k_1 = \left(\frac{g}{\alpha_2 + \alpha_3}\right) \cdot \left((1 - \alpha_4 - \alpha_5) - \frac{\alpha_1}{\beta_2}(1 - \beta_1 - \beta_3) \right)$$

$$k_2 = \left(\frac{1}{\alpha_2 + \alpha_3}\right) \cdot \left(\frac{\beta_7}{\beta_2} + \alpha_8\right)$$

Thus the terms in $(W - P)$ and $(E - W)$ on the RHS of the structural equations above may be interpreted as proportional correction aimed at ensuring convergence on to the path for real wages given by (16). In this model the movement of money wages is to ensure adherence with an estimated real wage trend or equilibrium path, and is subject to similar criticisms as those levelled against the real wage model in its more familiar partial adjustment form. A brief résumé of these criticisms now follows.

The most obvious problem which the real wage hypothesis raises is whether it is essentially different from the models described in (1) above, which attribute the major part of the explanation of wage movements to the excess supply of labour. The problem involves questions both of theory and of evidence. Parkin (1979) for example argues that the real wage model is (theoretically) indistinguishable from the excess supply model, because if real wages are high, according to neoclassical theory, this indicates excess supply for labour and hence downward pressure on wage rates. This argument thus rationalises the empirical finding of a negative relation between real wages and wage inflation within an excess supply framework. In early work on the real wage model, Kuh (1967) advanced an explanation similar to equations (1) and (6) above — the essence of the excess supply scheme. According to him the *net* real wage represents the supply side, and the time-trend the (average) productivity of labour. (See also Agarwala *et al.* (1972) for more recent work in the same vein.)

The first of these points raises the question of the *empirical* relationship between excess supply, unemployment, and real wages. The second point is quite different, and may be interpreted as an identification problem in an economic theoretic sense, here meaning that the particular theory of behaviour may admit more than one empirical representation.

On the empirical question a variety of views exist as to what the relationship may be expected to be. According to Barro and Grossman (1971), 'Cyclical variations in . . . the amount of employment *must* imply countercyclical variations in real wage rates' (p.82, my italics) in what they call 'conventional analysis'. This appears to attribute exogenous (cyclical) movement in the labour market entirely to supply shifts (where supply is assumed to respond positively to real wage increases). Perhaps a more operational approach would be to recognise that either or both demand and supply of labour may shift over time (cyclically or secularly), and the resulting pattern of real wages and employment will thus depend on the relative magnitudes of the respective shifts. One way to proceed with this question, without the full panoply of a simultaneous labour market model, is to establish as good a statistical relationship between employment (or unemployment) and real wages as possible, and identify the sign of the long-run relationship between the two. This exercise would be explicitly 'non-structural', both variables being regarded in some general way as endogenous, though procedures exist for establishing 'causality' in the relationship according to statistical criteria – for example, Granger causality as described by Granger (1977). Neftci (1978), for example, uses time-series filters on near-differenced, that is, $(1-0\cdot9L)$ measures of real wages and employment. In a general dynamic non-structural model with twenty-four lags he finds that the sum of lagged weights is significantly negative. Preliminary investigation of the time series for real wages and unemployment for the UK, using first-differenced data, reveals little lagged effect, and the correlation appears to be almost entirely in the contemporaneous period. (The cross-correlation co-efficient with zero lag for unemployment and real wages is $-0\cdot593$ and for unemployment and real earnings is $-0\cdot888$.) The effect, however, appears to be negative (real wages and unemployment), which is the opposite to Neftci's result.

The main point of this exercise, however, though limited, is not unimportant. This is that the argument that the real wage effect merely echoes an excess supply mechanism at work in determining wage inflation, where excess supply of labour may itself be approximated by measured unemployment, is simply not supported by the evidence of the time-series behaviour of unemployment and real wages.

The more fundamental question still remains, and this is the behavioural basis of the real wage model and the possibility of distinguishing it from an excess supply model. First, the performance of the alternative models in terms of their coherence with the data and the maintenance of *a priori* restrictions may be used to establish the empirical validity of the models at least in their usual incarnations. Thus, as demonstrated in Henry *et al.* (1976) excess supply models based on unemployment (Phillips curves) or, as shown in section 4, models based on simple neoclassical labour markets (Parkin, Sumner and Ward, 1976) are not supported by the evidence. The real wage model appears to have stronger empirical credentials, as is also illustrated in section 4. Second, the usual interpretation of the wage equation as a Walrasian adjustment equation does not carry over to the RNE version of the real wage model, because this version attributes the movement in basic rates to discrepancies in real net earnings. Thus, even if excess supply of labour depended simply on real earnings, Walrasian adjustment would not then imply that disequilibrium affected basic rates only.

I will conclude the discussion of real wage models with some comments on the exogeneity of the real wage target. If, for example, the real wage target is assumed to be a constant, or trend, then equilibrium in the labour market occurs only when real wages grow at that trend rate. This may be inconsistent with equilibrium elsewhere in the economy. An exogenous shock, such as the increase in oil prices in 1973, lowers domestic productivity, and growth in trend real wages, unless adjusted, will imply cumulative imbalance in the company sector. One aspect of this question, which is discussed further in section 4, is the evidence for an endogenous target, and in particular whether the target evolves over time.

3   Incomes policies

As in a previous paper (Henry and Ormerod, 1978) the method used to model incomes policy effects is to include dummy variables which operate on the wage equation for the duration of the policy period. One advantage of this procedure is that it allows for a potential direct effect of each policy, allowing for the possibility that the different policies may be quantitatively different from each other. (In this, the method is unlike that used by, for example, Lipsey and Parkin (1970), which treats the policies as if they were quantitatively the same.) On the other hand, there are well-known disadvantages. The choice of policy periods is largely judgemental, and use of dummy variables treats the policy as independent of wage price movements, which is obviously unrealistic (Wallis, 1971). These points are connected, and relate to the modelling of policies in the reaction-function form as used, for example, in the analysis of monetary policy. As already described in the first section, such a large undertaking is outside the scope of the present paper, and in what follows it will be assumed that the single equation estimates are not affected by simultaneous feedback from this source. Given that the incomes policy is likely to be based on previous wage and price movements, this assumption does not seem unreasonable.

In addition to incomes policy effects, the possibility of 'catch-up' or accelerating inflation following the relaxation of the policy is allowed for. First, some experiments use additional catch-up dummy variables, of the same length as the period for which the incomes policy operated (see Henry and Ormerod, 1978). Secondly, the possibility of catch-up is allowed for by using integral error correction (Hendry and Von Ungern-Sternburg, 1980), a device borrowed from classical servo-mechanic approaches to modelling systems.

The following table shows the historical periods chosen for incomes policies (Di) and their corresponding catch-up periods (Dio):

D1	=	196603 – 196702	D10	=	196703 – 196802
D2	=	197204 – 197301	D20	=	197302 – 197303
D3	=	197302 – 197401	D30	=	197402 – 197501
D4	=	196703 – 196902	D40	=	196903 – 197102
D5	=	197503 – 197702			

Briefly, the criteria involved in this selection are that they represent incomes policies of the statutory variety, including wage freezes. These are likely to be periods when the policy had its strongest effects, and hence the most useful for deciding whether the use of incomes policies have any impact on inflation. This is in the negative sense that if the policies in the table show little effect, then other, weaker, policies are unlikely to have had any influence at all.

4 Empirical results

All the models are estimated using unadjusted quarterly data, the definitions for which are shown in the appendix. Seasonal dummy variables were used in each case, but for brevity are not quoted.

In the tables, $\chi_1^2(\ \cdot\ )$ is a test of the validity of the autoregressive restrictions, $\chi_2^2(\ \cdot\ )$ the Box-Pierce test for a random correlogram and $\chi_3^2(\ \cdot\ )$ a test of constant parameters in a post-fitting sample. Figures in parentheses are t statistics. Unless otherwise stated, the sample period is 196301–197804, and variables are in log form.

(1) *Wage equations*
The models advanced here are of the real wage variety since it has been argued that excess supply models are more properly directed at earnings equations. The versions of the real wage model used are

(i) Partial adjustment model (Henry *et al.*, 1976)

$$\Delta W_t = \theta_1(L)\Delta W_{t-1} + \theta_2(L)\Delta P_{t-1} + \theta_3(\beta^t - RNE)_{t-2} + \theta_4(L)U_{t-1}$$

With certain exceptions (to be discussed below) the equation stands up reasonably well, and compares with the original result which was obtained over the period 1948–74 (Table 9, Henry *et al.*, 1976). The original estimates indicated a growth in target earnings of roughly 2·5

Table 2.1 Incomes policy effects and catch-up effects: partial adjustment model: selected examples

Dep. Var. $\Delta_4 W_t$	RNE_{t-2}	$\Delta^4 W_{t-1}$	$\Delta^4 W_{t-2}$	U_{t-1}	$\Delta_4 P_{t-1}$	t	C
	−0·126 (1·88)	0·786 (6·258)	0·183 (1·30)	−0·022 (1·573)	0·093 (0·806)	0·0012 (2·196)	0·539 (1·852)
	−0·129 (2·03)	1·119 (5·896)	−0·091 (0·424)	−0·017 (1·246)	—	0·0009 (2·159)	0·561 (2·02)
	−0·132 (2·099)	1·209 (7·912)	—	—	—	0·0004 (3·08)	0·571 (2·098)

D_1	D_2	D_3	D_4	D_5	D_{10}	D_{20}
−0·008 (1·25)	—	−0·015 (1·33)	—	−0·050 (4·762)	0·013 (1·839)	—
−0·008 (1·461)	—	−0·008 (0·824)	—	−0·033 (3·079)	0·012 (1·754)	—
−0·006 (1·13)	—	−0·001 (0·71)	—	−0·029 (3·097)	0·0076 (1·384)	—

D_{30}	D_{40}	$\chi^2_1(N)$	$\chi^2_2(16)$	R^2	p
0·025 (2·214)	—	$N=10$· 13·744	31·91	—	−0·518 (3·13)
0·025 (3·466)	—	$N=7$· 8·87	26·384	—	−0·410 (1·91)
0·029 (4·746)	—	$N=6$· 8·058	29·71	—	−0·469 (2·612)

per cent per annum, but in this re-estimate (third equation in the table) the implied growth rate is 3·8 per cent, which is hardly plausible. However, and this is where the new result differs from the earlier one, price inflation now appears to be insignificant. Artis and Miller (1979) have noted that real wage models typically produce a small effect for price inflation, though it might be added that the results in Henry *et al.* (1976), done on a series of samples, suggested that the price effect was increasing and not decreasing as the sample size was extended. Two points are involved here. The first is that real wage equations as described here assume that there is no money illusion in the long run, so the theoretical reason adduced by Friedman when introducing a price inflation term in the Phillips curve (that, as originally stated, the curve assumed labour market decisions were made in nominal instead of real terms) loses its force. Second, although the equation is homogeneous, there may still be an empirical role for price inflation in the real wage equation, it being, in Hendry's terminology, a 'derivative' error correction term. This possibility provides a rationalisation for the empirical finding of insignificant price inflation effects. Since 1974 real earnings have undergone substantial changes. This may be modelled by assuming that although longer-run objectives for real earnings are held, short-run deviations about this long-run trend take place. Adherence to longer-run objectives implies proportional correction will be important, whereas the short-run fluctuations around this trend suggest that derivative correction will not be important. (In Phillips's original application of servo-mechanic techniques to stabilisation policy, derivative control appeared to smooth out short-run fluctuations around desired paths.)

Change in the dynamic structure of the wage equation obviously produces changes in real wage behaviour, as the previous example illustrates. The alternative is to consider evidence for variations in the target itself. We next give illustrations of a number of ways in which this might be done; first by a moving target model, and second by using a moving average representation for the target.

(ii) Moving target model

$$\Delta W_t = \alpha_0 + \alpha_1 \Delta W_{t-1} + \alpha_2 RNE_{t-2} + \alpha_3 \Delta P_{t-1}$$
$$+ \alpha_4 \Delta P_{t-2} + \alpha_5 U_{t-1} + \alpha_6 U_{t-2}$$

which is produced by combining a partial adjustment model for W, i.e.

$$\Delta W_t = \lambda_1 (RNE^* - RNE)_{t-1} + \lambda_2 \Delta P_{t-1} + \lambda_3 U_{t-1}$$

with the adaptive scheme for the target

$$\Delta RNE^*_t = \downarrow (RNE^* - RNE)_{t-1} , \quad \downarrow > 0$$

Equation (ii) then is seen as a non-linear in parameters model, examples of which have been used in demand for money and stockbuilding. The version reported below is of an unrestricted linear form.

This moving target model (Table 2.2) does not achieve very satisfactory results and need not detain us. The model is probably best thought of as a relatively inferior way to model dynamics and target behaviour (as compared with the error correction model discussed below).

(iii) Moving average model

The moving average representation (Table 2.3) below does better, though the proportional correction term ($NE-P$) is not significant at the conventional level. This equation was arrived at after sequential testing of a general equation, and dropping those variables which proved insignificant. As in earlier equations, the price inflation terms

Table 2.2 Incomes policy effects and catch-up effects: moving target model

Dep.	RNE_{t-2}	$\Delta_4 W_{t-1}$	U_{t-1}	U_{t-2}	$\Delta_4 P_{t-1}$	$\Delta_4 P_{t-2}$	t
Var.	0·037	0·853	−0·022	−0·013	−0·021	0·217	0·0015
$\Delta^4 W_t$	(0·469)	(12·169)	(0·924)	(0·466)	(0·143)	(1·587)	(2·808)

	C	D_1	D_2	D_3	D_4	D_5	D_{10}
	0·149	−0·012	—	−0·024	—	−0·054	0·018
	(0·436)	(1·388)		(2·778)		(5·90)	(2·619)

D_{20}	D_{30}	D_{40}	$\chi_1^2(N)$	$\chi_2^2(16)$	R^2
—	0·011	—	$N=9$; 1·351	24·159	0·978
	(1·154)				

proved insignificant. In this model, the target (the moving average of lagged net real earnings) is endogenous, so, for example, cyclical factors which produce variations in actual earnings will be transmitted into revised targets, which in turn affect wage inflation. The net effect tends to amplify exogenous changes. Thus if there is an exogenous change in real net earnings due to, for example, a decrease in the average rate of income tax, money wage inflation will first decrease, as the discrepancy between desired and actual RNE targets decreases, and will then increase as the target is revised upwards extrapolatively. The parameter estimates in Table 2.3 indicate that the net effect is positive.

Table 2.3 Incomes policy effects and catch-up effects: moving average approach

Dep.	RNE_{t-2}	$\sum\limits_{i=2}^{10} RNE_{t-(i+1)}$	t	C	D_1	D_2
Var.	−0·16	0·287	0·0002	0·56	−0·008	−0·018
$\Delta_4 W_t$	(1·58)	(2·013)	(0·67)	(1·219)	(0·884)	(1·392)

D_3	D_4	D_5	$\chi_1^2(N)$	$\chi_2^2(16)$	R^2
−0·016	—	−0·053	$N=10$; 9·71	19·18	0·964
(1·558)		(7·234)			

(iv) Error correction models

These may be distinguished from partial adjustment models since, in principle, the possibility exists in these models to move rapidly to the region of equilibrium by use of derivative, proportional and integral error correction mechanisms. The examples taken here are Sargan's eclectic model,

$$\Delta W_t = \alpha_1(L)(W-P)_{t-1} + \alpha_2(L)(E-W)_{t-1} + \alpha_3(L)S + \alpha_4(L)U_{t-1}$$
$$+ \alpha_5 R + \alpha_6 t ,$$

and an elaboration of the RNE model,

$$\Delta W_t = \beta_1(L)(NE-P)_{t-1} + \beta_2(L)(E-W)_{t-1} + \beta_3(L)\Delta P_{t-1} + \beta_4 t$$

First, the Sargan model is shown in Table 2.4.

Table 2.4 Incomes policy effects and catch-up effects: the Sargan model

Dep.	$(E-W)_{t-1}$	$(W-P)_{t-1}$	$(W-P)_{t-3}$	ΔW_{t-1}	ΔW_{t-2}	S_{t-1}
Var.	0·023	−0·197	0·114	0·464	0·206	0·011
ΔW_t	(0·167)	(1·234)	(0·996)	(2·714)	(1·108)	(1·55)
	0·220	−0·068	−0·004	0·115	−0·257	0·015
	(2·93)	(0·80)	(0·046)	(1·07)	(2·58)	(3·06)
	0·451	0·389	−0·354	−0·359	−0·782	0·025
	(2·714)	(1·855)	(1·878)	(1·526)	(3·95)	(4·01)

R	T	C	$\chi_1^2(N)$	$\chi_2^2(16)$	R^2
0·003	0·004	−0·064	$N=5$; 6·728	30·007	0·574
(0·036)	(0·636)	(1·079)			
−0·383	−0·383	—			0·503
(3·94)	(3·94)				
0·140	−0·001	−0·059	$N=5$; 3·816	24·507	0·736
(2·053)	(0·703)	(1·26)			

The original estimate for the model over the sample 1952–197304 reported in Sargan (1980) is shown as the second row. A re-estimate over a sample beginning 196301 but ending, as his sample did, in 197304 is shown as the last row, while in the first row an estimate for 196301–197804 is depicted. The interest in this model is that it is a comprehensive error correction model with 'earnings drift' $(E-W)$ and real wage $(W-P)$ appearing as proportional factors. The equation also includes a number of ancillary variables such as working days lost (S) and the retention ratio (R), which other authors have found to be empirically useful ploys in wage equations.

Whilst the model appears to be fairly robust when the earlier part of the original sample is left out (compare row 3 with row 2), it appears to share the fate common to so many other wage equations when the later part of the sample is added (row 1). Noteworthy is the disappearance of a long-run or steady-state solution to the model, and the insignificance of the R and S variables. The insignificance of the real wage term echoes the results reported in Henry *et al.* (1976) on the original real wage model used by Sargan (1964), where it was shown that a real wage model appeared inferior to a real net earnings one.

A general error-correction model for the RNE hypothesis is illustrated in Table 2.5. This was initiated from the model

$$\Delta_4 \ln W_t = \sum_{i=1} \alpha_i \Delta_4 \ln W_{t-i} + \sum_{j=1} \beta_j \Delta_4 \ln P_{t-j}$$
$$+ \sum_{k=1} \delta_k (NE - P)_{t-k} + \sum_{m=1} \gamma_m (E - W)_{t-m}$$

and the quoted result is for a parameterised version of the model derived by omitting non-significant terms in sequence. In terms of statistical properties, this equation appears to be reasonably good.

Table 2.5 Incomes policy effects and catch-up effects: general error-correction model

Dep.	$\Delta_4 W_{t-1}$	$\Delta_4 W_{t-2}$	$\Delta_4 P_{t-3}$	RNE_{t-4}	$(E-W)_{t-1}$	$\Delta(E-W)_{t-2}$
Var.	0·748	0·348	0·334	0·167	0·244	0·412
$\Delta^4 W_t$	(10·834)	)2·93)	(3·743)	(2·409)	(2·241)	(2·837)

	D_1	D_3	D_4	D_5	D_{10}	D_{30}
	−0·009	−0·014	−0·013	−0·031	0·275	0·029
	(1·355)	1·851)	(1·956)	(3·320)	(3·426)	(4·311)

D_{40}	T	C	$\chi_1^2(N)$	$\chi_1^2(16)$	$\bar{R}^2$
−0·001	−0·001	−0·720	$N = 11; 20 \cdot 102$	25·241	0·982
(0·131)	(1·423)	(2·375)			

The long-run or steady-state solution of the model is of the form (in logs)

$$(E - W) = \gamma_1 (E - P) + \gamma_2 + \gamma_3$$

where $\gamma_1 = -0 \cdot 684$, $\gamma_2 = 0 \cdot 0009$ and $\gamma_3 = 2 \cdot 951$, but where for simplicity all inflation rates are assumed to be zero. This result would suggest a long-run tendency for growth in real earnings to compress earnings drift.

(2) *Earnings models*

(i) A respecified Parkin, Sumner and Ward model is

$$\Delta E_t = J_1(L)\Delta E_{t-1} + J_2(L)\Delta Pc_{t-1} + J_3(E(1+t_1) - P_E)_{t-1}$$
$$+ J_4(E(1+t_1) - P_F)_{t-1} + J_5(E(1-t_2)(1-t_3) - Pc(1+t_4))_{t-1} \quad (17)$$

where in this model the wage rate index is replaced by the earnings index to provide consistency with the implied measure of labour input in the model. Also the tax rates are estimated marginal rates, and the dynamics represented by a general lagged form around the steady-state equilibrium

$$J(E(1+t_1) - P_E) + J_4(E(1+t_1) - P_F) = J_5(E(1-t_2)(1-t_3) - Pc(1+t_4))$$

which represents an equality between simple linear demand and supply functions. Putting the model in the general dynamic form shown in (17) above avoids the logical problems which Parkin *et al.* have, and the model is sufficiently general to obtain a version of the model with data coherent dynamics (see Table 2.6).

Table 2.6 The Parkin, Sumner and Ward model: respecified estimates

Dep.	$\Delta^4 E_{t-1}$	$(E(1+t_1) - P_E)_{t-1}$	$(E(1+t_2) - P_F)_{t-1}$	$(E(1-t_2) \times (1-t_3) - Pc(1+t_4))_{t-1}$
Var.	0·556	0·371	0·143	−0·078
$\Delta^4 W_t$	(5·36)	(2·32)	(3·515)	(0·603)

$\Delta^4 Pc_{t-1}$	D_1	D_2	D_3	D_4	D_5	T	C
0·012	−0·026	−0·006	−0·041	−0·004	−0·047	−0·002	−0·089
(0·12)	(2·954)	(0·47)	(3·629)	(0·64)	(5·30)	(3·843)	(2·705)

$\chi_1^2(N)$	$\chi_2^2(16)$	R^2
$N=8$; 14·33	20·26	0·939

The quoted equation is the most successful from a range of dynamic alternatives as indicated by equation (17). Even so, it is clear that the model is largely a failure, with the demand and supply terms being wrongly signed. There does not seem to be any obvious way of respecifying the dynamics to improve the equation according to the $\chi_1^2(\cdot)$ statistic. (Note, however, that the quoted equation was derived from a general lagged version, following a 'general to specific' testing methodology.)

(ii) Sargan's earnings drift equation (1980) is

$$\Delta E_t = \beta_0 \Delta W_t + \beta_1 \Delta W_{t-2} + \beta_3 (E - W)_{t-1} + \beta_4 \Delta P_{t-1}$$
$$+ \beta_5 hr_{t-1} + \beta_6 S_{t-1} + \beta_7 \Delta U_{t-1} + \beta_8 t$$

Table 2.7 Sargan's earnings drift equation: re-estimates

Dep.	ΔW_t	ΔW_{t-2}	$(E-W)_{t-1}$	ΔP_{t-1}	HR_{t-1}	S_{t-1}
Var.	0·736	−0·077	−0·092	0·013	0·052	0·003
ΔE_t	(6·515)	(0·668)	(1·129)	(0·079)	(0·297)	(0·514)
	0·566	0·165	−0·396	−0·135	0·378	−0·007
	(7·751)	(2·254)	(5·647)	(1·915)	(3·788)	(2·685)

	ΔU_{t-1}	T	C	$\chi^2_1(N)$	$\chi^2_2(16)$	R^2
	0·020	0·000	−0·016	$N=6$; 20·159	14·764	0·703
	(0·859)	(0·227)	(0·408)			
	−0·014	0·0012	—	—		0·705
	(2·459)	(4·897)				

The first row of Table 2.7 shows a re-estimate of the Sargan earnings model, over the sample period 196301–197804. This is compared with his original estimate over the period 1952–197304. The equation signally fails in the more recent data period, with all variables except ΔW now becoming insignificant, and there being strong evidence of dynamic misspecification.

A further, also eclectic model is shown in Table 2.8. This arises from using RNE (measured from trend) as a disequilibrium term instead of the real wage. Although the empirical evidence is not completely convincing, this model does obtain a measure of support with only the price inflation term not obviously belonging in the equation.

Table 2.8 An eclectic model with RNE as a disequilibrium term

Dep.	$\Delta_4 E_{t-2}$	$(E-W)_{t-3}$	RNE_{t-2}	RNE_{t-4}	Δhr_{t-1}
Var.	−0·218	0·424	0·601	−1·001	0·399
$\Delta_4 E_t$	(1·456)	(2·758)	(3·199)	(6·382)	(1·326)

	$\Delta\Delta^4 P_{t-3}$	T	C	$\chi^2_1(N)$	$\chi^2_2(16)$	R^2
	−0·002	0·001	1·769	$N=6$; 3·098	26·56	0·549
	(0·006)	(1·629)	(2·410)			

5 Conclusions

These first discuss the empirical results and follow with comments on estimated incomes policy effects.

For the two main approaches described here, the excess supply and real wage, it has been argued that

(a)   there are deficiencies in the theory of the structural version by Parkin, Sumner and Ward of the excess supply model, and where these are corrected and the model applied, as it should be, to earnings movements, there seems little empirical support for it. This is of importance, since their study is one of the most comprehensive excess supply model applied to UK data.

(b)   As for real wage models, the results here (estimated by single equation methods) show that the RNE model is to be preferred on empirical grounds over the real wage model. Earnings as a regression variable in the wage equation was indicated by Henry *et al.* (1976), and the results here confirm that. The use of a net variable seems also recommended. (This is not directly tested here. But see Sargan (1980), where the implicit restriction on the real wage and the retention ratio is tested and not rejected.)

A more general question concerns the underlying behavioural hypotheses embodied in these models. Extreme views, namely a simple excess supply explanation of inflation (wage and/or earnings), whether of a Phillips curve or structuralist type, do not seem to hold. Neither, it should be added, does a target model for wages where that target is immutable and unaffected by cyclical conditions in the economy. The examples of evolving targets, whilst not decisive, are too suggestive to be ignored here. But it would be idle to pretend that the results given here provide a critical test of the two rival explanations of wage behaviour. However, the market-type explanations of the real wage hypothesis that have been put forward so far, such as Parkin (1979), have been shown to be inconsistent with the evidence of real wage movements.

Finally, we turn to the assessment of incomes policy effects. Unlike a previous paper (Henry and Ormerod, 1978), this one has tested for incomes policy influences in a variety of different wage models. Although the technique of testing for incomes policy effects by using dummy variables has been criticised and it still remains true that the modelling of incomes policy in a fully simultaneous setting of wage and price movements is a major objective of research in this area, none the less many widely different results have been claimed for incomes policy based on single equations and dummy variables like this present one. Here the outstanding feature is the significant effects for incomes policy generally observed, *whatever the basic model of inflation used*. This must make the quoted results of Parkin, Sumner and Ward (1976) and Minford and Brech (1979) highly doubtful. However, the results show that the policies have their planned effects only whilst in operation and tend to be followed by a period of restoration of real wage losses.

References: Chapter 2

Agarwala, R., Drinkwater, J., Khosla, D. and McMenomy, I. (1972), 'A Neoclassical approach to the determination of prices and wages', *Economica*

Artis, M. J., and Miller, M. (1979), 'Inflation, real wages and the terms of trade' in *Inflation, Development and Integration*, ed. J. K. Bowers (Leeds University Press)

Barro, R., and Grossman, H. (1971), 'A General Disequilibrium Model of Income and Employment', *AER* vol. 61

Elliott, R. F., and Shelton, H. C. (1979), 'The determinants of wage changes in the UK: a model of the size and frequency of settlements' (mimeo, University of Aberdeen)

Granger, C., and Newbold, P. (1977), *Forecasting Economic Time Series* (London: Academic Press)

Hart, R. A. (1979), 'Short run earnings changes and the excess demand for labour services' (mimeo, University of Glasgow)

Hendry, D., and von Ungern-Sternburg, T. (1980), 'Liquidity of Inflation Effects on Consumers' Expenditure' (mimeo, LSE)

Henry, S. G. B., Sawyer, M., and Smith, P. (1976), 'Models of Inflation in the UK: An Evaluation', *NIESR*

Henry, S. G. B., and Ormerod, P. (1978), 'Incomes policy and wage inflation: empirical evidence for the UK 1961–1977', *NIESR*

Henry, S. G. B. (1979), 'Forecasting Employment and Unemployment', paper presented to the Treasury, MSC Conference on Labour markets, Oxford

Henry, S. G. B., and Ormerod, P. (1979), 'Rational Expectations in a wage-price model of the UK', paper presented to SSRC conference on Rational Expectations, University of Sussex

Johnston, J., and Timbrell, M. (1973), 'Empirical Tests of a Bargaining Theory of Wage Rate Determination', *Manchester School*

Kuh, E. (1967), 'A productivity theory of wage levels – an alternative to the Phillips curve', *RES*

Lipsey, R. G., and Parkin, M. (1970), 'Incomes Policy: a Reappraisal', *Economica*

Minford, P., and Brech, M., 'The Wage Equation and Rational Expectations', SSRC – University of Liverpool Working Paper No. 7901

Neftci, S. (1978), 'A time-series analysis of the real wages–employment relationship', *JPE*

Nickell, S. (1979), 'The Effect of Unemployment and Related Benefits on the Duration of Unemployment', *EJ*

Parkin, M., Sumner, M., and Ward, R., 'The Effects of Excess Demand, Generalised Expectations and Wage Price Controls on Wage Inflation in the UK: 1956–71' in *The Economics of Price and Wage Controls*, ed. K. Brunner and A. Meltzer

Parkin, M. (1979), 'Alternative explanations of UK inflation: a survey' in *Inflation in the UK*, ed. Parkin and Sumner

Sargan, D. J. (1964), 'Wages and Prices in the UK: A study in econometric methodology' in *Econometric Analysis for National Economic Planning*, ed. P. E. Hart, G. Mills and J. K. Whitaker (London: Butterworth)

Sargan, D. J. (1980), 'A model of wage-price inflation', *RES*

Wallis, K. (1971), 'Wages, Prices and Incomes Policies: some comments', *Economica*
Wallis, K. (1980), 'Econometric Implications of the Rational Expectations Hypothesis', *Econometrica*, vol. 48, no. 1
Wickens, M. (1979), 'The efficient estimation of econometric models with rational expectations' (mimeo, University of Essex)

Appendix 2A   Data: definitions and sources

W Index of basic weekly wages of manual workers in the UK (1970 = 100)
        Source: *Economic Trends*, and *Economic Trends Annual Supplement*.

P General index of retail prices, all items (1970 = 100)
        Source: *Economic Trends* and *Economic Trends Annual Supplement*.

E Index of average earnings (1970 = 100)
        Source: *Economic Trends* and *Economic Trends Annual Supplement*.

P_E Export unit value index
        Source: *Economic Trends*.

P_F Wholesale price index
        Source: *Economic Trends*.

U Numbers unemployed in the UK, excluding school-leavers
        Source: *Economic Trends* and *Department of Employment Gazette*.

H_N Standard working hours in UK manufacturing
        Source: *Department of Employment Gazette*.

H Actual working hours in manufacturing
        Source: *Department of Employment Gazette*.

T_1 Total employers' contributions to national insurance funds as a proportion of total wages and salaries
        Source: *Economic Trends* and *Monthly Digest of Statistics*.

T_2 Total employees' NI contributions as a proportion of wages and salaries
        Source: *Economic Trends* and *Monthly Digest of Statistics*.

T_3 Average 'marginal' income tax rate
        Source: Blackaby, F. (ed.), *British Economic Policy* (p. 168).

T_4 Average indirect tax rate
        Source: *Economic Trends* and *Monthly Digest of Statistics*.

R Retention Ratio. Average for married man with two children under 11.
        Source: Jackson, D., Turner, H. A., and Wilkinson, F., 'Do trade unions cause inflation?', and *Inland Revenue Statistics*.

S Working days lost as a result of all stoppages.
        Source: *Department of Employment Gazette*.

Chapter 3

Public and Private Sector Pay and the Economy

ANDREW DEAN*

Introduction

The issue of public sector pay, in relation to pay in the private sector, is one that proved particularly controversial in the United Kingdom in the 1970s and one that continues to cause problems for British governments. The reasons for the concern about this issue are numerous, but three specific aspects are isolated and discussed in the present chapter: these are the question of relativities, the critical problem of public sector pay during periods of incomes policy, and the influence of public sector pay in public expenditure control. It is argued that each of these issues has had an important bearing on the success, or otherwise, of the economic policies of recent governments. In particular, it is argued that the problem of the control of public sector pay was an important contributing factor to the demise of two recent incomes policies, and that, subsequently, abnormally large increases in public sector pay were responsible for surges in public expenditure with serious implications for monetary and fiscal policy. In the process, these events have also been, in small part, a reason for the electoral defeat of two governments. These are serious matters, indeed, but they should perhaps not be overstressed. The sensible control of public sector pay, though important, is a necessary but by no means a sufficient condition for successful economic policies.

*The author was formerly at the National Institute of Economic and Social Research, London, from 1973 to 1979, where he conducted extensive research in labour economics, specialising *inter alia* on the issue of pay in the public sector. The research for the present chapter was undertaken whilst the author was at the National Institute but neither that organisation nor the OECD are in any way responsible for the views expressed here, which are the author's personal responsibility.

Public and private sector pay relativities: the facts

Researchers have found it remarkably difficult to obtain reliable data on the movement of pay in the public sector relative to that in the private sector. In recent years, the *New Earnings Survey* (*NES*) has provided a wealth of earnings data, although there are still certain problems with that data which are alluded to below. The usefulness of the *NES* data was realised by researchers in the mid-1970s and since 1977 the Department of Employment has been publishing its own breakdown of public and private sector pay, using special *NES* analyses (*Gazette*, December 1977). For the pre-1970 period, however, researchers have been forced to use a variety of ingenious adjustments and *ad hoc* methods to try to isolate public and private sector earnings movements from data intended for other purposes. The present author for instance used the April and October earnings inquiries together with a variety of other sources of pay for public sector groups (Dean, 1975), whilst Elliott (1977) used figures for wage rates in different industries. Both authors were thus faced with difficulties in allocating groups of workers to public and private sector categories, a typical problem being that of steelworkers, who in the post-war period have passed backwards and forwards between the public and private sectors and have thus proved difficult to classify.

Despite these data problems, it is nevertheless possible to get a fairly clear picture of how pay in the public and private sectors has moved over time. One of the most important limitations of the aggregate or sectoral data should however be mentioned straight away. All the figures presented below relate to average earnings for large groups of workers. The absolute levels of pay in the two sectors will be affected by the industrial, occupational and age *distributions* of the respective workforces. Attention should thus be focused on broad movements of pay over several years rather than on the precise details. However, over a very extended period, there will be *changes* in the composition of each workforce which will be large enough to affect even these comparisons, so that too much weight should not be given to minor movements in such relative pay series. The figures do not therefore indicate how pay for a particular job in the public or private sector has changed over time, matters which are explored in chapters 4 and 5, but indicate how the average level of pay has altered. The latter information is valuable in analysing how relative pay movements have affected the economy or have been affected by the economy or by, say, incomes policy. Both these topics are explored in later sections. This section concentrates on the facts about these broad pay movements, firstly concentrating on male manual workers' relative pay in the 1950s and 1960s, and then moving on to a consideration of the 1970s and non-manual and female pay.

Table 3.1 Relative pay of male manual workers, 1950 – 79[1]

		1950	1951	1952	1953	1954	1955	1956	1957	1958	1959
Public	£	7·22	8·01	8·77	9·24	9·68	10·56	11·58	12·05	12·61	12·99
Private	£	7·40	8·12	8·79	9·45	10·05	11·04	11·94	12·26	12·83	13·29
Ratio[2]		101·5	100·4	99·3	101·3	102·8	103·5	102·1	100·8	100·8	101·3

		1960	1961	1962	1963	1964	1965	1966	1967	1968	1969
Public	£	13·70	14·52	15·12	15·90	17·04	18·40	19·77	20·33	21·63	23·20
Private	£	14·29	15·29	15·87	16·31	17·84	19·13	20·47	20·79	22·52	24·16
Ratio[2]		103·3	104·3	103·9	101·6	103·7	103·0	102·5	101·3	103·1	103·1

		1970	1971	1972	1973	1974	1975	1976	1977	1978	1979
Public	£	25·4	28·2	32·0	37·0	42·7	58·1	67·2	72·7	81·2	93·0
Private	£	27·2	29·9	33·1	38·5	43·9	54·7	64·3	71·0	80·7	93·0
Ratio[2]		100·0	99·0	96·5	97·2	96·0	87·9	89·4	91·2	92·8	93·4

[1] Average gross weekly earnings (£) in April each year. Note that there is a break in the series in 1970 as the source for the earnings figures switches from the previous April inquiry into the earnings of manual workers to the *New Earnings Survey* and as the method of constructing the two series changes (for details, see the original sources). Although the absolute level of pay is slightly different as between the two sources, the movements in the two series give very similar results so that the ratio is a good indicator of changes in relative pay.

[2] Ratios are expressed here as private sector earnings divided by public sector earnings, with each series converted to an index based on 1970 = 100. A downward movement in the ratio therefore indicates a relative improvement in public sector relative pay, and vice versa.

Source: Dean (1975) for 1950 – 69, and *Department of Employment Gazettes*, December 1977, October 1978 and October 1979 for 1970—9.

The limitations of the long run of data for the period since 1950 produced by Dean are well known and were described in the original research (Dean, 1975). The author decided to allocate those industries that were *predominantly* within the private or public sector to that particular sector and concluded that 'the resulting series for the public and private sectors are therefore not ideal, but within the limitations of the data they are thought to be the best series that can be produced, the number of workers wrongly allocated being only a small proportion of the total.' With the benefit of hindsight, and with the advantage of now being able to use *NES* data for different groups of workers, one can see that one of the main disadvantages of the earlier data is that it was necessarily confined to *male manual workers* only. The *NES* data for 1970–9, which is described below, gives breakdowns for manual and non-manual male and female earnings and indicates that the relative pay movements as between public and private sector workers has moved in very disparate ways in the four groups. Nevertheless, this is the only source of data for earnings in the public and private sectors for the 1950s and 1960s. The only similar data is that provided by Elliott (1977) for wage rate movements for skilled and unskilled public and private sector workers for the period 1950–73, later being up-dated to 1975 by Elliott and Fallick (1980). The focus of the present chapter, however, is on movements in relative earnings and their interconnection with incomes policy and public expenditure control. The way in which public sector pay is actually determined and the details of how differentials have moved in the public and private sectors are explored in chapters 4 and 5 of this volume.

The long-term movement of public and private sector pay for *male manual* workers is indicated in Table 3.1. The table shows that the *average absolute* level of private sector pay has been higher than in the public sector for the whole of the period since 1950 with the exception of the years 1975 to 1978, with the absolute pay levels in the two sectors being by coincidence exactly the same in 1979. But little attention should be paid to the levels of absolute pay, since such a comparison will depend on the structure of the workforce in the two sectors and indicates virtually nothing about the relative remuneration for workers in similar jobs. For instance, there are virtually no nurses, teachers or policemen in the private sector, and similarly no farm labourers or shop assistants in the public sector. A preoccupation with absolute levels, as for instance in Beddoe (1978), may therefore be misleading, reflecting only compositional differences between the two sectors. The interest in these figures is provided by *movements* in the relative pay of the two sectors, as indicated, for instance, by the series for the ratio of private to public sector pay, here indexed at a level of 1970 = 100. The break in the series at 1970, with the change

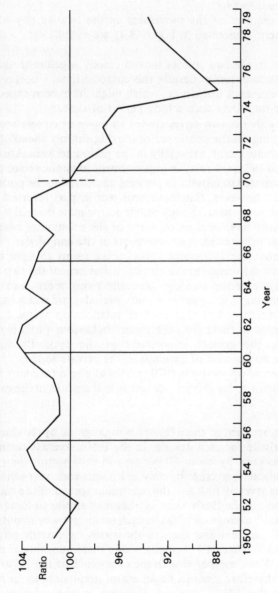

Figure 3.1 Ratio of private to public sector manual workers' earnings, 1950–79

Source: Dean (1975) and *Department of Employment Gazettes* (as in Table 3.1).

Note that downward movements in the graph indicate public sector earnings growing faster than the private sector, and vice versa. There is a break in the series in 1970, as described in the text, but this break will not have significantly affected the movement in the ratio of the two sectors, which is expressed as an index with 1970 = 100. The figures relate to average gross weekly earnings in April each year.

from the April manual workers' earnings inquiries to the *New Earnings Survey* provides another reason for paying little attention to the absolute levels of pay in the two sectors and for focusing on *relative pay movements*.

The main features of the movement in the relative pay of male manual workers, illustrated in Figure 3.1, are as follows:

(1) Earnings in the two sectors moved closely together throughout the 1950s and 1960s, despite the compositional changes in the structure of each workforce, which might have been expected to shift the ratio over such a long period of time.

(2) In the 1970s the two series ceased to move as closely together, with earnings in the public sector moving sharply ahead of those in the private sector, especially in the period between April 1974 and April 1975; the relative improvement in public sector pay by 1975 amounted to around 15 per cent compared to the position in the 1960s; however, this movement was in part reversed in the following four years, though public sector male manual workers still seem to have held on to much of the substantial advantage over their private sector counterparts at the end of the 1970s.

(3) Throughout the 1950s and 1960s, there seems to have been a significant difference in the cyclical behaviour of the two series, with private sector earnings generally rising more than public sector earnings during expansionary periods, and rising by less in the downturn – but this cyclical relationship seems to have disappeared in the 1970s; the earlier behaviour probably owed much to the greater importance of the cyclically sensitive overtime component of earnings in the private sector.

(4) In the period up to about 1970 there was also a tendency for the public sector to lag the private sector in the peaks in the earnings series.

The general movement of these figures is highlighted by looking at the summary statistics for each decade. In the 1950s, average earnings in nominal terms grew by about 80 per cent in each sector, the relative pay ratio changed on average by only 1·1 points each year (relative to the 1970 index level of 100) and the maximum spread of the ratio was only 4·2 points. In the 1960s, there is what may appear to some to be a surprising result; average earnings in each sector grew by about 70 per cent, over 10 per cent *less* than in the 1950s, whilst the pay ratio changed by an average of 1·2 points with a maximum spread of only three points. When compared with the experience of the 1970s, these two decades therefore seem to be an era of great stability in relative pay. During the 1970s, average earnings in the privatre sector increased by 242 per cent compared with 268 per cent in the public sector, reflecting the difference between two average annual compound growth rates of 14·6 per cent in the private sector and 15·5 per cent in the public sector. The average absolute change in the relative pay ratio was 2·2 points, with a maximum spread of 12·1 points, both much larger changes than in the 1950s or 1960s. In a period of higher inflation, one might expect the scope for relative pay movements to be rather larger and thus for either real or perceived 'problems' with relativities and differentials to arise. Nevertheless, the maximum movement for one year was as much as 8·1 points, the ratio moving (in favour of the public sector) from 96·0 to 87·9 between April 1974 and April 1975.

This large relative pay movement in 1974–5 was unprecedented. Throughout the previous twenty-five years there had been sizable swings in relative pay but nothing on anything like this scale. There had been a slow movement in favour of the public sector in most years since the late 1960s; with this sudden surge in pay in 1975 – public sector pay increased by 36 per cent compared with only 25 per cent in the private sector – public sector male manual workers were now in a position approximately 15 per cent more favourable to them *vis-à-vis* private sector manuals than compared with relative earnings levels in the 1950s and 1960s.

When the research showing these surprising figures was first published (Dean, 1975), the reaction from several commentators was that this movement was interesting but that it was dominated, if not entirely explained, by movements in the pay of mineworkers, who had received large pay increases following their two strikes in 1972 and 1974. Beddoe (1978), for instance, argued that once one took mineworkers and engineering workers out of the public and private sector series, on the grounds that the one group had achieved exceptionally large rises and the other unusually small rises during the period, then the pattern of pay in the two sectors looked rather different. This would, of course, be hardly a surprising result. But the important point to note was that whilst absolute pay levels in the two sectors did of course change once these adjustments were made, the relative movement of pay in favour of the public sector over the years examined (1970–7) was still substantial, particularly when compared with the previous two decades of relative stability, although less than the movements shown in the more comprehensive series. Examining other figures which excluded wages councils from the private sector series, Beddoe found that average earnings in the private non-wages-council sector moved from being 10 per cent higher than in the public sector in 1970 to only 2 per cent higher in 1977.

Other evidence that the favourable movement in the relative pay of public sector manual workers was indeed general, and was not due solely to aberrant increases for the miners or abnormally low increases in wage council industries, can be found by looking at the *NES* analyses of earnings by national agreement, which indicate that the improvement was achieved by the majority of groups of male manual workers in the public sector. There is further confirmation of this trend in the Department of Employment's own special analysis of the *NES* data provided in the December 1977 *Gazette*. The earnings of three different public sector groups – central government, local government and public corporations – are separately identified. It is noticeable that the deterioration of the pay of manual workers in the private sector *vis-à-vis* manual pay in each of these public sector groups in the period 1970–5 is in no case less than 10 per cent, and is indeed *least* in the private sector/public corporation comparison, despite the latter group including both the mineworkers and the electricity supply workers. The respective figures for the ratio of private to public sector earnings are shown in Table 3.2.

Table 3.2 Ratio of public sector to private sector pay, 1970 – 5 (male manuals)

	Central government	Local government	Public corporations
1970	123·9	127·9	97·8
1975	109·7	112·4	87·3
Change 1970 – 5 (%)	– 11·5	– 12·1	– 10·7

Source: *New Earnings Survey*. Calculated as in Table 3.1; a downward movement in the ratio (a negative sign for the change) indicates a relative improvement in public sector pay.

So far the earnings figures examined here have all related to *male manual* workers. For the period prior to 1970, the only information we have is restricted to that group of workers, for even the wage rate information provided by Elliott (1977) is restricted to male manuals. Given the relative stability of sectoral pay movements in the 1950s and 1960s, one might hypothesise that relative pay for other groups – in particular, non-manuals and females – may also have been relatively stable, but that can only be considered conjecture, in the absence of supportive evidence. For the period since 1970, however, we have the extensive *NES* material already referred to. *NES* public and private sector earnings data over the period 1970–9 for four groups of workers – manual and non-manual men and women – is summarised in Table 3.3 and Figure 3.2. The data for male manuals is the same material that has been discussed (for the 1970s) but it is instructive to see how other groups of workers have compared.

The *NES* data on private/public sector relativities for the period 1970–9 indicate that:

Table 3.3 Public and private sector pay 1970 – 9[1]

	1970	1971	1972	1973	1974	1975	1976	1977	1978	1979
Manual men:										
Public £	25·4	28·2	32·0	37·0	42·7	58·1	67·2	72·7	81·2	93·0
Private £	27·2	29·9	33·1	38·5	43·9	54·7	64·3	71·0	80·7	93·0
Ratio[2]	100·0	99·0	96·5	97·2	96·0	87·9	89·4	91·2	92·8	93·4
Non-manual men:										
Public £	35·6	39·4	44·7	48·4	55·7	71·4	87·4	92·9	101·3	112·4
Private £	34·8	38·9	42·8	48·0	53·8	66·4	78·0	86·3	100·3	113·5
Ratio[2]	100·0	100·9	97·9	101·4	98·8	95·1	91·2	95·0	101·2	103·3
Manual women										
Public £	13·3	15·5	17·8	20·2	25·0	35·5	42·5	45·9	50·5	55·1
Private £	13·3	15·2	16·9	19·6	23·2	31·0	38·3	42·9	49·0	55·2
Ratio[2]	100·0	98·1	94·9	97·0	92·8	87·3	90·1	93·5	97·0	100·2
Non-manual women										
Public £	21·2	23·2	26·6	28·7	33·3	46·5	58·2	62·5	66·8	73·7
Private £	15·1	17·1	18·7	21·4	25·1	33·1	40·0	45·2	51·6	58·6
Ratio[2]	100·0	103·5	98·7	104·8	105·9	100·0	96·5	101·5	108·4	111·7

[1] Average gross weekly earnings (£) for adult workers whose pay for the survey pay period in *April* each year was not affected by absence. Minor qualifications to these results, because of under-representation of certain public sector employees in 1971 and 1974 and for other reasons, are given in the original sources.

[2] Ratios are expressed here as private sector earnings divided by public sector earnings, with each set converted to an index based on 1970 = 100.

Source: New Earnings Survey data as reported in *Department of Employment Gazettes*, December 1977, October 1978 and October 1979.

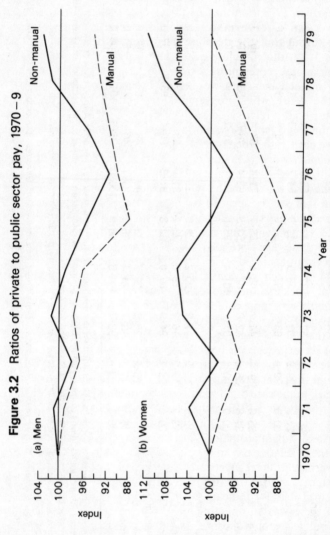

Figure 3.2 Ratios of private to public sector pay, 1970–9

Source: New Earnings Survey data as reported in *Department of Employment Gazettes* (and shown in Table 3.3).
Ratios of average gross weekly earnings for adult workers in the private sector relative to the public sector for April each year are expressed as an index based on 1970 = 100. Note that downward movements in the graph indicate public sector earnings growing faster than the private sector, and vice versa.

(1) Only public sector *manual men* were better off *vis-à-vis* their private sector counterparts at the end of the 1970s than they had been at the beginning (Figure 3.2); *manual women* were back to roughly the same relativity as in 1970, whilst both men and women *non-manual workers* in the public sector were relatively worse off in 1979 than they had been at the start of the decade; however, an assessment of the relative performance of each group throughout the decade really requires that one look in Figure 3.2 at the cumulative area between the graphed line and the horizontal representing 1970 = 100, and on this basis public sector manual men and women have unequivocally done well over the 1970s, whilst non-manual women in the public sector have suffered a relative deterioration.

(2) Both male and female *manual* workers in the public sector seem to have done rather better relative to private sector workers than *non-manual* workers (as represented in Figure 3.2 by the dotted lines always lying below the solid lines).

(3) *Non-manual women* in the public sector, in contrast to manual men in that sector, seem to have experienced a deterioration in their relative pay over much of the period amounting by 1979 to around 12 per cent compared with the situation in 1970.

(4) Despite these disparate movements, it is clear that each public sector group achieved a substantial improvement in relative pay in 1974–5, which was continued in 1976 for non-manual but not manual workers; this movement was very clear, general and apparently very large compared to the previous movements in the 1950s and 1960s witnessed by manual males.

(5) Since the 1974–5 'wage explosion', which was so marked in the public sector, there has been a movement back in favour of the private sector for all four groups in each of the years since 1975 (manual men and women) or 1976 (non-manual men and women), in the case of all groups except manual males more than offsetting the mid-1970s public sector gains.

In the case of manual males, we have already noted that the improvement of relative pay in the period 1970–5 was very similar for central government, local government and public corporations. This is not the pattern, however, for the other three groups of workers, as the NES data in Table 3.4 indicate. It is only in the *local government* sector that there was an unambiguous improvement for all the four groups of public sector workers, this being most marked for manual workers.

In *central government*, on the other hand, there would appear to have been an actual deterioration in relative pay for non-manual women and virtually no improvement at all for males, whilst manual women

Table 3.4   Percentage changes in private/public sector relative pay, 1970–5

	Central government	Local government	Public corporations
Manual men	−11·5	−12·1	−10·7
Manual women	−16·8	−12·6	+2·2
Non-manual men	−0·9	−6·5	−9·3
Non-manual women	+0·1	−3·5	−4·4

Source: *New Earnings Survey*. Calculated as in Table 3.1; note that a minus sign indicates a deterioration in private sector relative pay, or an improvement for the public sector.

achieved the largest improvement of any group. In this case, however, there is undoubtedly a data problem. As has been pointed out elsewhere by Dean (1980), there can occasionally be problems in analysing recorded *NES* data when settlements are either brought forward to before or put back beyond the mid-April survey date for the *NES*. This can happen very easily if pay negotiations with a settlement date in March or April are protracted because of disagreements and are eventually concluded in the latter half of April or May, even though such settlements may be backdated to the prior date. A classic example of this occurred in 1975 when non-industrial civil servants received an extremely large pay award, of the order of 30 per cent, following the revival of the Pay Research Unit exercises after the period of suspension during the Heath incomes policy. This pay award was finally agreed after the date of the *NES* survey in mid-April 1975, even though the award was in two parts, backdated to the previous January and the start of April. This very large award does *not* appear in the April 1975 *NES* so that the earnings figures for non-manual workers in central government are lower. If the pay rises had been reflected in the 1975 data then the comparison for 1970–5, rather than showing virtually no change (as in the table above), would undoubtedly show a very large relative pay improvement for central government non-manuals.

In the *public corporations*, the significant movement was the deterioration of the earnings of manual women over this period, in contrast to the gains achieved by other groups. Male workers in the public corporations, both manual and non-manual, achieved much larger relative improvements than women.

In the years following this 1974–5 surge of pay in the public sector, the improved positions were gradually reversed. The impact of incomes policy in the later years, as discussed in the separate section below, was felt more strongly in the public sector. The large rises in the public sector in 1974 and 1975 were, in part, political in origin.

There is little evidence in the early 1970s, including the period of the Heath incomes policy, that the public sector had been unduly 'squeezed' by the effects of pay policies, except perhaps for non-manual women (see Figure 3.2). There was therefore no special justification on those grounds for any particularly strong improvement in public sector pay in 1974–5. However, the political situation in 1974 is relevant. The Heath incomes policy and the Conservative government were defeated in the February general election, which took place against the background of the miners' strike and the three-day week. The defeat, albeit an extremely narrow one with the Conservatives actually winning more votes but less seats than Labour, was in part a judgement against formal incomes policy and in favour of the Labour Party's 'Social Contract' with the unions. The policy on incomes of the new government was to rely on the unions to exercise restraint, in exchange for a generous programme of industrial relations and social policy legislation (see Appendix to this volume for full details). In practice, the first action of the government was to concede the miners' very large pay claim virtually *in toto* and then to agree to large settlements for the other groups of public sector workers, such as electricity supply workers and railwaymen, who followed on with large claims of their own. In the next year, the government allowed what was effectively a free-for-all for workers in the public sector. Although the private sector followed in with some exceptionally large settlements, there was no bottomless purse for private sector workers, especially with companies suffering both from the recession and from price controls and a profits squeeze. Thus, in the year to April 1975, public sector pay rose by around 10 per cent more than pay in the private sector. The effect on inflation, on public expenditure control and on the general economic situation was inevitably adverse, and arguably coloured economic policy and performance throughout the rest of the decade. The effect of this public sector pay explosion on the control of public expenditure, which was particularly damaging, is examined in more detail below.

The period from 1975 to 1979, during which time the Labour government's successive phases of incomes policy were in force, was marked by a slow movement of relative pay back in favour of private sector workers (see Figure 3.2). This is one period for which the evidence clearly indicates that pay in the public sector was controlled much more tightly than in the private sector. The way in which incomes policies have affected relative pay in the two sectors is examined in detail in the following section.

An overview of incomes policies in the public sector

Throughout nearly the whole of the postwar period, successive governments have intervened fairly heavily in pay negotiations in an attempt to restrain the rate of growth of incomes. Although there have been periods of time when a government has abjured intervention in pay matters, such periods have usually been extremely short (as indicated in the Appendix). The latest attempt to 'stand back' from pay negotiations, that being pursued by the Conservative government from 1979 onwards, may, judging from the apparent determination of its proponents, last longer than most. But even this non-interventionist stance is to a certain extent tinged with elements of involvement. For the government is directly involved in pay matters through its planning of public expenditure, through the operation in recent years of cash limits, and through control over a wide variety of aspects of manpower in the public sector. As George Brown once said, 'it is impossible for a government not to have an incomes policy, even if it has no policy'.

In reality it is inevitable that governments will be involved to some extent in matters of pay, if only because nearly one-third of all workers are in the public sector. Furthermore, if a government wishes to actively intervene to try to reduce the level of pay settlements, it is only natural that it should try particularly hard to apply such policy to its own labour force. Successive episodes of both voluntary and statutory policy have witnessed particularly intense attempts to apply such policies to the public sector, even though governments have on occasions professed that no discrimination in the application of policy is intended. It is only natural, however, that the public sector should be better 'policed' than the private sector, where any central control cannot help but be less than direct. Winchester (1975) concluded that

> experience over the last 15 years has proved conclusively that any government policies to restrain wages can be applied more effectively in the public sector than elsewhere. Clearly if a government decides that wage restraint is desirable in the interest of national economic policy, it is not surprising that it should apply such restraint to the pay of its own direct or indirect employees.

However, the evidence cited in chapter 5 below does not suggest that the conclusion is quite as clear-cut as that: incomes policies do not appear to have been invariably more effective in the public sector, although the public sector unions clearly strongly feel that to be the case.

The postwar history of incomes policies indicates that discrimination against the public sector has been common but not general. Despite the suspicion that the government would attempt to intervene behind the scenes, there was no stated policy of trying to control public sector pay in either the Stafford Cripps pay freeze of

1948–51 or the Macmillan wage and price plateau of 1956. In 1961–62, however, during the Selwyn Lloyd pay pause, the government openly declared that it would intervene in public sector awards where it thought necessary, relying only on exhortation in the private sector. During the next episode of incomes policy, between 1965 and 1970, there was no explicit discrimination against the public sector, but it is noticeable that the inquiries of the National Board for Prices and Incomes were disproportionately directed towards public sector groups, several of which were investigated on more than one occasion. There then followed, in the period 1970–2, the most deliberate attempt to hold back pay in the public sector, presumably as an example and possibly as encouragement to private sector workers. This was the so-called 'N–1' policy of the Heath government. The policy was an attempt to de-escalate wages by leaning more and more heavily on public sector settlements and attempting to reach agreement for each successive group at 1 per cent less than the preceding settlement. The theory behind the policy was that if downward pressure could be exerted in public sector settlements, then private sector settlements would follow them down, but the way in which the government sought to influence negotiations was not clear. The policy was soon superseded by a formal policy anyway as a pay freeze was imposed at the end of 1972 to halt the continued escalation of settlements. In principle the ensuing Heath incomes policies of 1972–4 (Stages I to III) were applied across the board. In the end, the intransigence with which the government applied the policy to one particular group of public sector workers, the coalminers, led to the demise of the pay policy and of the government. But this was not before the Pay Board had already spelt out the case for special anomaly awards to civil servants and government scientists (Pay Board, 1973).

The strange interim period between the advent of the new Labour government in March 1974 and the reintroduction of pay controls with the £6 limit in the summer of 1975, the period of the 'Social Contract', was or was not a period of incomes policy depending on how one defines that term. Although the incoming Labour government claimed that it had a 'Social Contract' with the unions, whereby concessions on such matters as industrial relations legislation and higher pensions would be traded off against wage restraint, the latter was not achieved to any noticeable extent. The annual increase in the growth of average earnings accelerated from around 15 per cent in early 1974 to nearly 30 per cent within a year. Although one ingredient of this surge in earnings was the payment of thresholds inherited from the Heath Stage III policy, an important element was the explosion of pay of a large number of public sector groups. The procedure was started off by the extremely large pay award granted to the miners (who were at that time on strike). This was followed by large settlements for many other public sector workers, which the Labour government did virtually nothing to prevent. The Pay Research Unit's work, which had been disregarded for several years under the Heath incomes policy, was now used to give exceptionally large pay rises to half a million civil servants. On whatever measure one takes, the relative pay of public sector workers increased significantly faster than that of private sector workers during this period.

The 1974–5 pay explosion, which was essentially generated by the government's willingness to buy industrial peace in the public sector by agreeing to extraordinarily large settlements, whilst letting the private sector settle however it wished, showed up the 'Social Contract', which had been a major plank in the government's victories in the two 1974 elections, to be little more than a sham. Whilst the government pushed through much of the promised legislative programme, virtually no wage restraint was secured in return. The combination of price controls and wages free-for-all meant both a squeeze on profits and a sudden expansion of real wages, which can have been nothing but detrimental to employment prospects. The resulting surge in inflation was extremely damaging to the British economy and the subsequent surge in public expenditure eventually led to the IMF visit and cutbacks of 1976–7.

The £6 limit, introduced almost as an emergency measure though with TUC acquiesence in July 1975, served to reduce earnings increases very rapidly back down to around 15 per cent from the 30 per cent area that had been reached in 1974–5. But the limit, plus the succeeding stages, also, in principle, served to freeze a set of relativities that, *ex post*, seem to have been rather favourable to the public sector. The new limits were voluntarily agreed with the TUC, which supported the first stages but then withdrew support in 1978. There was not necessarily any sectoral discrimination in the pay limits or guidelines but the reality was that the policy was more strictly enforced in the public sector, with the exception of a concession on productivity provisions which was used in the later stages to justify increases outside the agreed pay limits for miners and electricity workers. Although price controls and sanctions against companies paying over the limits served to moderate increases in the private sector to a certain extent, the policy was only loosely policed and there was no doubt much evasion of the limits by private employers. Furthermore, the government was seen to be using sanctions (such as the blacklisting of companies for government contracts) against minnows rather than against some of the big fish like Ford which were nevertheless paying over the limits. Indeed, when the government finally tried to use sanctions against Ford in the autumn of 1978, it only ended up being defeated in the Commons on the sanctions issue, thence finding itself having to drop the sanctions entirely.

The government meanwhile tried to 'hold the line' in the public sector, backed by newly introduced cash limits on budgeted expenditures. However, with private sector firms flouting the government's prescribed 5 per cent limit at will by the winter of 1978–9, this only led to a series of strikes by successive public sector groups attempting to preserve differentials or to keep up with the rate of inflation. The apparent breakdown of Labour's special relationship with the unions, which had arguably brought it victory in the 1974 elections, was an important reason for the May 1979 general election defeat. The government had, however, bought industrial peace by agreeing to a series of supplementary awards which were to depend on comparability exercises carried out by a new Standing Commission on Pay Comparability under Professor Clegg. This was on top of special arrangements already agreed for the firemen, linking them to average earnings following their strike in the winter of 1977–8, for doctors and dentists, for university teachers, for the armed forces, for the police and for civil servants. Although all these awards came under the general heading of special cases, it is clear, as argued in the next section, that their proliferation was a major reason for the need for a renewed series of public expenditure cuts in 1979–80. It was the history of the mid-1970s experience repeating itself. A feeling amongst public sector workers that their pay had been unjustifiably held back during several years of pay policy, a large increase in the number of days lost in strikes in the public sector, being met eventually by a sudden surge in public sector pay and a subsequent crisis of public expenditure control.

This review of the various periods of incomes policies indicates that there has inevitably been a certain amount of discrimination against the public sector. This discrimination has not always been explicit and on many occasions it has occurred simply because policing of such policies is likely to be more effective where the government is the paymaster and where settlements are for large numbers of workers and are highly visible. Therefore one would expect, as a general rule, that one might detect a deterioration in the relative pay of public sector workers during incomes policy periods.

One of the problems in analysing earnings data of the sort described in the first section, in order to investigate the effect of incomes policy on relative pay, is that the 'timing' of the data (generally annual) is not in sufficiently short periods or over the right periods for one to make an entirely satisfactory distinction between policy-on and policy-off periods. The study of manual workers' pay over the period 1950–75 (Dean, 1975) concluded that even the six-monthly data used (April and October each year) was 'not discriminating enough to be able to provide conclusive evidence either way in judging the effects of incomes policies'. In fact, the evidence suggested that the one very explicit policy aimed at restraining public sector settlements, the N−1 policy of 1971−2, far from de-escalating public sector settlements and forcing them below those in the private sector, may actually have had the opposite effect. The evidence on the relative wages of public sector workers provided by Elliott (1977) tends to confirm the fairly neutral findings on the effects of incomes policy up to 1973, and also suggests that the effects of the N−1 policy may have been perverse.

The *NES* data for the period since 1970 gives no clear indication of how the Heath policies (1972−4) affected relative pay, but suggests that the incomes policies of the later 1970s may indeed have been adhered to less strongly in the private sector. The *NES* data shown in Figure 3.2 indicates that an improvement in private sector manual workers' relative pay occurred in each of the four years following April 1975, this improvement being general for non-manual workers as well after April 1976 (this latter result being affected, as described above, by a delayed settlement for civil servants after the *NES* survey in April 1975). The improvements varied from about 6 per cent for manual men (1975−9) to 16 per cent for non-manual women (1976−9), with movements of 13 per cent for non-manual men and 15 per cent for manual women. These large movements in favour of private sector workers which followed the 1974−5 public sector pay explosion, took place under periods of incomes policy − initially the £6 limit from July 1975 and then the three succeeding stages of the Labour government's incomes policy.

A review of the effect of incomes policy on the public sector by Thomson and Beaumont (1978) concluded that 'the overall figures do not suggest that the public sector has been badly mistreated in the actual outturn of incomes policies, which may be rather different to government intent'; and that 'contrary to many arguments, the public sector has not been unduly harshly treated by incomes policies'. These findings should perhaps be qualified, since they only examined the period up to 1976. In the three following years, there does appear to have been *de facto* discrimination against the public sector, although in the case of male manual workers this represented only a partial unwinding of the unprecedentedly advantageous position of 1975. The unfortunate fact is that particular public sector groups do feel very keenly that they have been discriminated against, and they react against this by demanding special case treatment. The series of disputes in the public sector in the winters of 1978−9 and 1979−80 all owed something to a sense of a grievance about being maltreated, whether the reality was so or not. The staged awards, comparability studies and high settlements that these 'catch-up' claims produced have had serious consequences for the control of public expenditure, as discussed in the following section. Furthermore, in the case of the police and the firemen, the government committed itself to the unprecedented and extraordinary step of linking the pay of these workers directly to an earnings index (see chapter 5), thus encouraging any wage/price spiral to be more intense and further exacerbating attempts to contain public spending.

Public sector pay and the control of public expenditure

The long-term secular rise of the share of public expenditure in GDP is well known and well documented. At the end of the 1970s, this movement has been halted, at least temporarily, following a series of public expenditure cuts by governments of both persuasions. This period of retrenchment, however, followed a period of several years, especially in the mid-1970s, when public expenditure had become very much out of control. The rapid rise in public expenditure at that time can be attributed very largely to exceptionally large pay increases in the public sector, but it is argued here that these were only a by-product of a system of public expenditure control which has tended to generate rises in public expenditure which have normally been such as to lead to an increasing share of resources being employed by the public sector. Whilst 'abnormal' rises in public sector pay may therefore be seen to lead to surges in public expenditure, these episodes are really just a symptom of the overall lack of control inherent in the system of public expenditure.

The idea that there might be some natural or inbuilt reason why public expenditure might grow faster than national product, as it has done in virtually all industrialised countries in the postwar period, is one that has been common for some time. Baumol (1967) was one of the first to specifically model this procedure. He posited a simple model of 'unbalanced' growth, where there were basically two sectors, with disparate productivity growth rates. One sector of the economy is technologically progressive and thus generates high productivity growth, whilst the other sector achieves only limited productivity gains. It is then fairly easy to show that, if output growth in the two sectors remains relatively constant, then the non-progressive sector will absorb an increasing share of employment, which will also entail a declining rate of growth of overall productivity. The only strong assumption required to get this result is that output growth in the two sectors should be comparable.

The Baumol model has been applied to the case of the public and private sectors of the economy. Spann (1977) and Skolka (1977), for instance, have argued that the public sector can be described as a non-progressive sector, with lower productivity growth than the rest of the economy, so that the Baumol model would suggest an increasing share of public sector employment over time. This result would seem to accord with the statistics that Martin (1980) has documented, which show a strong trend towards a growing share of public sector employment in nearly all OECD countries. In the case of the United Kingdom the share of the public sector in total employment has increased from 22½ per cent in the early 1960s to around 29 per cent in 1978 (Table 3.5).

Given the rising share of public sector employment in total employment, it is not then surprising that public expenditure should also be absorbing an increasing share of national product in most of the industrialised countries. Although the public sector wage and salary bill represents only one part of public expenditure, it typically amounts to at least half and in some countries up to three-quarters of Government final consumption, so that pay movements play a dominant role in movements of public expenditure. If public sector pay moves exactly in line with pay in the private sector, then a rising share of public sector employment, barring unusual movements in other expenditure components, will entail a rising share of public expenditure in GDP. If pay in the two sectors moves erratically from year to year, but over a period of several years movements in the two sectors are equivalent, then the path of this rising share will itself be erratic, especially when cyclical considerations are taken into account, and this pattern of erratic movements may induce corrective governmental action which is itself erratic and destabilising for the economy. The course of public sector relative pay outlined in the first section above indicates that whilst relative public/private sector pay movements tended to be fairly stable in the 1950s and 1960s, they became extremely large and erratic in the 1970s. This made the control of public expenditure extremely difficult, and in the mid-1970s in particular the public sector pay explosion led to a rapid rise in the share of public expenditure in GDP.

The assumption of the Baumol model of equivalent output growth in the two sectors has rarely been met, at least *ex post*, in the case of the United Kingdom. The way in which governments have sought to plan and control public expenditure in Britain since the 1960s has been in the form of detailed five-year plans set out in annual Public Expenditure White Papers. Although these expenditure plans have generally been drawn up in the light of some overall projection of the growth of resources, the outcome has more often than not been disappointing, with less output growth than expected. Although the plans may have provided for no or only very minor growth in the share of public expenditure in GDP, the under-achievement on GDP has rarely been matched by a downward revision of public expenditure. It has proved rather difficult to make short-term

Table 3.5 Employment in the public sector, 1960–78

	Total employment[1] (thousands)	Public sector thousands	Public sector % of total employment	of which: Central government %	Local government %	Public corporations %
1960	23,660	5,325	22·5	6·9	7·7	7·9
1965	24,780	5,549	22·4	5·5	8·7	8·2
1970	24,381	6,117	25·1	6·3	10·5	8·3
1971	24,031	6,232	25·9	6·5	11·0	8·4
1972	24,020	6,308	26·3	6·7	11·5	8·0
1973	24,610	6,417	26·1	6·7	11·7	7·7
1974	24,715	6,568	26·6	7·1	11·5	8·0
1975	24,596	6,932	28·2	7·7	12·2	8·3
1976	24,429	6,981	28·6	8·1	12·4	8·1
1977[2]	24,551	7,066	28·8	8·1	12·2	8·5
1978[2]	24,610	7,065	28·7	8·1	12·2	8·4

[1] Total employees in civilian employment plus self-employed persons.
[2] Provisional.
Source: Economic Trends, November 1979.
Components may not add due to rounding.

adjustments to public expenditure plans to match lower growth prospects and of course certain elements of expenditure, such as unemployment and social security benefits, have moved in the opposite direction. This element of insensitivity of public expenditure to changes in the longer-term growth of the economy has been mirrored by the movement of public sector employment (although much of this was in part-time employment), which has proved far less responsive to general economic conditions, and has therefore fluctuated much less than private sector employment. These circumstances have therefore led to what has virtually been a ratchet effect in both the growth of public expenditure and public sector employment. In the last twenty years there have been very few occasions when employment in the public sector has actually fallen. This has also meant that when governments have attempted to rein back the growth of public expenditure they have often had to do so in the most draconian fashion, since the cumulative effect of growing public sector numbers and increased expenditure programmes proves extremely difficult to reverse.

There is another factor, however, which has made public expenditure control rather erratic and haphazard, and which highlights the importance of public sector pay movements in this process. This other factor is the long-term structural phenomenon known as the 'relative price effect', an effect which is related to Baumol's unbalanced growth concept. In recent work on the latest (1979–80) series of expenditure cuts, Price (1979) has argued that 'the recurrent crises of financial control which have afflicted public spending plans in the last decade and a half', which have led to the need for periodic cutbacks, whichever administration has been in office, 'have been a response to an increase in the relative price of providing public services'. The author argues that the reason why there is constant pressure to increase public spending lies in the fact that output in the public sector, and hence productivity, is not properly measured. By convention the output of public services is nearly all measured by indicators of labour input so that there is *by definition* virtually zero productivity growth. Increases in the volume of services can therefore occur only through increases in employment. Because there is no productivity offset, increases in wages and salaries in the public services are reflected directly in the price of those services, as conventionally measured in the national accounts, so that the price of such services rises more rapidly than prices in general. This phenomenon, the relative price effect, will therefore be positive in the longer run so long as pay in the public services tends to move in line with pay in other sectors and so long as productivity in the economy generally continues to grow. If public service pay increases faster than other pay then the relative price effect will be more strongly positive and public expenditure as a proportion of GDP will grow even more rapidly. It is important to note that *any* growth in public services, as conventionally measured, can only occur through increased employment, in which case the share of public expenditure in GDP will rise. Price shows that: 'the share of public spending in GDP increases in proportion to the relative price change (or productivity disadvantage) *vis-à-vis* the economy as a whole'. One thus gets the result that even if the volume of public services is unchanged, so that government spending falls as a share of GDP in volume terms, nevertheless the share of government in GDP in value terms will remain virtually constant.

Until the advent of cash limits, governments had for many years exercised control in volume terms; any increase in the price of public spending over and above what was already catered for was met by supplementary estimates. A pay increase in the public sector over and above the average level achieved in the private sector, less the non-governmental productivity increase, would not increase planned expenditure volumes, but would nevertheless increase public expenditure as a share of GDP, and as a by-product would necessitate a higher level of taxation. The move to cash limits whereby public expenditure in the current or forthcoming year is budgeted for in current price terms (rather than Public Expenditure White Paper survey prices) offers the chance that expenditure can be controlled in value as well as volume terms. Such limits appeared to work reasonably well at a time when a pay policy had been accepted in the public sector, but begs important questions when the outcome of public sector pay bargains is less easily determinable. In such circumstances are cash limits really a public sector incomes policy in disguise, or are they meant to be flexible and thus ineffective?

The problem of the relative price effect which, given the way government sector output is currently measured, tends to be significantly positive and thus tends to create problems of expenditure control, is exacerbated whenever public sector pay moves erratically relative to the private sector, as happened in the 1970s. If public sector pay increases less rapidly than private sector pay in any period, so that the relative price effect is reduced, but then rises faster as public sector wages and salaries catch up, then this causes problems in the catch-up period. Public expenditure increases rapidly, causing pressures to cut spending volumes, especially in an era of cash limits and public sector borrowing targets. The 1979–80 series of public expenditure cuts reflected this pattern.

During the 1978–9 'wage round', which was marked by a series of industrial disputes in the public sector through the winter, several groups of workers made settlements which included second-tier delayed payments to be based on the work of the Standing

Commission on Pay Comparability which the Labour government set up under Professor Clegg in the spring of 1979. The effects of 'catching-up' awards of various sizes recommended by the Clegg Commission, when taken with the large awards given to the Armed Forces, doctors and dentists, and the police by other review bodies, and the sizeable staged award granted to civil servants following the revival of the Pay Research Unit, meant that public sector pay increased especially rapidly in 1979 and 1980, following a period of years when it had risen less fast than pay in the private sector. The inevitable result was that the relative price effect (as measured by the difference between the GDP factor cost deflator and the general government consumption deflator), which between financial years 1975/76 and 1978/79 had been virtually flat, suddenly became strongly positive in 1979/80 and is projected to be about 7 per cent in 1980/81 as the full year impact of catch-up payments and staged settlements in the public sector is felt (Figure 3.3).

This extraordinarily strong relative price effect in the period 1979–81, reflecting increases in the relative cost of public spending during this catching-up phase, is a major reason for the series of cuts in the volume of public expenditure by the new Conservative government. In the circumstances just described, it is necessary to make substantial cuts in the volume of public expenditure in order to maintain a constant share of such expenditures in GDP – the stated aim of the new government. Examination of the chart indicates that this is not the first time that this has occurred. In the 1960s, there was a fairly stable positive relative price effect. This was a period when, apart from normal mild cyclical fluctuations, public and private sector pay appears to have moved in a rather similar fashion (see Figure 3.1), but with productivity gains in the private sector meaning that the price of public sector output increased at a faster rate. In the early 1970s, this effect was very muted, but then emerged very strongly again in the mid-1970s, at a time when relative public sector pay rose strongly. After a further period of virtually no relative price effect, from roughly 1976 to 1979, there was a further catching-up period with a strongly positive effect in 1980.

It is instructive to note that the two most significant periods of public sector pay catch-up, in 1974–5 and 1979–80, have immediately preceded the two most drastic episodes of public expenditure cuts – those introduced by the mid-1970s Labour government in 1976–7, following the IMF team visit, and those introduced by the new Conservative government in 1980–1. These series of cuts, although in one sense necessitated by the lack of expenditure control inherent in this system, have arguably been disruptive and destabilising in their effect on the economy and, as Price has argued, must surely be 'second best to a policy of planning so as to prevent the necessity for

Figure 3.3 Relative rates of inflation and the relative price effect, 1962/63 to 1980/81

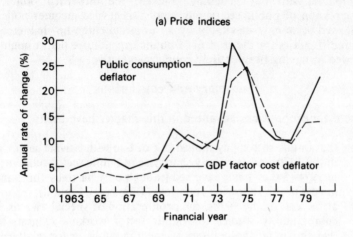

(a) Price indices

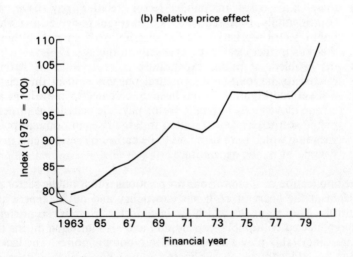

(b) Relative price effect

Source: *Economic Trends Annual Supplement* (1979) and *Price* (1979).
Note that 1979/80 and 1980/81 are forecast figures from the latter source, and that the dates refer to financial years starting in April.

cuts'. The reason why public expenditure control has proved so unsuccessful is that the relative price effect has not been treated as a long-term structural phenomenon. The problem has been exacerbated by the erratic way in which public sector pay has been allowed to move compared with pay generally. Indeed, the unwritten policy of suppression of public sector pay, under successive incomes policies, followed seemingly inevitably by an eventual catch-up, has created such difficulties for the control of public expenditure that it might be viewed as having been entirely counterproductive.

Summary and conclusions

The main propositions advanced in this chapter have been:

(1)   that public sector pay moved out of line with private sector pay in the 1970s, an especially sharp rise in public sector relative pay in 1974–5 then being reversed (though only partially for manual males) in the following four years (Figures 3.1 and 2);
(2)   at the end of the 1970s, the proliferation of special awards and comparability studies for public sector workers suggests that there might be another improvement in public sector relative pay in the period 1979–81, although not on the scale of 1974–5;
(3)   these large rises in public sector relative pay have, not coincidentally, followed periods of incomes policy during which public sector workers have felt discriminated against, although this was in fact clearly the case only in the late 1970s;
(4)   the problem of public expenditure control, which is strongly related to the long-term structural phenomenon of the relative price effect (Figure 3.3), has been exacerbated by these large and erratic movements in public sector pay; the occasional surges in public sector pay have resulted in large rises in nominal public spending which have then had to be curbed by serious cuts in the volume of public expenditure.

The implication of these various propositions is that public sector pay is right at the heart of both incomes policy and public expenditure control. The way in which public sector pay is so strongly interconnected with public expenditure and also inflation means that it must inevitably play a central role in economic policy. The lack of planning and control of public sector pay has arguably been the recurring and unsolved problem for British governments in the 1970s and has created great difficulties in the control of the economy. The enormous swings in public sector pay in this period have been reflected in destabilising movements of public expenditure, with control only being re-established subsequently by means of large and unplanned cuts in expenditure volumes. The remark made in the introduction to this chapter therefore bears repeating; namely, that the sensible control of public sector pay is a necessary but by no means a sufficient condition for successful economic policies.

References: Chapter 3

Baumol, W. J., 'The macro-economics of unbalanced growth; the anatomy of urban crisis', *American Economic Review*, vol. LVII, June 1967, pp. 415–26

Beddoe, R., 'The improvement in public sector pay; fact or illusion?', Trade Union Research Unit, Technical Note no. 41, 1978

Beenstock, M., and Immanuel, H., 'The market approach to pay comparability', *National Westminster Bank Review*, November 1979

Dean, A. J. H., 'Earnings in the public and private sectors 1950–1975', *National Institute Economic Review*, no. 74, November 1975, pp. 60–70

Dean, A. J. H., 'Public and private sector manual workers' pay 1970–1977', *National Institute Economic Review*, no. 82, November 1977, pp. 62–6

Dean, A. J. H., *Wages and Earnings*, vol. 13 of RSS/SSRC Reviews of U.K. Statistical Sources (Oxford: Pergamon, 1980)

Department of Employment, New Earnings Survey results in issues of December 1977, October 1978 and October 1979, *Gazette*, HMSO

Elliott, R. F., 'Public sector wage movements, 1950–1973', *Scottish Journal of Political Economy*, vol. XXIV, no. 2, 1977, pp. 133–51

Elliott, R. F., and Fallick, J. L., *Pay in the Public Sector* (Macmillan, 1980)

Hawksworth, R. I., 'Private and public sector pay', *British Journal of Industrial Relations*, vol. XIV, no. 2, July 1976, pp. 206–13

Martin, J., 'Public sector employment trends', paper presented to the Congress of the International Institute of Public Finance, Jerusalem, August 1980

Pay Board, *Advisory Report no. 1; Anomalies arising out of the Pay Standstill of November 1972*, HMSO, 1973

Price, R. W. R., 'Public expenditure: policy and control', *National Institute Economic Review*, no. 90, November 1979, pp. 68–76

Skolka, J. V., 'Unbalanced productivity growth and the growth of public services', *Journal of Public Economics*, vol. 7, April 1977, pp. 271–80

Spann, R. M., 'The macro-economics of unbalanced growth and the expanding public sector: some simple tests of a model of government growth', *Journal of Public Economics*, vol. 8, December 1977, pp. 397–404

Thomson, A. W. J., and Beaumont, P. B., *Public sector bargaining: a study of relative gain* (Farnborough: Saxon House, 1978)

Winchester, D., 'Labour relations in the public sector in the United Kingdom', in Rehmus, C. M. (ed.), *Public Employment Labour Relations: An Overview of Eleven Nations*, Institute of Labour Studies and Industrial Relations, Ann Arbor, 1975

Chapter 4

Incomes Policy and the Private Sector

KEN MAYHEW

1 Introduction

This chapter is concerned with the potential and actual impact of incomes policies on the private sector. We assess the extent to which they distort differentials within plants or firms and relativities between plants and occupations. We consider the allocative importance of relative pay and we discuss other ways in which the disruption of established pay relationships might affect the private sector; for example if comparability is an important factor for bargainers, there might be severe industrial relations problems. Even if pay relationships are not much affected, behaviour may be influenced in other ways by an incomes policy, and this is our final area of concern.

There are various possible types of incomes policy, and any impact will depend on the policy's construction and implementation. The following features are important:

(i)   whether the policy limit is in flat-rate or in percentage terms;
(ii)   whether the limit applies strictly to individuals or whether it is used just as the basis for settling the increase of the paybill of the whole bargaining group;
(iii)   the size of the limit and the rigour with which the limit is viewed as a maximum rather than a norm;
(iv)   the allowance or not of exceptions, and the nature of these exceptions – for example, productivity deals, low pay, comparability;
(v)   the extent to which accidents of timing cause the introduction of a pay policy to have unintended effects on pay comparisons between those groups which have settled before implementation and those which have yet to settle.

Whatever the objective features of a policy, its impact will ultimately depend on the rigour and success with which it is applied, and also on whether its application is evenly spread throughout industry.

2   The role of relative pay

The allocation of labour between plants
If incomes policy distorts differentials and relative pay, then it might make labour markets less efficient. This notion rests on a neoclassical model of supply and demand for factors of production. Relative prices act as signals, and factor flows are the responses.

There is plentiful evidence to indicate that for any particular occupation in any area, the average earnings of plants show great differences (Mackay *et al.*, 1971; Robinson, 1968; Robinson, 1970). In addition there is substantial dispersion within each plant, and the ranges of earnings of the plants overlap each other (Mayhew, 1977). These features, together with imperfect information and the apparent lack of correlation between recruitment rates and relative earnings (Mackay *et al.*, pp. 144–7 and pp. 149–51), are what commentators have identified as the critical issues in the debate about whether pay matters or not. As Brittan and Lilley (1977, chapter 8) have correctly argued, merely to point to such features is not to deny the importance of pay. Before any conclusions can be drawn, these findings have to be put into a more general context. This involves an exploration of search theory and of internal labour market theories. Briefly, the argument is that if internal labour markets exist, then much search can take place only *inside* firms.

On a strict definition an internal labour market[1] is one with limited ports of entry; there are only a few job grades which can be filled by recruits from outside the firm. Other jobs are filled by the promotion or upgrading of existing workers and by offering non-pecuniary, non-transferable benefits. A less strict definition would be one where an employer attempts to reduce turnover by rewards for length of service. He incurs fixed costs in searching for, selecting and training employees and he naturally wishes to amortise these over as long a period as possible. Particular stress has been put on the costs of training (see, for example, Oi, 1962). If the training is for a skill which is specific to the firm, then the employer will pay both the direct and indirect costs of such training. He can later recoup these costs by paying the worker less than the value of his marginal product. The worker will not leave, because his highest alternative wage outside the firm will be lower, since if he left he would not be able to sell his specific skills elsewhere, by definition. In a world of imperfect capital markets the employer might also have to pay for general training, and he would therefore have to construct an internal job structure which would encourage workers to remain in his service.

Internal labour markets are thought to be a feature of many parts of the public sector in Britain, but only very scattered information exists on private firms. Mackay *et al.* found little evidence of limited ports of entry in their sample of engineering firms, but recently Mace (1979) has suggested that a broader set of criteria should be used. These include turnover rates, the existence of promotion ladders, the nature of the training provided by a firm, the extent to which pay is determined by reference to internal differentials, the nature of adjustment mechanisms to changes in economic conditions.[2] On such criteria it seems clear that there exists a substantial degree of internalisation in British industry and commerce.

Crucial for the worker are the implications of this for his ability to acquire information.[3] Imagine a worker who arrives in a particular town. He has no trade, but believes (correctly) that he would (given time) be able to perform most of the semi-skilled jobs available in the area. He searches for wage offers until the marginal costs of search equal the marginal gains. Stigler (1962) demonstrated that even if the ranking by earnings of firms remained constant over time, so that the gains could be discounted over a long period, there would never be enough search to eliminate all dispersion, so long as the marginal costs of search were positive. Thus the employer is partly relieved from one external labour market pressure — the supply responses of individual workers. Further, if changes in product demand conditions or the entry of new firms means that rankings of firms do not remain constant, then the gains from search can be discounted over only a short time-period, with the result that there will be very little search. The fact that for any grade of labour plants have widely dispersed ranges of earnings which overlap each other complicates the matter still more. A searcher will have information about only a limited number of points on each range. Even if he could acquire information about the whole range of each and every firm, he would not have a reliable basis on which to choose his employer. For he would have little prior information as to where he would be in any particular year in any particular firm; this he could acquire only when in a job. Therefore he would be irrational to discount his gains from search over any but the shortest time-period. Thus his amount of search would be small and so the forces which might equalise wages are weak. In other words, the very existence of internal labour markets generates forces which give them large margins of discretion in which to operate.

It seems likely, therefore, that the potential impact of the sort of incomes policies Britain has had on the allocation of similar grades of labour between firms is strictly limited. Following the logic of our analysis of search in local labour markets, the area where we ought to look for greatest impact is in the rate of quitting. More workers who search on the job will be disappointed in their findings, and leave to search other firms. In other words, the argument is that a worker has to enter a firm before he can obtain much of the information necessary for him to decide whether it is offering a 'good' job.

Further, wages are only one element in the package of rewards. Even if incomes policy acts to restrict the employer in his use of non-wage pecuniary benefits to attract or retain workers, the use of non-pecuniary benfits often remains open to him. In addition, of course, adjustments to the required labour force can be achieved through changes in hours worked or changes in production techniques. However, the possibility that incomes policies do encourage a switch from straight wage rewards to non-pecuniary and indirect pecuniary ones has two important, but often ignored, implications. First, presumably such rewards are not costless to the employer; and thus any study which analyses the impact of a particular policy on wages would be likely to overstate the extent to which it reduced pressures on cost inflation. Second, in so far as information is harder to obtain on non-wage as opposed to wage benefits, then the amount of search undertaken – and along with it the discipline of the external market – will decrease still further.

The allocation of labour between occupations

There are a number of dimensions to be considered here. They include the allocation of labour within firms, its allocation between firms, the readiness of individuals in the labour market to switch skills, and the response to pay signals of those not yet in the labour market when making their decisions about general education and training.

Much relevant evidence has emerged from the recent concern with skill shortages. The evidence comes partly from questionnaires, partly from statistical analysis and partly from general impression. Though there is some doubt as to the prevalence of such shortages, there is no doubt that they are very important for some employers, especially in the engineering sector. The occupations particularly affected are skilled manual occupations, draughtsmen, computer operators and electrical engineers.

A number of studies have asked those involved why there are skill shortages.[4] The DE/MSC quarterly survey[5] asks local employment offices, some studies ask employers while yet others ask employees. It is obviously difficult to place great reliance on such surveys. For instance, in the case of employers the respondents are likely to be those experiencing difficulty, whilst it is hard to be confident that respondents' opinions as to the most important causes correspond with the reality. Indeed there are those who believe that it is impossible to rank the factors responsible for skill shortages. Nevertheless it is useful to report some of the results.

The most recent DE/MSC surveys indicate that general shortages in the locality for a particular occupation are the major reason for vacancies in any establishment remaining unfilled. Difficulties over housing provision are frequently reported as an important contributory factor. Pay, employers' selective requirements and non-acceptability of skill-centre trainees are also mentioned.

A NEDO (1978) study, sampling workers who left their jobs in 1978, found that poor prospects for advancement were mentioned by 46 per cent of those interviewed, whilst 30 per cent mentioned low pay. Pay figured as a much less important factor in an earlier study concerned with workers who left their jobs in 1976 and 1977. Three skill shortage studies undertaken at the end of 1978 in Reading, Portsmouth and the Central Region of Scotland (the first two concentrating on engineering) found that pay was not generally regarded as a major factor in causing skill shortages. Nor did employers feel that pay provided the most likely *solution* to the problem. More reliance was placed on increased internal flexibility together with the introduction of new technology to obviate labour shortages. Studies for the MSC (1976, 1977, 1978) found that an increase in overtime provided an excellent short-term solution, and that in the longer term shortages could be eased by more training, by the use of part-time workers or by the use of labour-saving equipment.

Thus work on the recent skill shortages indicates that there are many factors other than pay regarded as being responsible, and, more revealing, that employers place faith in many measures other than pay to remedy the shortages. Beyond this very little information exists on the relationship between occupational mobility and pay. In the same way, we know little about the impact of pay on educational decisions and occupational choice before entry into the labour market.[6]

In the foregoing we are not arguing that pay is unimportant in allocating labour. What we are arguing is that there are alternative adjustment mechanisms, and that the short- and long-run effects of any given change in relative pay are vastly uncertain. To the extent that incomes policy has altered differentials or relativities, we should not be surprised if this fails, particularly in the short run, to be reflected in general shortages of particular types of labour. Rather, we should be looking for increased turnover rates and for recruitment problems in specific firms.

Pay and comparability
Leaving aside the allocative function of relative pay, we need to

consider a rather different point. Many relativities and differentials tend to be maintained by convention as expressed through collective bargaining or by official conciliation and arbitration. Disruption of them might cause severe industrial relations difficulties.

The sorts of comparisons made by workers and their representatives may change from time to time. For example, Brown and Sisson (1975), studying engineering workers in Coventry and print workers in Fleet Street, found that in the engineering industry the period 1964–71 saw forces external to the plant assume increasing importance, only for internal forces to reassert themselves after 1971. By contrast, in Fleet Street it was forces external to the plant which were predominant from 1961 to 1964, with internal forces taking over from 1964 to 1970. Brown and Sisson try to link such developments with changes in the bargaining structure, but most importantly for our purposes, they find that since

> it is likely that it is... common for workforces to retain their previous reference groups in addition to any fresh groups gained; ... effective comparisons are to some extent cumulative.

In a 1975 survey, PEP (Daniel, 1975) found that people tended to evaluate their position largely against that of members of their own social group, and that, as far as comparisons could be made, this had changed little since Runciman's (1966) famous survey of 1962. After a further survey of management and union negotiators (Daniel, 1976a) PEP reported that the latter's attitudes were very similar to those of the population as a whole. Table 4.1 summarises the main considerations in the minds of management and union when preparing for wage negotiations. It records the percentage of respondents spontaneously mentioning the various factors listed.

Table 4.1 Management and union considerations in preparing for negotiations

	Management %	Union %
Cost of living	36	75
Comparability	51	51
Firm's/establishment's ability to pay	61	15
Changes to the system of pay	30	41
Others	39	44

Source: Daniel (1976b), p. 23.

From this we can see that comparability was an important

consideration for management and unionists alike. In Table 4.2 we record the groups mentioned by each party as those whose earnings had been taken into account in preparing for negotiations.

Table 4.2 Comparison groups in negotiations

	Management %	*Union* %
Local groups of workers	51	41
Groups of workers in the same establishment	22	22
Groups in the same industry	14	16
Groups employed by the same company in different establishments	6	10
Other groups	8	10

Source: Daniel (1976b), p. 24.

The similarity of ranking by employers and managers is particularly noteworthy. Both sides regard local comparisons as easily the most significant, and second in importance for both were comparisons with different occupational groups at the same plant.

There is a further important consideration concerning comparability. That is the extent to which people are concerned with absolute or with percentage differentials. The evidence of both PEP and of Hilde Behrend (1973) indicates that it is the former which are regarded as important. This seems to be an odd finding. If considerations of equity are behind concern for comparability, then it seems obvious that workers would be concerned with *relative* differentials. Otherwise individuals would regard a one-pound difference when earnings are £2 and £1 as being as equitable as when earnings are £1,000,001 and £1,000,000. In their responses to questionnaires individuals may well convert (consciously or unconsciously) proportionate differences into absolute ones at current rates of pay.[7]

More generally, the evidence confirms that comparability has to be an important consideration in the design of a policy, and further that many different types of comparisons are commonly made. In particular any policy which disturbs local relativities or differentials within the plant is likely to run into difficulties.

3   The impact of incomes policy on relative pay

Commentators have concentrated on the post-1970 experience when exploring this question. To a large extent this is for want of adequate data before the annual publication of the *New Earnings Survey* from 1970. A further consideration, however, has been that whereas some of the post-1970 policies incorporated a flat rate element, the 1964–70 policies were couched in terms of percentage limits. A commonly applied percentage increase will not alter percentage differentials, but the matter is more complicated than that. Such a policy might prevent changes in differentials which would have taken place in unconstrained circumstances. Accidents of the relative timing of settlements during the freeze and period of severe restraint did cause particular anomalies, whilst the ability to gain exceptional treatment varied from group to group. Conversely the fact that limits were applied to groups rather than to individuals in Stages II and III of the Conservative policy and from August 1977 of the Labour policy imparted an extra element of flexibility. Though such group limits were not an *explicit* feature of the 1964–70 period, the NBPI did appear to encourage them,[8] thus giving scope for changes in differentials not at first obvious in the formal statements of the norms. In other words, it is not as clear as at first it seems that commentators are right to concentrate their attention on the post-1970 period.

The aggregate econometric studies (Henry and Ormerod, 1978) imply that incomes policy has had relatively little long-run success in holding down absolute pay levels below what they would otherwise have been. Such studies are the subject of Chapter 2 in this book, and so here we shall content ourselves with the observation that such studies can be regarded as at best inconclusive, and at worst as tilting at windmills. Their results are only as good as the models of inflation they employ; and there is still substantial disagreement in this field. Bearing this very severe qualification in mind, this writer would tentatively conclude that in certain periods, for a short time, policy has acted to hold down aggregate earnings increases below what they would otherwise have been. It is also clear that there is a rebound effect, but there is no reliable evidence to indicate that it is more than 100 per cent. In other words, at worst incomes policies have at certain periods played what might be regarded as the useful role of altering the timing of earnings increases. Even if aggregate earnings inflation was not much altered, this, of course, is not to say that there have been no distributional implications, and it is to these that we now turn.

Tables 4.3 and 4.4 examine changes in the overall distribution of male and female earnings respectively. Among manual men there was very little change over the 1970–9 period as a whole. The lowest decile and lower quartile moved slightly closer towards the median as did the upper quartile. The highest decile moved further away. Both because we do not know what other influences were at work and also because the *NES* figures are for April each year, it is difficult to infer much about the influence of incomes policy. The biggest improvement in the relative position of the lowest decile and lower quartile came between April 1973 and April 1974, this together with further improvement in the following year perhaps being attributable to threshold payments (see Appendix for details of how these operated). From April 1977 the

Table 4.3 Quantiles of the earnings distribution as a percentage of the corresponding median, 1970–9 (males)

	Lowest decile	Lower quartile	Upper quartile	Highest decile
Manual men				
1970	67·3	81·1	122·3	147·2
1971	68·2	81·8	122·1	146·5
1972	67·6	81·3	122·3	146·6
1973	67·3	81·4	121·6	145·3
1974	68·6	82·2	121·0	144·1
1975	69·2	82·8	121·3	144·4
1976	70·2	83·4	120·8	144·9
1977	70·6	83·1	120·3	144·4
1978	69·4	82·4	121·2	146·0
1979	68·3	81·7	122·2	148·5
Non-manual men				
1970	61·8	77·1	130·8	175·1
1971	61·7	76·5	131·2	174·4
1972	61·7	76·8	131·3	173·7
1973	61·6	76·7	130·9	172·7
1974	62·9	77·6	130·2	171·6
1975	62·6	77·5	129·6	166·7
1976	62·5	77·8	130·5	167·5
1977	63·6	78·4	128·8	164·5
1978	62·9	78·4	126·9	163·9
1979	63·4	79·0	127·3	163·0
All men				
1970	65·4	79·7	126·7	160·6
1971	66·1	80·3	126·5	160·7
1972	65·5	79·7	126·4	160·9
1973	65·6	79·9	125·3	158·5
1974	66·8	80·7	124·6	157·0
1975	67·0	81·0	125·3	157·6
1976	67·6	81·3	125·6	159·5
1977	68·1	81·4	125·6	157·7
1978	66·8	80·6	125·1	157·9
1979	66·0	80·3	125·1	156·9

Source: Figures taken from Table 15, *New Earnings Survey 1979*. They refer to the gross weekly earnings of those whose pay was not affected by absence.

Table 4.4 Quantiles of the earnings distribution as a percentage of the corresponding median, 1970 – 9 (females)

	Lowest decile	Lower quartile	Upper quartile	Highest decile
Manual women				
1970	69·0	83·0	120·1	144·8
1971	70·2	83·6	120·4	143·0
1972	68·9	82·5	121·6	145·9
1973	69·2	82·8	121·4	144·4
1974	69·1	83·0	119·8	143·4
1975	68·4	83·3	119·6	141·4
1976	67·8	82·6	119·6	140·6
1977	70·3	83·3	118·3	137·8
1978	70·8	83·2	119·6	140·9
1979	70·4	82·8	119·5	140·6
Non-manual women				
1970	64·2	78·3	129·4	173·7
1971	65·0	78·8	128·2	169·9
1972	64·0	78·2	129·1	170·9
1973	65·6	79·2	129·0	169·5
1974	66·5	79·4	127·9	162·0
1975	66·5	80·3	127·2	171·5
1976	65·1	79·9	128·6	172·9
1977	68·1	81·7	126·8	165·6
1978	68·8	81·9	127·4	164·7
1979	69·5	81·8	126·4	160·7
All women				
1970	66·4	79·8	129·3	170·4
1971	66·6	80·2	127·3	165·8
1972	65·6	79·6	128·6	167·1
1973	67·4	80·7	127·6	164·7
1974	67·7	81·0	126·4	159·1
1975	67·4	81·5	125·2	164·5
1976	66·1	80·2	125·9	165·9
1977	68·6	82·1	124·7	162·1
1978	69·1	82·2	125·3	161·4
1979	69·4	82·1	124·7	158·6

Source: As for Table 4.3.

relative position of these two groups worsened, reflecting the weakening hold of incomes policy. The deterioration in the relative position of the highest decile of manual workers between 1972 and 1974 might reflect the penalties against the higher-paid which were part of Heath's policy. Perhaps the most notable change over the period as a whole was the decline in the relative position of the top decile of non-manual men. The most dramatic movement in any single year was between April 1974 and April 1975. Part of this may be the result of settlements made during the last months of Stage III of Heath's policy, which continued after he left office until July 1974. Part may also be the result of the lingering impact of threshold arrangements.[9] But figures at this end of the earnings scale may be misleading in so far as the importance of non-pay and fringe benefits in the total reward package has increased during the 1970s.

Table 4.5 Quantiles of the earnings distribution as a percentage of the corresponding median; private sector, 1971 – 9 (males)

	Lowest decile	Lower quartile	Upper quartile	Highest decile
Manual men				
1971	67·5	81·5	122·3	146·8
1972	66·9	81·0	122·5	147·0
1973	67·5	81·7	121·8	146·1
1974	68·4	82·3	120·7	144·0
1975	68·9	82·8	120·6	143·6
1976	69·4	83·0	120·9	144·9
1977	69·9	82·9	120·4	144·5
1978	68·6	82·2	121·0	145·8
1979	67·9	81·5	122·0	148·5
Non-manual men				
1971	62·0	76·8	132·7	180·4
1972	62·2	77·3	132·5	180·0
1973	61·7	77·1	132·3	180·2
1974	62·7	77·6	130·0	175·6
1975	63·0	78·2	129·9	174·5
1976	62·4	78·1	130·4	174·0
1977	63·6	78·8	130·2	174·1
1978	62·0	78·1	131·2	173·9
1979	62·1	78·5	130·8	171·6
Total				
1971	66·0	80·2	125·8	159·3
1972	65·3	79·8	125·5	159·3
1973	65·9	80·2	124·7	157·8
1974	66·8	81·0	123·8	155·2
1975	67·1	81·5	124·3	156·4
1976	67·2	81·3	124·4	157·2
1977	67·7	81·4	124·0	157·0
1978	66·3	80·7	124·6	159·1
1979	65·6	80·5	125·7	159·9

Source: For 1971 – 7, Department of Employment, 'Earnings of employees in the private and public sectors', *Gazette*, October 1977; for 1978 – 9, Department of Employment estimates.

The picture for women is similarly inconclusive. For the lower reaches of both the manual and non-manual labour force the biggest improvement came later than for men — between April 1976 and April 1977. For the upper quartiles and for the top decile of non-manuals there were two particularly bad years, 1973–4 and 1976–7; for the top decile much the largest fall came in 1976–7. As with men, over the period as a whole there was a particularly marked deterioration in the position of the top decile of non-manuals. But

Table 4.6 Quantiles of the earnings distribution as a percentage of the corresponding median, private sector, 1971 – 9 (females)

	Lowest decile	Lower quartile	Upper quartile	Highest decile
Manual women				
1971	69·6	83·5	119·9	141·7
1972	68·1	82·5	121·8	145·7
1973	67·9	82·3	120·9	143·9
1974	68·6	82·8	119·9	143·5
1975	67·7	82·2	118·7	139·8
1976	66·7	81·7	120·2	140·9
1977	68·5	82·8	118·1	137·6
1978	69·3	82·6	120·1	142·1
1979	69·3	82·5	120·2	140·6
Non-manual women				
1971	68·3	81·5	125·3	156·3
1972	68·8	82·6	125·6	157·0
1973	70·0	82·3	124·9	156·1
1974	70·8	82·8	124·2	153·8
1975	71·0	83·0	123·5	151·0
1976	70·3	82·3	123·8	151·5
1977	72·4	83·9	121·7	150·2
1978	71·1	83·2	124·4	154·1
1979	71·5	83·0	123·9	152·7
Total				
1971	68·8	82·5	123·0	152·0
1972	68·4	82·7	123·7	152·7
1973	69·1	82·4	123·0	150·7
1974	70·0	82·9	122·5	150·2
1975	69·6	82·9	121·3	146·3
1976	69·0	82·1	122·2	147·2
1977	71·3	83·6	120·2	145·0
1978	70·5	83·0	122·5	149·2
1979	70·8	83·0	122·3	148·6

Source: As for Table 4.5.

there was a more marked improvement in the position of the lowest decile of that group.

It may be objected that the above exercise includes the impact of developments in the public sector. In Tables 4.5 and 4.6, therefore, we present figures for just the private sector. The picture for the private sector is similar to that for the economy as a whole. There are, however, a few noteworthy differences. For both non-manual men and women, 1973–4 saw a marked deterioration in the position of the

Table 4.7 Ratios of female to male earnings

	Lowest decile	Lower quartile	Median	Upper quartile	Highest decile
Manual workers					
1970	51·2	51·0	50·0	49·2	49·1
1971	53·1	53·0	52·0	51·3	50·7
1972	53·3	52·9	52·4	52·0	52·1
1973	53·3	52·7	51·6	51·5	51·3
1974	54·7	54·7	54·3	53·8	53·9
1975	57·6	58·5	58·3	57·5	57·0
1976	59·6	61·2	61·8	61·1	59·8
1977	62·2	62·6	62·5	61·3	59·6
1978	63·1	62·6	62·0	61·2	59·8
1979	62·2	61·2	60·4	59·1	57·1
Non-manual workers					
1970	52·6	51·2	50·6	50·1	50·2
1971	55·2	54·0	52·3	51·2	51·0
1972	54·4	53·4	52·2	51·5	50·0
1973	55·3	53·8	52·1	51·3	51·1
1974	57·0	55·1	53·8	52·9	50·9
1975	61·8	60·1	58·1	57·0	59·7
1976	62·3	61·4	59·8	59·0	61·8
1977	65·0	63·3	60·7	59·8	61·1
1978	64·3	61·4	58·7	58·5	59·0
1979	64·4	60·8	58·7	58·3	57·9
All workers					
1970	54·5	53·5	53·7	54·5	56·8
1971	55·8	55·4	55·7	55·8	57·3
1972	55·7	55·6	55·7	56·6	57·9
1973	56·0	55·0	54·4	55·5	56·5
1974	57·3	56·5	56·4	57·3	57·3
1975	61·3	61·4	61·0	60·9	63·7
1976	62·9	63·6	64·4	64·5	67·0
1977	65·3	65·5	64·9	64·4	66·8
1978	65·3	64·5	63·2	63·4	64·5
1979	65·6	63·5	62·2	62·0	62·9

Source: *New Earnings Survey 1979*, Table 15.

top decile, whilst higher-paid women lost out more appreciably in 1974–5 than did their counterparts in the public sector.

Movements in the overall dispersion can occur in three separate ways. First, differentials between the groups which make up the population to be studied can change. Secondly, dispersion within some or all of the groups may change. Thirdly, the relative weightings of the groups may alter. A study of the overall dispersion may, therefore, miss offsetting developments at the less aggregate level. First, we turn to an examination of differentials.

The most striking change in the 1970s has been in the relationship

Table 4.8 Ratios of female to male earnings – private sector

	Lowest decile	Lower quartile	Median	Upper quartile	Highest decile
Manual workers					
1971	52·9	52·4	51·5	50·1	49·3
1972	52·4	52·3	51·4	51·0	51·0
1973	51·4	51·3	51·2	50·7	50·4
1974	53·1	53·3	53·1	52·7	52·9
1975	56·8	57·1	57·6	56·8	56·0
1976	58·5	59·9	60·8	60·5	59·2
1977	60·7	61·9	61·9	60·7	59·0
1978	62·0	61·7	61·4	60·9	59·8
1979	61·5	61·0	60·3	59·4	57·2
Non-manual workers					
1971	51·9	50·0	47·0	44·6	40·9
1972	51·7	49·7	46·5	44·3	40·6
1973	53·5	50·3	47·1	44·4	40·7
1974	55·4	52·3	49·2	46·9	43·1
1975	59·2	55·7	52·6	49·9	45·4
1976	60·4	56·6	53·7	51·1	46·8
1977	62·7	58·5	55·2	51·5	47·5
1978	61·6	57·2	53·4	50·9	47·6
1979	61·5	56·5	53·4	50·5	47·5
Total					
1971	53·3	52·5	51·2	50·0	48·7
1972	53·2	52·7	50·8	50·0	48·7
1973	53·2	51·8	50·7	49·9	48·3
1974	55·0	53·8	52·6	52·0	50·7
1975	58·5	57·5	56·5	55·0	52·8
1976	60·1	59·1	58·4	57·4	54·7
1977	62·8	61·3	59·7	58·0	55·2
1978	62·5	60·6	58·9	57·9	55·2
1979	62·9	60·0	58·2	56·7	54·2

Source: As for Table 4.5.

between male and female earnings. Table 4.7 gives details for the whole economy, and Table 4.8 just for the private sector. Comparisons are made at various quantiles of the distributions. In each case female earnings are expressed as a percentage of male earnings. For example, the first figure (52·6) in that section of Table 4.7 referring to non-manual workers indicates that in 1970 those at the lowest decile on the distribution of female manual earnings earned 52·6 per cent of those at the lowest decile on the male manual distribution.

For manual workers there was some closing of the gap between 1970 and 1971, but the most sustained narrowing was between 1973 and 1976. This continued for another year at the median and below, but by 1977 the narrowing had ceased, and by 1979 there had been some slight widening. A similar pattern emerges for non-manual workers, except that widening started somewhat earlier. For both manual and non-manual groups the most substantial compression took place between April 1974 and April 1975.

Stages II and III of the Conservatives' policy exempted from the limits progress towards equal pay under the Equal Pay Act of 1970. But it would be perverse to describe this as an 'effect' of incomes policy. Independent of this provision, it is possible that incomes policy had some impact – for example in 1974–5 the threshold payments, as well as a last-minute rush to meet the provisions of the Equal Pay Act, which was meant to be fully in force by the end of 1975. But it is impossible to disentangle the effects of incomes policy on the one hand, and of Equal Pay and of trade union bargaining behaviour under inflation on the other. Most commentators assign the major role to the equal pay legislation.[10] This made it illegal for an employer to pay different rates to men and women doing the same job. Two considerations throw doubt on its efficacy. First, occupational segregation is an important source of earnings disadvantage for women; and it is generally agreed that, whatever its long-term role, equal opportunities legislation, which also came fully into force at the end of 1975, could have done very little by this stage to significantly alter such segregation. Secondly, the Act has many exceptions. It applies only to those women covered by collective agreements and to males and females 'employed by the same employer or associated employer at the same establishment or establishments at which common terms and conditions of employment are observed either generally or for employees of the relevant classes' (Chiplin and Sloane, 1976, p. 93); yet women appear to be concentrated in low-paying firms.

It might then be that but for the presence of incomes policy and the exceptional treatment of women, the Equal Pay Act would not have had such a great impact. A further possibility remains, and that concerns the role of trade union bargaining priorities in an era of high inflation, about which we shall have more to say later.

An examination of differentials between occupations is rendered difficult by the lack of readily accessible time-series data. Even the *New Earnings Survey*, which anyway provides an annual run only from 1970, has a discontinuity in 1973, caused by a change in occupational classification. Largely for this reason attention has been concentrated on the results of the Department of Employment June occupational survey.[11] This is limited to manual workers and to three sectors – engineering, shipbuilding and ship-repairing, and chemicals. Details are given in Table 4.9. The table gives the ratio of the hourly earnings of skilled workers to the earnings of labourers. Earnings exclude overtime premia, and the results are presented separately for timeworkers and payment-by-results workers.

In engineering, differentials for timeworkers were fairly stable through the 1960s. From 1971 there was some compression. The years 1971–2, and 1972–3 saw substantial narrowing, with even more taking place in 1974–5 and 1975–6. The first of these four periods was not one of incomes policy. The second included Heath's 'freeze' and Stage II, whilst 1975–6 coincides largely with the year of the £6 limit.

Table 4.9 Skill differentials in three industries

| | Timeworkers | | | Payment-by-results workers | | |
	Engineering	Ship-building	Chemicals	Engineering	Ship-building	Chemicals
1963	143	134	114	146	138	111
1964	144	138	113	148	137	114
1965	143	140	114	148	140	109
1966	145	125	114	150	143	107
1967	145	144	111	152	146	109
1968	144	137	113	150	146	108
1969	144	132	110	151	148	110
1970	144	126	109	148	147	111
1971	144	133	109	149	148	107
1972	141	131	107	148	142	108
1973	138	128	108	143	136	107
1974	137	129	106	138	134	108
1975	132	122	104	132	131	108
1976	128	119	105	131	130	108
1977	128	124	105	133	125	109
1978	129	113	105	133	125	109
1979	130	125	107	131	118	107

Source: see text.

The remaining period, 1974–5, coincides with the Social Contract Mark I, a period of no effective restraint, though threshold payments continued to be paid. None of the incomes policies of the 1960s appear to have had any impact. This reflects three factors – they were generally expressed in percentage form; they usually operated on rates rather than on earnings; particularly in the latter part of the 1960s they were not rigorously applied or observed. Nor at the end of our period did incomes policy prevent differentials from stabilising or even widening. The same general conclusions hold for pieceworkers, whose differentials widened somewhat until 1967, fell back slightly until 1972, and then during the next three years narrowed appreciably, only to stabilise at the end of the period.

The skill differential for timeworkers in chemicals declined pretty steadily (though not by a large amount) from 1968 until 1975, after which it stabilised. Again it is difficult to pick out any obvious connection with incomes policies. Indeed for pieceworkers in chemicals it is hard to discern any real fall in the skill differential at all.

The skill differential in shipbuilding was much more volatile than in the other two industries. Over the period 1963–79 as a whole, it fell substantially for both timeworkers and pieceworkers. Though there were sizeable falls between 1967 and 1970 and again between 1974 and 1976, there is no obvious consistent relationship with incomes policy.

To sum up, there was indeed a fall in the skill differential during the 1970s. This narrowing was not as sharp as that experienced during the two World Wars. What it did do was to undo the widening which had taken place in the 1950s and early 1960s. Some of the narrowing took place during periods of incomes policy, and, it is not unreasonable to believe, somtimes as a direct result of the policy. However the timing is such as to suggest that other forces were at work. Given that, there is some suspicion that even during periods when incomes policy appeared to be exercising an influence these other forces were prime causal factors.

A caveat has to be entered here. The skilled category is composed of an aggregate of different occupations. At any one time there are great differences in the earnings of these occupations as well as differences in the course of their earnings over time. A variety of 'weighting' changes, therefore, may effect movements of the skill differential. These include changes in occupational composition, in the relative numbers of timeworkers and payments-by-results workers, and in the relative importance of small and large firms. To give two examples. In small engineering firms (with 25–99 employees) fitters accounted for 11·7 per cent of all timeworkers in 1970, buy by 1978 they accounted for 17 per cent. In all three industries small firms gained a greater weighting in the survey over the decade, and especially from 1975. In particular the apparent widening of the skill differential during the later part of our period may well reflect a shift towards the higher-paying occupations within the skilled group. The greater representation of smaller firms, where skill differentials are generally lower, may have caused an understatement of the improvement in the position of the unskilled.

Elliott and Fallick (1979) constructed series which allowed them to compare the earnings of manual and non-manual workers over the period 1951–75. Table 4.10 gives details. As we can see from column 3 of the table the relationship was very much the same in 1975 as it had been in 1950, but this masks some quite large changes which occurred during the intervening years. From 1955 to 1963 there was an uninterrupted improvement in the position of salaried workers. The years

Table 4.10 Earnings of manual and non-manual workers

	(1) Manual workers' earnings (1950 = 100)	(2) Non-manual workers (1950 = 100)	(3) (2)/(1) · 100
1950	100·0	100·0	100·0
1951	110·1	112·3	102·0
1952	118·9	119·7	100·7
1953	126·6	127·3	100·6
1954	135·6	134·1	98·9
1955	148·7	144·2	97·0
1956	159·8	158·7	99·3
1957	166·4	167·3	100·5
1958	172·3	183·9	106·7
1959	180·1	200·6	111·4
1960	193·3	220·3	114·0
1961	205·2	234·6	114·3
1962	212·6	246·3	115·8
1963	222·0	257·2	115·9
1964	241·0	269·8	112·0
1965	259·6	285·4	109·9
1966	273·6	300·8	109·9
1967	282·9	319·8	113·0
1968	305·3	335·4	109·9
1969	328·8	355·2	108·0
1970	371·5	395·0	106·3
1971	409·8	440·8	108·0
1972	474·5	484·9	102·2
1973	541·9	528·5	97·5
1974	643·8	616·8	95·8
1975	788·7	793·8	100·7

Source: Elliott and Fallick (1979).

after 1963 saw a gradual, but by no means smooth decline; though the impact of this was only to unwind the earlier improvements. Some of these changes may well have reflected the influence of incomes policies. To give some examples. The temporary improvement in the position of salaried workers in 1967 might have reflected the fact that incremental salary systems protected them from the rigours of the period of severe restraint in the first half of that year. Equally the deterioration of the following two or three years might have been a consequence of their inability to benefit from the sort of productivity deals which were so common for manual workers.

Given, however, the state of knowledge about the general determinants of differentials of this sort and given the importance of fringe benefits at the top end of the salaried range, it is impossible to venture beyond weak conclusions such as these.

The Royal Commission on Income Distribution and Wealth (1979, especially chapter 6) came to similar conclusions about differentials between the following occupational classes: higher professional; lower professional; managers and administrators; clerks, foremen; skilled manual; unskilled manual. Movements of such differentials led to a narrowing of the overall dispersion of earnings in the 1970s. A tendency towards a reduction in the dispersion of earnings within many occupations contributed further to this. But an offsettting factor was a change in occupational composition away from the manual classes towards the higher paid professional classes.

The general picture, then, is one of relatively slow change, with incomes policy playing only a shadowy role. Certainly the sharp reduction of differentials in engineering was the exception rather than the rule.

A problem with work of this kind is that it deals with highly aggregate data. A closer study of the impact of incomes policy on local labour markets or even on the structure of earnings within the plant is needed. William Brown's work (1976 and 1979) represents one of the few attempts at such a study. He was concerned with forty engineering factories in the West Midlands, employing some 80,000 people. He analysed the earnings of a number of occupational groups: machinists, electricians, storekeepers, and labourers among manual men; machinists/assemblers among manual women; Grade D male clerks, female secretaries and female Grade B clerks. Brown analysed hourly or weekly earnings excluding overtime. During Stage I of the Conservatives' policy the standstill was observed fairly closely. The three groups who gained the most were male and female machinists (2.29 per cent and 3.26 per cent respectively) and female clerks (2.14 per cent). High proportions of the first two groups were on payment-by-results schemes, whilst the third group benefited from age-related incremental pay scales. Under Stage II the male grades experienced overall pay increases that were very close to the norm. Between one third and one quarter of the firms exceeded the norm by over 2 per cent. More or less the same proportion undershot it by over 2 per cent. This indicates that the norm did not universally become a minimum entitlement. Women did far better than men, largely because of movement towards equal pay, which was exempt from the limit. They also did far better in Stage III, when again the men by and large kept close to the policy norm. During the Social Contract Mark 1, by contrast, all occupational groups received very substantial increases, exceeding the 20 per cent maximum of the Social Contract. The return to a better defined policy in August 1975 (the £6 limit followed in August 1976 by the 5 per cent policy) saw a return to conformity. Clerical workers exhibited a very close conformity in both phases. With regard to manual workers, a very substantial proportion of plants (a quarter of them for all but storekeepers) settled significantly below the limit, which again, therefore, was not treated as a minimum entitlement. Depending on the occupational group, between 26 per cent and 42 per cent of plants had earnings increases above the 15p limit. But the overall average exceeded it by only 2p. In the succeeding phase of policy a smaller proportion of firms undershot, and a higher proportion overshot the limit. Nevertheless the overall earnings increase probably exceeded it by less than 1 per cent.

A picture emerges, therefore, of general conformity. Yet because of the design of the policy in terms of group limits, there was scope for flexibility in the way increases were distributed within each factory. A qualification needs to be entered here. Brown's analysis concerns earnings. It could be that the norm was added to everyone's pay as an entitlement; but that earnings varied around the norm as a result of variations in overtime or incentive payments.

Brown analyses the movement of skill differentials from October 1972. Over the period as a whole there was a compression. There was relatively little change during the first two stages of Tory policy and even through to the fall of the government in February 1974. This was followed by a very sharp compression from early 1974 until the middle of 1975. Wilson's Phases One and Two were strongly redistributive in intent. During Phase One the compression of differentials continued, but during Phase Two there was some widening of differentials.

Brown concludes from this that incomes policy did not have a great impact on skill differentials in the firms he studied. The major year of narrowing was the relatively free bargaining period of the first version of the Social Contract (August 1974 – July 1975). Indeed during Phases One and Two (August 1975 – July 1977) bargainers seem to have used what flexibility they had to partially restore differentials. This was in spite of this being a policy couched nominally in terms of individual limits. Obviously the policy was not very closely adhered to by the firms involved, though the excess was not large and the limits were not generally regarded as minimum entitlements.

Brown is inclined, therefore, to discount the importance of incomes policy as an explanation for the squeezing of differentials. To some extent, he overstates his case since during the year of substantial narrowing the hangover of the Conservatives' Stage III, threshold payments, were an important contributory factor. Nevertheless the relative lack of impact remains startling.

Brown also considered the effect of incomes policy on inter-factory differentials of workers of the same skill or occupation. He found that the policy did not radically alter the ranking of firms, though under Stage III they were forced closer towards paying alike. To some degree this process was reversed under the Social Contract Mark 1, only for the narrowing to resume as a stricter policy came in to force from the summer of 1975.

If the timing of incomes policy makes it unlikely that it is the major influence on the narrowing of skill differentials, then it is incumbent upon us to suggest other possible reasons. One common explanation is the so-called Reder hypothesis. This starts from the premise that, when faced with a general shortage of labour, employers may prefer to use the internal rather than external labour market as a means of adjustment. To increase the number of skilled employees, an employer promotes from within by training his less skilled men and perhaps simultaneously relaxes skill standards or alters production techniques. Similarly he upgrades workers into the semi-skilled ranks, so that he is left with a shortage at the unskilled end of the spectrum. To fill this grade he has to turn to the external market, and if there is enough excess demand for labour to exhaust the reserve of unskilled manpower, then unskilled rates will be bid up, thus reducing the skill differential. This explanation fits well to the periods of significant narrowing during the two World Wars. Quite obviously it does not fit the 1970s, a period of general excess supply of labour.

An alternative theory, put forward by Brown, involves trade union bargaining behaviour under inflation. The unusually high inflation rates of the 1970s had two effects on attitudes — 'the charity effect' and 'the illusion effect'. The first of these, it is contended, meant that a bargainer felt that, since everyone in his bargaining group — well-paid and poorly-paid alike — was suffering equally from rising prices, everyone should be compensated equally. There was thus a natural preference for flat rate deals. At the same time, the highly-paid, unused to thinking in terms of the large money amounts involved, were slow to realise that such deals were eroding their differential. Proponents of this view point to the ending (or even reversal) of the narrowing at a time when price inflation was moderating as an indication that the charity effect was evaporating and that time had corrected illusions. Though the approach is an attractive one, it remains untested (and possibly untestable) in any formal sense. Recently Elliott (1980) has persuasively suggested that the preference for flat-rate increases reflects the majority power of unskilled workers in certain large unions such as the AUEW. He further argues that there is a limit to which market forces can be overridden in this way, and that therefore one might expect a widening of the skill differential.

PEP conducted a study (Daniel, 1976) of a sample of manufacturing establishments in the late autumn of 1975. In this they interviewed managers, leaders of management negotiating teams, and leaders of union negotiating teams. Among the questions asked were some concerning the impact of the £6 pay limit. The sorts of problems which the PEP investigators expected to uncover were the following: the effect of the limit on internal payment systems; tailoring it to fit in with existing incentive schemes and with systems for determining the hierarchy and size of differentials within enterprises.

The general finding was that the policy was causing surprisingly few problems. The large majority of increases granted were within the limit, and many were less. Employers reported little difficulty in gaining acceptance of increases by either manual or non-manual workers. A quarter of the establishments studied had already concluded their negotiations. In these establishments 38 per cent of employers reported that no problems had been caused. The largest single difficulty mentioned by employers were the consequences for differentials. Union negotiators were rather less happy – only about half professed themselves to be satisfied with increases achieved. This was a much less favourable response than that to the increases received in the previous round. The authors stressed, however, that the incidence of industrial action relating to negotiations about increases under the policy was much less frequent than that relating to the previous round of bargaining.

Less than half of the union negotiators felt that the policy would benefit their own members but nearly three-quarters felt it would benefit the national economy. In the same way the majority of managers felt that what was good for the country was not necessarily good for their company. With regard to incomes policy generally, 32 per cent of union negotiators were opposed to it in principle, 44 per cent were prepared to accept it as a short-term measure, whilst 21 per cent would accept it as a permanent item in the management of our economy. This figure of 21 per cent compares to 47 per cent of management negotiators.

4   Non-pay influences of incomes policy

There are other directions in which incomes policy may have had an influence. It may be that the inability of employers to exercise maximum flexibility in their wage negotiations or that concern over comparability might increase industrial unrest. To test precisely for the relationship between incomes policy and strike activity requires the production of a sound theoretical econometric model. No such model exists, and therefore one has to interpret with caution the conclusions of the various writers on this subject.[12] Using simple on-off dummies, Pencavel (1970) found some evidence that incomes policy reduced stoppage frequency, whereas Hunter (1973) and Shorey (1977) found no significant effects. Hunter tried to distinguish between 'hard' and 'soft' policies, but again without finding any significant result. Davies, covering a later period (1966–75) than these other three authors[13] and using 'hard' and 'soft' dummies, found that incomes policy reduced strikes over pay issues, but that there was an upsurge of industrial action once a policy was removed. There was also, he argued, an increase in stoppages over non-pay issues, particularly during the hard phases of policy.

Indeed it is impossible to generalise. Different policies will have different effects. This depends not only on the size of the limit and on the rigour with which it is enforced, but also on the degree of 'acceptability' of the policy. Thus the period of the £6 limit and the early months of the succeeding phase of policy saw an unusually low frequency of stoppages and relatively few working days lost because of industrial disputes. By contrast Heath's attempts at income restraint probably caused there to be more stoppages than there would otherwise have been.

It is possible that incomes policy causes people to act as individuals rather than collectively. It might thus increase absenteeism or even increase the quit rate, in so far as a worker might feel that the only way to achieve a substantial increase in his pay is to find a new job. Unfortunately evidence on such matters is sadly lacking. But again there is little reason to expect consistency of effect from policy to policy.

More generally policy might well influence trends of thinking in industrial relations. Each era has its fashions, and in the context of incomes policy it is fair to say that the 1960s were the age of productivity bargaining, whilst the 1970s were more the era of comparability, and to a lesser extent during the early 1970s of maintenance of the real wage. The concern of incomes policies with such things is bound to some degree to be a reflection of the general concerns of the time. But it is also likely that the stress placed upon them by the policies would itself influence attitudes and behaviour.

The fashion for productivity bargaining had started before the advent of the Labour government in 1964. Productivity bargaining has been defined as 'the negotiation between management and workers' representatives of changes in working practices leading to more efficient working, at the same time as the re-negotiation of levels of earnings to give workers a share of the savings brought about by the change' (Daniel and McIntosh, 1973, p. 3). There seems little doubt that incomes policy increased the incidence of productivity bargaining particularly after 1966. Generally it has been argued that most such bargaining was a sham, simply a device to get round restraint whilst achieving no real gain in efficiency. Daniel and McIntosh (1973) dissent from this view. They studied a sample of 62 of the 3,000 cases on the DEP register.

The NBPI laid down the following guidelines for a productivity agreement:

(i)   it should be shown that workers were making a direct contribution towards increasing productivity by accepting more exacting work or a major change in working practices;
(ii) forecasts of increased productivity should be derived by the application of proper work-standards;
(iii) an accurate calculation of the gains and the costs should normally show that the total cost of output, taking into account the effect on capital, will be reduced;
(iv) the scheme should contain effective controls to ensure that the projected increase in productivity is achieved, and that payment is made only as productivity increases or as changes in working practice take place;
(v)   the undertaking should be ready to show clear benefits to the consumer through a contribution to stable prices;
(vi) an agreement covering part of an undertaking should bear the cost of consequential increases elsewhere in the same undertaking.

Daniel and McIntosh claim that just under half of the agreements they studied 'were substantial agreements conforming to the principles of the policy'. Many of the managers and unionists they interviewed stressed that, leaving aside the specific content of agreements, they had a beneficial effect on labour relations more generally, a boost being given to orderly collective bargaining and joint regulation.

Criticisms can be made of this study. In particular, it might be argued that it relies overmuch on the impressions of the parties to the agreements, and that it was conducted too soon after the event to allow one to be sure that long-term gains had been achieved. Nevertheless Daniel and McIntosh have raised the important possibility that substantial beneficial effects may have stemmed from the 1964–70 incomes policy. In a sense NBPI may have been having the impact of a superior management consultancy firm.

Finally incomes policy may, it has been pointed out, create tendencies towards greater centralisation within unions. This could lead to great strains within some unions, where the decline of multi-employer national bargaining has shifted power towards the plant. This is particularly true of a policy such as the post-1974 one which not only had active TUC co-operation, but which involved some element of bargaining about macroeconomic strategy generally. In such circumstances national officers may find more attractions in the policy than do the rank-and-file. Despite the potential dangers, there is little evidence to suggest that incomes policy has had much long-lasting impact on the changing power structure of unions.

5   Conclusions

The conclusions of this chapter are largely negative. We argued that relative pay sets wide margins within which employers can operate. If, therefore, incomes policy prevents movements in relative pay that would otherwise have taken place, in the short run this is unlikely to cause severe allocative problems. However, firms may be pushed into using non-pay rewards more intensively. This implies cost increases which conventional studies of incomes policy will not pick up. It also implies that searchers will find it harder to acquire information about the relative merits of firms, and thus that the margins within which firms operate might be even wider. There is in fact little evidence to suggest that differentials or relativities were disturbed for anything other than the short run. Whatever problems individual plants faced in maintaining or developing appropriate pay structures, it is hard to believe that incomes policies were anything other than a temporary irritant, though it is in this area that hard information is most difficult to come by.

We showed that concern about comparability is strong, and particularly comparability at the local level. It is possible that because of this incomes policy may have a deleterious effect on the conduct of collective bargaining. Yet we argued that it is difficult to find consistent, long-lasting effects here. In the same way there seem to have been no profound influences on the structure of unions or on the distribution of power within them. Finally, we suggest that there may be positive benefits to be derived from the conduct of a policy, giving as an example the influence of the NBPI on the workings of individual companies.

Notes: Chapter 4

1 Still the best work on internal labour markets in Doeringer and Piore (1971).
2 On this particular aspect, see Thomas and Deaton (1977).
3 For a more detailed analysis, see Mayhew (1977).
4 For a recent survey, see Department of Employment (1979).
5 See Department of Employment (1979) for details of these surveys.
6 As is often the case, better evidence exists for the US than for the UK. For example Gallaway (1971) found a significant positive correlation between relative earnings and net flows of workers between occupations. Interestingly, however, he could not find any relationship between earnings and new entries into occupations. Willis and Rosen (1979) found that expected gains in lifetime earnings influence the decision to attend college, whilst Freeman (1976) showed that worsening prospects for college graduates were to a large extent responsible for a decline in the number of students progressing beyond high school. In Britain there was recently a marked swing to technological subjects in universities and polytechnics in the face of deteriorating labour market prospects for graduates as a group.
7 Of course, as with all such investment decisions, it is absolute differentials that matter for the supply of labour to a particular occupation or firm.
8 See, for example, the NBPI reports on civil engineering, construction and building industries (Reports Nos 91–3), in which the Board recommended comprehensive programmes of reform of pay and occupational structures.
9 Elliott and Shelton (1978) provide some evidence on the impact of settlements on negotiated rates.
10 A thorough discussion of equal pay and equal opportunities legislation is to be found in Chiplin and Sloane (1976).
11 See Dean (1978). Attempts to use the *NES* data include Ashenfelter and Layard (1979) and the Royal Commission on the Distribution of Income and Wealth (1979).
12 For a critique of econometric work on strikes, see Mayhew (1979).
13 Pencavel and Shorey both covered the period 1950–67. Hunter continued a little later (until 1971) thus capturing the strike wave at the end of the 1960s.

References: Chapter 4

Ashenfelter, O., and Layard, R., 'The effects of incomes policy on relative pay', Centre for Labour Economics, LSE, Discussion Paper No. 44 (1979)

Behrend, H., *Incomes Policy, Equity and Pay Increase Differentials* (Edinburgh: Scottish Academic Press, 1973)

Brittan, S., and Lilley, P., *The Delusion of Incomes Policy* (Temple Smith, 1977) Chapter 8

Brown, W., 'Incomes policy and pay differentials', *Oxford Bulletin of Economics and Statistics*, vol. 38, no. 1 (1976), pp. 27–49

Brown, W., 'Engineering Wages and the Social Contract, 1975–7', *Oxford Bulletin of Economics and Statistics*, vol. 41, no. 1 (1979), pp. 51–61

Brown, W., and Sisson, K., 'The use of comparisons in workplace wage determination', *British Journal of Industrial Relations*, vol. XIII, no. 1 (1975), pp. 23–51

Chiplin, B., and Sloane, P., *Discrimination in the Labour Market* (Macmillan, 1976)

Daniel, W. W., 'The PEP Survey on inflation', *PEP Broadsheet* no. 553 (1975)

Daniel, W. W., 'Wage determination in industry', *PEP Broadsheet* no. 563 (1976a)

Daniel, W. W., 'The next stage of incomes policy', *PEP Broadsheet* no. 568 (1976b)

Daniel, W. W., and McIntosh, N., 'Incomes policy and collective bargaining at the workplace', *PEP Broadsheet* no. 541 (1973)

Davies, R. J., 'Economic activity, incomes policy and strikes: a quantitative analysis', *British Journal of Industrial Relations*, vol. XVIII, no. 2 (1979), pp. 205–23

Dean, A., 'Incomes policies and differentials', *National Institute Economic Review*, no. 85 (1978), pp. 40–8

Department of Employment, 'Earnings of employees in the private and public sectors', *Gazette*, vol. 85, no. 12 (1977), pp. 1335–40

Department of Employment, 'Skill shortages in British industry', *Gazette*, vol. 87, no. 5 (1979)

Doeringer, P., and Piore, M., *Internal Labour Markets and Manpower Analysis* (Lexington, Mass.: D. C. Heath, 1971)

Elliott, R. F., 'Union wage policy, inflation and skill differentials' (mimeo, 1980)

Elliott, R. F., and Fallick, J. L., 'Pay differentials in perspective: a note on manual and non-manual pay over the period 1951–75', *Economic Journal*, vol. 89, no. 354 (1979), pp. 377–84

Elliott, R. F., and Shelton, H. C., 'A wage settlements index for the United Kingdom 1950–75', *Oxford Bulletin of Economics and Statistics*, vol. 40, no. 4 (1978), pp. 303–19

Fallick, J. L., 'The growth of top salaries in the post-war period', *Industrial Relations Journal*, vol. 8, no. 3 (1977), pp. 4–13

Freeman, R. B., *The Over-Educated American* (New York: Academic Press, 1976)

Gallaway, L. E., *Manpower Economics* (Homewood, Ill.: Irwin, 1971)

Henry, S. G. B., and Ormerod, P. A., 'Incomes policy and wage inflation: empirical evidence for the UK 1961–77', *National Institute Economic Review*, no. 85 (1978), pp. 31–9

Hunter, L. C., 'The economic determination of strike activity', *Glasgow University Discussion Papers in Economics*, no. 1, 1973

Mace, J., 'Internal labour markets for engineers in British industry', *British Journal of Industrial Relations*, vol. XVII, no. 1 (1979), pp. 50–63

Mackay, D. I., Boddy, D., Brack, J., Diack, J. A., and Jones, N., *Labour Markets under Different Employment Conditions* (Allen & Unwin, 1971)

Manpower Services Commission, *The Merseyside Study*, 1976

Manpower Services Commission, *The Borders Study*, 1977

Manpower Services Commission, *The South Essex Study*, 1978

Manpower Services Commission, *Labour Shortages and Manpower Policy* (HMSO, 1978)

Mayhew, K., 'Earnings dispersion in local labour markets: implications for search behaviour', *Oxford Bulletin of Economics and Statistics*, vol. 38, no. 2 (1977), pp. 93–107

Mayhew, K., 'Economists and strikes', *Oxford Bulletin of Economics and Statistics*, vol. 41, no. 1 (1979), pp. 1–19

National Board for Prices and Incomes, *Pay and Conditions in the Civil Engineering Industry*, Report No. 91 (HMSO, 1968)

National Board for Prices and Incomes, *Pay and Conditions in the Building Industry*, Report No. 92 (HMSO, 1968)

National Board for Prices and Incomes, *Pay and Conditions in the Construction Industry other than Building and Civil Engineering*, Report No. 93 (HMSO, 1968)

National Economic Development Office, *Engineering Shortages and Related Problems* (NEDO, 1978)

Oi, W., 'Labour as a quasi-fixed factor of production', *Journal of Political Economy*, vol. 70, no. 6 (1962), pp. 538–55

Pencavel, J., 'An investigation into industrial strike activity in Britain', *Economica*, vol. 37, no. 147 (1970), pp. 239–56

Robinson, D., *Wage Drift, Fringe Benefits and Manpower Distribution* (Paris: OECD, 1968)

Robinson, D. (ed.), *Local Labour Markets and Wage Structures* (Gower Press, 1970)

Royal Commission on the Distribution of Income and Wealth, Report No. 8 (HMSO, 1979)

Runciman, W. G., *Relative Deprivation and Social Justice* (Routledge & Kegan Paul, 1966)

Shorey, J., 'Time series analysis of strike frequency', *British Journal of Industrial Relations*, vol. 15, no. 1 (1977), pp. 63–75

Stigler, G., 'Information in the labour market', *Journal of Political Economy*, vol. 70, no. 5, part 2 (1962), pp. 94–105

Thomas, B., and Deaton, D., *Labour Shortage and Economic Analysis* (Oxford: Blackwell, 1977)

Willis, R. J., and Rosen, S., 'Education and self-selection', *Journal of Political Economy*, vol. 87, no. 5, part 2 (1979)

Chapter 5

Incomes Policy and the Public Sector

J. L. FALLICK and R. F. ELLIOTT*

Introduction

In chapter 3 above, two important aspects of public sector pay are identified. The control of public sector pay during periods of incomes policy (and at other times) is of importance to governments because of the implications of the rate of growth of pay for the rate of growth of public expenditure. More importantly, the dual role of employer and regulator of the overall level of economic activity provides government with a unique opportunity, and responsibility, to ensure the success of incomes policies. If the government does not enforce the provisions of an incomes policy in the public sector, then the chances of success for that policy are severely diminished via the 'spillover' effects from public sector pay settlements to private sector settlements and because of the possible impact of the growth of public expenditure. Taking these two arguments as our starting-point, this chapter provides a detailed examination of the behaviour of the public sector during periods of incomes policy, adopting an analytical treatment which concentrates on the way in which pay is determined in the public sector. A central feature of the approach adopted below is the hypothesis that it is only by examining and understanding the mechanisms which govern pay change that we can hope to discover how pay growth might be controlled. In the light of this we will be able to demonstrate the considerable problems which one encounters in trying to control public sector pay via incomes policy, and these general, inherent, problems will be illustrated by reference to the

---

* The authors would like to thank the other contributors to this volume for their helpful comments on an earlier draft. Not all the advice offered was acted upon and the authors alone bear responsibility for the final version.

successes and failures of the various periods of incomes policy since 1950.

The determination of public sector pay

The problem

Table 3.5 above shows quite clearly that public sector employment rose in both absolute and percentage terms in both the 1960s and the 1970s. By the end of the 1970s approximately 29 per cent of all employment was accounted for by public sector employment. The composition of this employment, by occupation, by sex and by sub-sector within the public sector, has changed quite markedly over the last two decades, the two main trends being the growth of non-manual employment and the growth of part-time female employment.[1] Table 3.5 also indicates that the combined share of total public sector employment accounted for by central and local government has risen from 64·9 per cent to 70·5 per cent, with a concomitant fall in the share of the public corporations (35 per cent to 29·5 per cent). This change in the composition of the labour force is of far more than mere statistical interest. Whereas the majority of the employees in the public corporations are involved, directly or indirectly, in the production of goods and services which are for sale to the public at large, those in both central and local government are not.[2] This means that a large and growing proportion of public sector employees are obliged to rely on what might be called 'indirect' methods of pay determination because of the absence of a directly determined market price for their output. Admittedly, the Corporations operate under different conditions from most of their private sector counterparts as a result of their wider social welfare targets, their element of monopoly power, and also as a result of the availability, during the 1960s and 1970s at least, of government subsidies to cover their losses. None the less, the distinction made above is still valid, in that the role of the market in price formation is at least potentially viable in the case of the public corporations, and as such it provides an important guide to pay determination, whereas with the remainder of the public sector no such guide exists. In consequence we are forced to fall back on a much more circuitous and difficult set of procedures for determining appropriate levels of pay.

Frequently, the public sector is the sole or majority buyer of specific types of labour in the market – such is the case, for example, with teachers, doctors, the police and coalminers, while on the other side the price, and in some extreme cases the quantity of labour supplied, may be controlled to a greater or lesser degree by trade unions and professional associations. Bilateral monopoly is, therefore, an appropriate description of the labour markets in which much of the public sector operates. Within such markets the prevailing conditions of labour supply and demand merely establish a range of possible wage and employment solutions. The eventual outcome is determined through the process of bargaining and reflects the differing economic, political and other pressures operating on the two parties to the negotiations. The differing institutional frameworks within which bargaining occurs will also modify and perhaps even distort the economic pressures which should lead to a solution to the bargaining process. Consequently, it is important to study both the process of collective bargaining and the nature of the institutions in the public sector, in order to fully understand the wage and employment decisions that result.

The principle of comparability – of levels of pay based on those which obtain in outside employment – has provided the focus for much of the postwar public sector collective bargaining and the determination of 'appropriate' comparisons has strongly influenced the development of the various institutions. For most civil servants, for example, a sophisticated machinery has been established for determining pay through a process of 'fair comparisons', while for manual workers the principle of comparability, although less institutionalised, is none the less of paramount importance. Although the process of collective bargaining and the precise importance of comparability vary across the public sector, one can identify a few principal variants of the general concept, and it is to a description and analysis of these that we now turn.

Pay determination in practice

The Machinery[3]

The pay of most manual workers in the public sector is determined through industry-wide negotiations. The Whitley Committee of 1916 recommended 'the establishment for each industry of an organisation, representative of employers and workpeople, to have as its object the regular consideration of matters affecting the progress and well-being of the trade from the point of view of all those engaged in it'. The legislation nationalising coalmining, civil aviation, transport, electricity, gas, atomic energy, and steel, imposed a statutory obligation on the Boards responsible for operating these industries to enter into joint consultation with the workers' organisations as to the establishment and maintenance of joint machinery for the settlement of terms and conditions of employment. Similar 'Whitley Councils' had been established shortly after 1916 for manual and some junior non-manual employees in the civil service, local government and the

Post Office, and these were introduced for the health service upon its inception in 1948. In all cases rates of pay and other conditions of employment were established through national negotiations which were subject to a few minor local additions or adjustments.

The significance of the principle of comparability for manual workers' pay in the public sector was emphasised by the passing of the Fair Wages Resolution which was adopted by the House of Commons on 14 October 1946. The Resolution specifically required that government contractors observe 'fair' conditions of work as well as 'fair' wages, and it obliged contractors to apply these to all persons employed in every factory, workshop, or place where the contract was being executed.

Although the Resolution was designed to apply to outside employers engaged on government contracts, this established the concept of a fair wage by reference to other employment and formed the basis for the specific procedures which were established for industrial civil servants. The original resolution dates from 1891 and in 1910 the government of the day undertook to apply the terms of the Resolution to its own employees. With the passage of the current version, the government reconfirmed its undertaking to its own employees in a statement by the then Chancellor of the Exchequer in the House of Commons in January 1948.

Some attempts have been made to move away from comparability. In particular, the National Board for Prices and Incomes (NBPI), which was established in 1965 to assist with the implementation of the prices and incomes policy of that period, identified large areas of inefficient labour utilisation in the public sector and they advocated increased use of productivity-linked incentive payment schemes for manual workers, to improve efficiency. Despite numerous reports on local government manual employees, and manual employees in the nationalised industries and public corporations, which put forward schemes designed to reduce overtime and link pay growth more closely to the growth in productivity, the NBPI was forced to conclude, in 1971, that progress towards relating earnings to performance had been slow, with only a few notable exceptions (such as electricity supply) and even in these cases further scope remained. In an earlier article by one of the authors (Elliott, 1977) it was shown that for public sector manual workers in general, and unskilled manual workers in particular, the whole postwar period has been characterised by remarkably similar-sized settlements across the various manual groups in the public sector, and a highly stable set of occupational and industrial rankings. Elliott also indicates that comparability exercises take place between manual groups in different industries within the public sector, to the extent that 'the size of wage increases received by an extremely large number of public sector employees depends on the outcome of perhaps two key bargains' (Elliott, 1977) and the importance of these comparability exercises during periods of incomes policies will be highlighted below.

While the National Joint Councils and Whitley Councils existed for manual, and some junior non-manual, employees in the public service, the pay of the majority of non-manual employees was determined by an entirely different procedure.

The most sophisticated mechanism for establishing rates of pay for public sector non-manual workers, by reference to levels of remuneration in outside work, is the Civil Service Pay Research Unit (PRU). In 1955 the Priestly Commission (Priestly, 1955) recommended that the primary principle governing the pay of non-industrial civil servants should be fair comparison with the current levels of remuneration of outside staffs employed on broadly comparable work. As a result the PRU was established in 1956 and since that date it has conducted regular pay surveys to establish the rates of pay of certain key grades in the civil service. Linked to each of these key grades are a large number of grades known as 'consequentials', containing smaller numbers of employees whose pay rates are automatically adjusted in line with those of the key grades.

A tripartite steering committee, comprising representatives of the Civil Service Department, the Pay Research Unit and the general secretaries of each staff association, is responsible for the overall direction of the PRU. It considers major issues of policy and any modification of the Unit's role, together with agreeing the master list of firms to be surveyed. The master list comprises most major employers in the private and public sector who operate salary scales and who engage in collective bargaining with the representatives of their white-collar staff. Originally this list was based on *The Times*'s list of the top 500 British firms, and it seems to have remained relatively stable ever since.[4] As chapter 3 above indicated, on a number of occasions during the early 1970s the results of these exercises led to large increases in pay for civil servants and indeed to them overtaking the private sector. This somewhat paradoxical outcome is of considerable interest and importance, and will be discussed in detail later in this chapter. The activities of the PRU were 'suspended' between 1975 and 1978, firstly as part of the 1975 incomes policy and subsequently because the government of the day rightly feared the implications of reinstating the process of comparability in the light of the improvements in private sector non-manual pay after 1976 (see Figure 3.2 above). However, it was revived in 1978, and in consequence pay levels in the private sector are once again direct inputs into the negotiations which determine the level of pay in this important part of the public sector.

Although not as formally developed as the PRU system,

comparability plays a major role in determining the pay of the vast majority of non-manual workers in the middle ranks of the NHS, local government and the other non-civil service sections of the public sector. Indeed, the rates established by the PRU are frequently taken as guidelines or targets by these non-manual groups outside the civil service, although this system of establishing non-manual pay by comparisons *within* the public sector itself has no formal status and is consequently extremely difficult to pin down.

The final set of arrangements governing the determination of non-manual pay in the public sector are the various review bodies. These can usefully be divided into two categories, namely the standing review bodies and the *ad hoc* or specially commissioned review bodies (although many of the former types arose as the result of recommendations made by the latter type). Examples of standing review bodies are the Top Salaries Review Body, which was established by the Priestly Commission on the Civil Service (Priestly, 1955) to determine appropriate rates of pay for the most senior posts in the civil service, for government ministers and MPs, for board members of nationalised industries and for the senior officers in the armed forces; and the Review Body on Doctors' and Dentists' Remuneration, which was established on the recommendation of the Royal Commission on Doctors' and Dentists' Remuneration 1957–60 (the Pilkington Commission). The most important specially commissioned review body in the postwar period has probably been the Houghton Committee (Committee of Inquiry into the Pay of Non-University Teachers) of 1974, although a very large number of special reports have been commissioned. In all cases where these reports dealt with the pay of public sector non-manual workers, the principle of comparability played a crucial role, and the terms of reference of the standing review bodies all include explicit recognition of the central role of external comparisons. Perhaps the best illustration of the importance of the concept can be gained from the annual reports of the influential Prices and Incomes Board. Established in 1965 as part of the incomes policy of that period (see the Appendix for details), the PIB began with an extremely hostile attitude to the principle of pay changes based largely on comparability, but as Thompson and Beaumont (1978) have pointed out, by 1969 the PIB had been forced to recognise that comparability was 'deeply rooted and cannot entirely be discarded' (PIB report no. 122, quoted in Thompson and Beaumont).

In the period since 1976, the principle of comparability has been strengthened by two important developments in public sector pay determination. The activities of a further set of specially commissioned *ad hoc* committees of inquiry into the pay of specific sub-groups within the public sector have again been heavily based on the notion that public sector pay should be linked directly to pay in the private sector. Most notable of these special inquiries is that conducted by a committee under the chairmanship of Lord Edmund-Davies, which reported on police pay in 1977. Although this report attempted to take supply and demand factors into account the final award was principally designed to bring police pay back into line with pay in the private sector, and more importantly, from our standpoint, the government of the day accepted the committee's recommendation that in future, police pay should be linked to the Department of Employment index of average earnings, and should be adjusted upwards automatically in line with the movements in the index. This ties the basic pay of a large number of public employees directly to earnings changes in the private sector (and it should be noted here that the earnings index includes overtime pay, bonus, payments by results, and so on), thus establishing the notion of comparability permanently, in a way which will prevent these public employees from ever falling behind the private sector. The second important development of the late 1970s was the creation by the Labour government of the Clegg Commission. Although at the time of writing the new Conservative government has still to 'show its hand' on the commission, it has so far abided by the recommendations made by the commission on the pay of certain public sector groups and since the election some additional public sector pay claims have been referred to Clegg. The terms of reference are quite explicit in according a leading role to comparability, and although the work of the commission must be seen in the context of the 'cash limits' regime, which requires that 'excessive' pay awards be financed by reductions in total employment for the public sector workers concerned, we cannot avoid the conclusion that comparability, principally with the private sector, is the dominant mechanism for determining pay in the public sector at the outset of the 1980s, as it was at the outset of both the 1960s and 1970s.

Limitations and drawbacks

Even in the absence of incomes policies, the problems inherent in the use of comparability as the major mechanisms for determining pay levels in the public sector are considerable. At the most fundamental level, it can be argued that although pay is a central element in determining the relative 'attractiveness' of an occupation, it is only one component of total remuneration. Other factors, such as security of employment, working conditions, holidays, fringe benefits and pension provision play an important part in the individual's choice of job; and although some attempts have been made to introduce some of these factors into comparability calculations, the general tendency has been for comparability to be based exclusively on pay levels.

Although many public sector workers would argue that private sector fringe benefits, particularly company cars, are of considerable financial value, the tendency throughout the 1970s has been for more and more 'perks' to be subject to taxation, with the Inland Revenue increasing tax liability to allow for these non-pay items in private sector total remuneration. On the other hand, public sector unions have effectively resisted attempts to allow security of employment and index-linked pensions, probably the two most valuable 'perks' associated with public sector employment, to be 'costed' realistically in comparability exercises, with the result that on balance, for a given pay level, it is extremely difficult to say definitively which group of employees has the better total remuneration package. For example, although the security of employment traditionally associated with public sector jobs increasingly came under pressure in the late 1970s and early 1980s, in the 1960s and early 1970s security of employment was more or less guaranteed. As Adam Smith pointed out in 1776, wages vary with (among other things) the 'agreeableness' of the employment and with the 'constancy' of employment, the general rule being that the more unpleasant the job and the higher the probability of unemployment then the more an employer will have to pay to secure a given number of workers of a given quality.[5] To the extent that these factors have been undervalued or ignored in the comparability exercises, it can fairly be said that public sector employees have been getting pay settlements significantly different in size from those which would be produced under the operation of a properly functioning competitive labour market.

Economists argue that one of the main functions of pay differentials and relativities is to allocate labour efficiently among competing alternative occupations. When the 'marginal product' of labour is high, the employer can attract the desired quantity of labour by paying high wages, yet still make a profit. However, if comparability exists along the lines outlined above, private sector employers may be unable to obtain the number of employees they desire by conventional wage signals. Moreover, unless public sector productivity growth is consistently kept in line with productivity growth in the private sector, comparability will inevitably lead to a reduction in the rate of economic growth and the cumulative problems outlined in Baumol's model of unbalanced growth, referred to in chapter 3 above.

It would be possible to go on outlining the problems inherent in the comparability approach to public sector pay *ad nauseam*. However, the most important aspects have been touched upon and these will suffice for the purposes of the present discussion. A far more difficult question is what to put in place of comparability: both at the conceptual/methodological level and at the more practical level of pay determination mechanisms, this question remains largely unresolved. However, before we can begin to deal with it, some further facets of comparability in practice are worthy of consideration. In particular, how has the comparability concept and the associated mechanisms performed during the successive periods of incomes policy?

The impact of incomes policies

The first rule which must be observed when discussing the behaviour and experience of the public sector under any of the postwar periods of incomes policy is that generalisation can be dangerously misleading. The public sector is made up of a wide range of occupations dispersed over more than fifteen industrial groupings, and to refer to the experience of this heterogeneous labour force during incomes policies as if it were largely uniform is to overlook or disguise the very complexity which makes control of public sector pay the thorny practical problem it is. The significant fact to note is that not only did the public sector perform differently under successive incomes policies, but for any given policy period we can identify a range of settlement sizes within the public sector. As a result of this we must treat statements referring to average settlement size with caution and devote a significant part of our attention to analysing the nature and significance of those settlements which breached the policy rules or guidelines. Tables 5.1 and 5.2 provide some illustrative aggregate increase data for the majority of the policies implemented up to the fourth quarter of 1975. Interpreted cautiously these provide a useful first approximation to the analysis of the public sector under incomes policies. They enable us to conclude that if governments sought to enforce incomes policies by example, that is by holding their own employees strictly to the increases permitted by the various policies (as is often suggested in popular discussion of incomes policies) then their wishes would seem to have been disappointed. That is not to say that incomes policies were not successful in the public sector or even that they were not more harshly applied there. Evidence has already been presented in chapters 2 and 3 above which suggests that within limits they were relatively successful and also that they do appear to have been more vigorously applied in the public sector. Rather, the aggregate data demonstrate quite clearly that from the outset we can reject the notion that the government can readily determine *a priori* the level of settlements which it will permit its own employees to obtain in a given bargaining period. With this point firmly established we can move on to the more complex but more important issue of where and how policy breaches took place, which we believe provides the key to an understanding of past policy 'failures' and provides a guide to the scope (if any) for running a successful incomes policy in the future.

Table 5.1 The average size of wage settlements for public sector manual workers during periods of incomes policy, 1950–75

Year/Quarter	Policy[1]	Skilled Size	Skilled Number	Semi-skilled Size	Semi-skilled Number	Unskilled Size	Unskilled Number	Females Size	Females Number
		The average size and the number of wage settlements for:							
1950 I and II	Zero norm	7·0	(2)	9·9	(1)	14·9	(1)	—	—
1956 I–IV	No norm	7·0	(25)	7·6	(24)	7·9	(24)	6·9	(9)
1961 III and IV–1962 I	Zero norm	3·5	(15)	3·2	(11)	3·4	(14)	3·8	(4)
1962 II–1963 I	2–2·5% norm	3·9	(29)	4·7	(26)	4·1	(27)	5·4	(10)
1963 II–1966 II	3–3·5% norm	4·9	(91)	4·6	(75)	5·0	(80)	5·3	(29)
1966 III and IV	Freeze	—	—	—	—	—	—	—	—
1967 I–1968 II	Zero norm	5·5	(37)	5·1	(27)	5·1	(35)	9·7	(14)
1968 III–1969 IV	3·5% ceiling	6·8	(44)	6·8	(39)	6·7	(44)	5·9	(16)
1970 I and II	2·5–4·5% norm pa	17·6	(13)	14·2	(12)	9·9	(11)	11·3	(4)
1971 IV–1972 III	'N–1'	12·0	(27)	11·9	(24)	16·1	(24)	13·2	(12)
1972 IV–1973 I	Freeze	—	—	—	—	—	—	—	—
1973 II and III	£1+4%	7·6	(12)	8·5	(12)	10·0	(13)	7·8	(5)
1973 IV–1974 II	£2·25 or 7%	12·6	(30)	11·7	(26)	12·1	(27)	9·8	(14)
1975 III and IV	£6 per week	17·3	(15)	17·6	(11)	14·9	(16)	15·8	(9)

[1] See the Appendix for full details of the various policies.

Source: R. F. Elliott and J. L. Fallick, *Pay in the Public Sector* (Macmillan, 1980).

Table 5.2 The average size of salary settlements for public sector clerical workers during periods of incomes policy, 1967 – 75

Year/Quarter	Policy[1]	Public Corporations		Local and National Government	
		Min.[2]	Max.	Min.	Max.
1967 I – 1967 II	Severe Restraint	5·3	4·8	8·1	7·6
1967 III – 1968 II	Zero norm	3·9	3·6	4·2	9·0
1968 III –	3·5% pa	4·4	5·0	5·8	5·0
1969 IV		6·1	5·8	7·1	3·7
1970 I and II	2·5 – 4·5% norm pa	9·0	9·9	16·3	8·5
1970 III – 1971 III	'Free Collective Bargaining'	10·9	11·1	15·3	11·1
1971 IV – 1972 III	'N – 1'	12·8	11·2	10·4	9·9
1972 IV – 1973 I	Freeze	–	–	–	–
1973 II and III	£1+4%	14·2	9·3	24·8	8·2
1973 IV – 1974 II	£2·25 or 7%	17·0	16·0	19·5	17·4
1974 III – 1975 II	Stage IV Threshold and further compensation for RPI	35·0	25·0	41·4	30·6
1975 III and IV	£6 per week	19·7	19·6	–	–

[1] See the Appendix for full details of the various policies.
[2] Min. and max. here refer to the average settlement size, calculated for those on the minimum and maximum points respectively of the relevant incremental salary scale.
Source: R. F. Elliott and J. L. Fallick, op. cit.

The impact of incomes policy on the wages of manual workers in the public sector

As we have already seen in chapter 2 above, it is difficult to isolate the effects of incomes policies on wage movements. Evidence that the average size of pay settlement was greater during periods of incomes policy than the policy aimed for is clearly not evidence of the total ineffectiveness of the policy. Without it, pay settlements may have been even greater. To estimate the effectiveness of pay policies it is necessary to engage in some speculation or estimation of how pay settlements were likely to have behaved in the absence of such policies.

In an earlier attempt to test for the impact of the various incomes policies that existed over the period, the present authors followed the example of Brechling and constructed a wage equation[6] which included a set of dummy variables which operated during periods of incomes policies (Elliott and Fallick, 1980). It is quite clear from the results of the wage equation approach that incomes policies have enjoyed a rather mixed success over the period.

The 1961–2 'pay pause' was specifically aimed at restraining public sector pay growth and it met with a degree of success during 1961. By the beginning of 1962, however, pressures began to build up, and in the first quarter of that year over fifteen different public sector settlements occurred. They largely took the form of hourly, and not weekly, wage increases due to a fairly widespread reduction in the standard working week that occurred at this time. It has been suggested (Clegg, 1971, p. 2) that this policy was only effective in the public sector, and this is confirmed by our evidence. While only two public sector agreements implemented settlements during the last half of 1961 around forty private sector (non-wages council) agreements were implemented at an average level of between 5 and 8.5 per cent on hourly wages for different skills.

The electricity supply settlement of February 1962 was an important turning-point in the development of this policy, for it was one of the few straight increases in weekly wages negotiated at this time. Furthermore, the settlement had been concluded in November 1961 under threat of national strike and was therefore very much in the public eye. It represented the first major break in the public sector, which had hitherto appeared to conform to the policy, and it led to a series of associated demands from local authorities and gas which resulted in several settlements being implemented at the beginning of April 1962. The sequence of events which led to these settlements in April 1962 provides a very good illustration, from one of the earliest periods of incomes policy, of how a single settlement which breached the policy almost inevitably leads to a further more damaging set of breaches, via comparability claims and, as in the present case, via informal linkages between settlements within the public sector. The electricity supply settlement was implemented in February 1962, and was therefore in direct contravention of the 'zero norm' which was intended to run from July 1961 until March 1962. Although the associated settlements of April 1962 were strictly speaking outside the zero norm period, they were in general above the recommendations of the 'guiding light' which followed the zero norm 'wage pause'; and more importantly they were justified by reference to (and comparison with) a settlement negotiated during the zero norm policy, and in contravention of that policy. In this way a single settlement, obtained after the threat of strike action, was the trigger for a more major breach, largely as a result of internal comparability. The significance of this early example is, first, that the pattern of events described was to be repeated frequently during subsequent periods of incomes policy; and, secondly, that the initial policy breach sets the scene for subsequent increases, and as such it takes on considerable importance.

The 'standstill' of 1966 prevented all increases, and in the first six months of the period of 'severe restraint' that followed several increases which had been deferred because of the standstill were implemented. In fact, either because of this or because they qualified for exceptional treatment under one of the four criteria established in the White Paper,[7] 20 per cent of all public and private sector bargaining groups managed to implement settlements, and the level of these settlements was somewhat higher than the government would have liked, at around 5·5 per cent on average.

As was widely acknowledged at the time, the norm of 3·5 per cent which was to apply between March 1968 and December 1969 was not strictly enforced; and, as Table 5.1 reveals, settlements were averaging between 6 and 7 per cent over the period from the middle of 1968 to the end of 1969. In fact some groups did abide by the norm in 1968 but they soon found themselves left behind by others who paid less regard to norms. The result of this differential adherence to the March 1968 to December 1969 policy provides the next simple illustration of comparability effects in practice. If we analyse the behaviour of a number of groups the implications of the failure of all groups to adhere to the 3·5 per cent 'group ceiling' quickly become apparent. The settlements for government industrial and Post Office manipulative grades in 1968 and the early 1969 iron and steel settlement were within the norm. However, in the middle of 1969 government industrials received between 10 and 12 per cent depending on skill and iron and steel received over 27 per cent! In fact the 1969 settlement for Post Office manipulatives only just exceeded the norm, and of all the public sector groups they came closest to adhering to the norm during this period. This probably explains why the manipulative grades sought and achieved large rises early in 1971, after industrial action.

Any vestige of pay restraint that remained broke down in 1970 under the 'wage explosion' of that year. What caused this and what was the role of the public sector during this period? To answer this we must reiterate the importance of comparability; during this period, the relationship between private and public sector pay clearly played an important role. Certainly the price effects of the 1967 devaluation were making themselves felt in 1969 and 1970 and large increases seemed likely to result. But the increases that occurred in 1970 were much larger than could have been expected on these grounds alone. Rather, as chapter 3 above shows, 1968 and 1969 had witnessed smaller increases in wage rates in the public sector than had been achieved by the private, non-wages council sector. Large additions to basic pay had been granted in the private sector in 1968 and 1969 and as a result public sector wages fell behind. Prior to the actual wage explosion there is evidence of discontent in the outburst of strikes in the public sector, and in 1969 the dustmen (local authority manuals) received a large settlement as a result of strike action. None the less, not all large wage increases were achieved as a result of industrial action, as large increases had already been achieved by several groups towards the end of 1969 through normal bargaining. Negotiations in electricity supply resulted in a large settlement towards the end of 1969 – at about the same time as the dustmen settled – and it has been suggested that these negotiations were influenced by the pay settlements that had occurred in the private sector (Edwards and Roberts, p. 231). The settlement in electricity led once again to a number of large settlements in early 1970 for those industries in the utilities/local authorities group of agreements.

This particular group of settlements provides a further example of how the comparability process has operated in practice. In particular, they demonstrate quite dramatically how comparability exercises between one group of public sector employees and a private sector group can have wide-ranging consequences for a much larger number of public sector groups, whose occupational and industrial composition, not to mention their productivity performance, bears little or no relation to the private sector workers with whom the initial comparison was made. By obtaining a highly favourable settlement, via direct comparisons with the private sector, the electricity supply workers acted as a pace-setter for the other utilities (gas and water workers) and for local authority manual workers in general. The formal and informal linkages which exist between the basic rates paid to these groups meant that once one favourable settlement was made on the basis of comparison with the private sector, the maintenance of agreed or established differentials and relativities necessitated similar-sized settlements for a much larger number of workers, over a wide range of industries and occupations. It is important to re-emphasise that the conditions in the sub-labour markets (both geographic and skill) in which these other groups operated, may have borne little or no resemblance to those obtaining for electricity workers. None the less, the initial comparison with the private sector, and the large settlement which it produced, formed the basis for the series of large increases which occurred in the public sector at that time.

Undoubtedly, post-devaluation price and, we should add, tax increases suggested that larger-than-average wage increases would occur at the end of 1969 and during 1970. None the less, it does appear that an additional factor fuelling public sector demands was the level of wage settlements achieved in the private non-wages council sector in 1968 and 1969. Perhaps these private sector settlements were in themselves a reaction to the wage restraint of the previous years. This remains to be fully explained, but it now seems clear that they initiated the 'wage explosion' of this period. Moreover, it is important to note that they did so during these two years by focusing attention on wage rate and not earnings advances, as had been the case in the earlier part of the sixties. Although the distinction between wage rates and earnings was mentioned in the introduction to the present volume, their precise significance in this context requires further elaboration. Clearly, when attempting to negotiate a public sector pay claim on the basis of a comparison with private sector employees, the negotiators will be obliged to choose either rates or earnings as the basis of the comparison, unless the distribution of total hours worked between normal hours and overtime hours is identical in the two sectors and unless the structure of earnings in terms of bonus payments, shift premia and the like are also broadly similar in both sectors. If the make-up of pay differs between the two sectors for either or both of these reasons, then claims based on wage rate comparisons, for example, will result in a divergence of final earnings between the two sectors despite the similarity in their basic wage rate. The significance of this technical distinction should not be underestimated. During the period under discussion, one of the present authors has argued (Elliott, 1977) that certain important groups in the public sector were able to negotiate significant increases by basing their comparisons on increases in private sector wage rates which were themselves designed to remedy the effects of a protracted period of wage drift in the private sector. This set of comparisons and claims based on private sector rates broke with the previous tradition of comparisons based on private sector earnings, and because of this rather clever manoeuvre many public sector manual groups were able to obtain increases considerably above the target level suggested by the government pay policies then in operation.

After the 'wage explosion' and the spell of free 'collective bargaining' that accommodated it in the period to the third quarter of

1971, the policy of 'N–1' was instituted. Once again this was a policy which was to be applied with particular rigour in the public sector, where each settlement was to be 1 per cent lower than that group's previous settlement. However, there is no evidence of a successive de-escalation of settlements. The freeze which was introduced upon the failure of the 'N–1' policy prohibited all settlements and was in turn followed by a second phase which restricted rises to £1 + 4 per cent of the average pay bill over the preceding twelve months.[8] This phase of incomes policy, in fact, extended beyond the third quarter of 1973 to November 1973 and therefore the figures in Table 5.1 are only approximations. Despite fairly substantial increases during this period, all agreements appear to have conformed to the policy, while the wage equation approach mentioned above suggests that this and the following phase were successful in reducing settlements by 2·5 per cent below what would have occurred in their absence. The next incomes policy to be introduced in the period covered by Table 5.1 came on the heels of the very large wage rises that resulted both from the threshold provisions of the final stage of the Conservative government's incomes policy and under the first phase of the new Labour government's 'social contract'. The 'social contract' Mk II – the £6 pay limit – was adhered to by the public sector but still resulted in substantial wage rises, as Table 5.1 reveals. None the less, as a first estimate, the wage equation suggests that this was probably the most effective policy of all, reducing wage settlements by more than 3 per cent below the level they would otherwise have attained. However, there is considerable merit in considering the performance of the public sector after 1974 as a separate issue, due to the change in the way in which incomes policies were conducted from the period of the 'social contract' onwards, and due to the increasing importance of government attempts to reduce public expenditure after that date. Accordingly we will look at the public sector as a whole, after 1974. However, before moving on to the most recent period, we present some results on the impact of incomes policies on non-manual groups between 1950 and 1975.

The impact of incomes policy on the pay of non-manual workers in the public sector
In contrast to the many studies of the impact of incomes policies on the pay of manual workers, there exist very few similar studies for white-collar workers. One of the principal reasons for this was the absence of suitable data prior to the introduction of the *New Earnings Survey* in 1970, but even after that date problems remain which cast considerable doubt on the usefulness of aggregate studies of pay changes for non-manual workers when taken in isolation. Whereas the manual labour force may be subdivided into a few relatively

homogeneous skill groups with ease, and without imposing unrealistic or unjustified assumptions on the study, the situation in non-manual labour markets is quite different. The range of skill levels or human capital endowments covered by the term 'non-manual' is clearly considerable, from a shorthand typist requiring perhaps one or two years of informal post-school training, to professors of surgery, requiring up to ten years' formal post-school training and perhaps as many years informal 'on-the-job' training. Over and above these human capital considerations, the recent development of more complex models of the labour market such as internal labour market theories, which would seem to have particular relevance for the UK public sector, lead us to suggest that the approach to the analysis of the impact of incomes policies which has been adopted in most studies using manual wage and earnings data may require some modification when we move on to study non-manual labour markets, and particularly the public sector non-manual labour force. In the analysis presented below we have taken the experience of clerical workers in the public sector as illustrative of the general experiences of the non-manual group. Because of the range of skills and occupations already mentioned, no one group of non-manuals can be said to be typical of the group as a whole. However, the clerical group does provide the best illustrations of the general experience, and in the limited space available it would not be possible to do justice to all the individual non-manual groups.[9]

By and large, clerical occupations in central and local government reveal a considerable degree of disparity in their performance during the several incomes policies that occurred over the period. Incomes policies at the start of the period were relatively 'straightforward', but during the 1970s several contained the complicated flat rate plus percentage provisions (as detailed in the Appendix). Clearly, this presents problems for estimating the extent to which the settlements of the different groups analysed here complied with the policies of this period.

The 'wage pause' of 1961 and the early part of the prices and incomes policy of 1965–6 met with considerable success and with few exceptions all those non-manual settlements in 1965 received increases which conformed to the 3–3·5 per cent norm of that period. The local and central government sector, in particular, adhered to the norm during 1965, although it is apparent that in the last months of this policy the norm was exceeded with increasing frequency by the agreements in both local government and the public corporations. By 1966 the modal size of settlement had risen to around 5 per cent.

The 'standstill' of 1966 effectively prohibited all increases during the last half of that year. During the period of 'severe restraint' which followed, only local government, British Rail, and the Port of London implemented settlements which qualified for exceptional treatment.

These settlements had been due to be implemented in 1966 but had been deferred until 1967 as a result of the 'standstill'. The post-'standstill' picture for clerical settlements is revealed in Table 5.2, and it is immediately clear that the few settlements implemented during the 'period of severe restraint' were of a similar order of magnitude to those implemented by manual workers at this time. It has been suggested elsewhere (Elliott and Fallick, 1980) that the large size of manual settlements implemented in 1967 may have prejudiced the climate of restraint being fostered at this time and it would appear that the settlements of some groups of non-manual public employees played their part in this process. None the less, it is important to note that throughout 1968 the settlements of non-manual workers were much lower than those for manual workers and indeed the majority of settlements in the period up to the end of 1968 were around 3·5 per cent. Although this meant that those implemented before April 1968 exceeded the ineffective zero norm of that period, most fell in the last months of that year and therefore conformed to the new norm. Public corporations adhered most closely to the norm over this period while in the local and central government sector several agreements which are traditionally linked to the local government agreement received large 'catching-up' increases. After 1969, the restraint began to break down and in 1970 increases around 10 per cent appear to have been typical. None the less, it is worth noting that while in the subsequent brief period of 'free collective bargaining' manual workers in the public sector achieved settlements which averaged around 20 per cent, the majority of settlements for clerical workers remained around 10 per cent. Furthermore, it is important to recognise that only in local government and coalmining (those sections in which manual workers had already achieved large increases as a result of industrial action) did clerical workers receive settlements in excess of 20 per cent.

In principle, there is no reason to expect the large awards being paid to public sector manual workers at this time to have any influence on the awards of clerical workers in the public sector. If the comparability exercises of the PRU, for example, keep strictly to their accepted guidelines, as laid down by Priestly (Priestly, 1955) then the relevant variable on which to focus attention would be the movements in pay of clerical workers in some or all of the private sector. However, the experience in local government and coalmining, where the relatively rigid procedures of the PRU do not apply directly but where we would expect the awards achieved by equivalent groups in the civil service to be a major determinant of the size of settlement achieved (as had been the trend up to this point in time), reveals an important departure from the accepted, though strictly informal, procedure. A claim based on the erosion of the differential between skilled manual workers and junior non-manuals was likely to (and in the two cases mentioned did) lead to a superior settlement to that based on comparability. In this way, by varying the weight attached to comparability and in particular by designing claims based on exemption clauses in the various policies, such as the 'pay relativities' clause in the early 1970 'range policy' (see Appendix for details) some groups of non-manual employees, such as those in local government and coalmining in the period under discussion, were able to exceed the average settlement size for public sector non-manuals by a significant amount.

From October 1971 the policy of 'N−1' was introduced in an attempt to de-escalate the size of settlements. In general it appears to have met with some success in de-escalating non-manual settlements with the exception of non-manuals in the public corporations. Its success was confined to specific areas of non-manual pay and, partly as a result of this mixed response, it was succeeded by the 'freeze' of 1972−3. Stage II, which followed the 'freeze', involved a straightforward addition of £1 + 4 per cent to the salaries of the majority of non-manual workers covered here, with the sole exception of local government. In their case, increases at the bottom point of the scale considerably exceeded the pay limit and this may well be a result of the limited industrial action these workers engaged in at this time.

Most groups appear to have opted for £2.25 per week under Stage III in 1973−4 and for most this resulted in increases which were well in excess of 7 per cent. In fact the civil service received two substantial increases during this phase of the policy, as a result of the Pay Board report, *Anomalies* (1972), while clerical workers in the National Coal Board also enjoyed a very large rise. The latter settlement once again resulted directly from the large increases awarded to manual workers in the mines after the 1974 industrial action and subsequent Pay Board report on *The Relative Pay of Mineworkers* (1973).

The report of the Pay Board on pay 'anomalies', which arose out of the pay standstill of November 1972, provides a useful example of the problems which have almost invariably followed incomes policies. Although the specific details of the report need not concern us here, the principle is important. Recognising that differentials and relativities had been seriously disrupted by the way in which the policy had been operated in practice, the government was forced to grant considerable retrospective increases in order to restore 'balance' to the formal integrated salary hierarchies which characterise the public sector non-manual labour market and in order to avoid industrial action in support of claims for redress. Significantly, much of the discussion which surrounded these claims for 'redress' suggested that the relatively poor performance of certain non-manual groups, which arose precisely because they adhered to the policy while others did not, was in some sense unfair. The redress seems to have come in the form of a secondary pay settlement for those who had adhered to the policy, designed to bring them back into line with those who had managed to breach it, rather than an attempt to penalise those who had breached the policy in the first place. The significance of this set of awards would seem to be, first, that it provided a precedent for a retrospective claim based on comparisons with groups which had breached the policy; second, that it granted a type of legitimacy to the breaches themselves; and finally, that it gave considerable further formal support to the notion that the violation of established relativities was sufficient grounds for a pay claim. Although the Pay Board attempted to undermine or remove this impression by its report on *Relativities* (1974) which was produced more or less in conjunction with the *Anomalies* report and which arose from the same initial reference from the Secretary of State, their efforts were largely in vain. The precedent set by the 1972 *Anomalies* report has been followed repeatedly and has undermined the effectiveness of almost every subsequent period of incomes policy.

One method of circumventing the restraints of incomes policy which is open to many employers is to 'restructure' salary scales so that employees move on to new, higher salary levels. It would appear that such practices were not adopted in the public sector as a way of avoiding the restraints of the middle and late 1960s and early 1970s. Furthermore, the expenditure cuts and restraints of this latter period prevented local and central government, in particular, from avoiding the restraints by regrading individual employees. Restructuring of salary scales and regrading of staff occurred in the late 1950s and early 1960s but the reorganisation was largely completed before the incomes policies of the middle 1960s and after.

So far our discussion has concentrated on those non-manual employees whose salaries are determined by conventional collective bargaining and by the PRU. The remainder of the non-manual group, who come under some variant of the standing or special review procedure, are even more dispersed in terms of their experiences during the various periods of policy. The substantial intervals between major pay reviews for most senior public servants, particularly those covered by the Top Salaries Review Body, meant that for long periods the illusion that these groups were complying with incomes policies was sustained. Small increases in line with incomes policy were awarded but as a result the salaries of most of these groups failed to keep pace with the general movement in salaries, particularly where others managed to break the policies. After the infrequent pay reviews, large increases have therefore been awarded, but by virtue of this they have effectively received increases which have broken if not the letter, certainly the spirit of the earlier pay policies. Here, once again, we encounter the dilemma of establishing salaries by means of comparability exercises. Infrequent pay reviews inevitably result in large infrequent salary increases which not only compensate the senior public employees for the deterioration in their position relative to their private sector comparison group (allowing, of course, for the fact that backdated settlements are not full compensation, due to the losses generated by price increases in the intervening period) but which also legitimise, to a certain extent, the earlier incomes policy-busting settlements and may even prejudice future attempts at restraint.

The period since 1974

The period since 1974 provides a range of policies and reactions to policy which in many ways exemplify the whole set of problems which successive postwar incomes policies have generated. The public sector experience since the imposition of the £6 limit in July 1975 illustrates what are arguably the three central problems of pay in the public sector. First, although the £6 limit achieved considerable success, bringing average earnings increases down from around 30 per cent to nearer 15 per cent, the 'Social Contract' which followed, and which depended on voluntary restraint by the unions on the basis of a formula agreed between the government and the TUC, appears to have succeeded only in the public sector. Whereas the government was able to influence the size and nature of settlements for its own workers, it is clear that in the private sector both unions and employers regarded the Social Contract as only a minor constraint, if any constraint at all, on their behaviour. Although, as indicated in chapter 3, during the early 1970s public sector employees had obtained some of the largest earnings increases in the economy as a whole, the Social Contract once again produced conditions which gave the private sector employees the greatest scope for circumventing both the spirit and the letter of the government's pay policy.

The second principal feature of the period since 1974 has been the use of arguments other than the conventional comparability approach in order to achieve special treatment or status during a period of pay restraint. Large increases were obtained by the miners and the electricity supply workers, by putting forward pay claims based on productivity agreements. The importance of these claims is that they show how some public sector groups, particularly manual workers in the nationalised industries and public corporations, have altered their bargaining strategy to suit the terms and provisions of successive policies. In the case of the miners, the whole notion of productivity bargaining had been strongly resisted by both union leaders and rank-and-file members throughout the period in the late 1960s during which the PIB had sought to promote this principle. Although there were some sections of the labour force, and some members of the union's national executive, who opposed the introduction of productivity-linked increases, the principle was eventually accepted by the miners, and formed the basis for their better-than-average pay award.

The third feature of this period, which once again highlights the special problems of the public sector under incomes policies, arose as a result of the special arrangements which govern the pay of certain public sector groups. Doctors and dentists, the armed forces, university teachers and the police all obtained some measure of special treatment during the currency of the social contract. In each instance, some variant of the 'special case' argument was adopted by the employees' side, although in the case of the police and university teachers this claim had to be backed up with threats of disruptive industrial action before the special inquiry was finally called. Although the outcomes of these special inquiries have varied considerably, the principles adopted have tended to be highly similar, if not identical. The employees in each of the claims based their argument on a combination of manpower shortage, length of time since the last claim, deterioration in their comparative position (vis-à-vis external and internal comparators), and finally their 'worth' to the community. The final mix, which was more a question of which of these elements to give maximum weighting to, as all the claims to be treated as a special case contained all four elements to some extent at least, depended largely on what the employees' representatives felt would sway the body set up to hear the case. The net outcome of the succession of special case awards was that even within the public sector the Social Contract was of limited success, although the enormous settlements of 1974–5 which were secured by almost all the public sector manual and junior non-manual groups were not repeated, even as the Social Contract began to disintegrate with the withdrawal of TUC support in 1978. Despite Labour's attempts to proceed as if it was still pursuing an incomes policy through the winter of 1978, public sector settlements grew steadily as the government faced a mounting series of industrial disputes. In an attempt to reduce the settlement size, the Labour government instituted the Standing Commission on Pay Comparability in early 1979 (under Professor Hugh Clegg). The mechanism which the government sought to promote involved a modest award, or at least an award more modest than the original claim, which would be paid 'now', with the promise of a supplementary award later based on a report by the Clegg commission. As the Clegg reports have so far relied heavily on the principle of comparatibility,[10] both internal and external, the process seems to have come full circle by the beginning of the 1980s.

Analysis and conclusions

The historical evidence on the rate of growth of pay in the public sector from 1950 to 1980 suggests a number of fairly simple propositions. Although the evidence as presented indicates that the experience of the public sector employee sub-groups is complex and heterogeneous, the basic principles and forces which govern the eventual outcomes are less complex; and, moreover, the experiences of the period since 1974 suggest that these forces and principles have remained fairly constant throughout the period of our analysis. We have argued that the key to an understanding of the impact of successive incomes policies on pay differentials and relativities in the public sector lies in the analysis of the mechanisms which govern and control pay determination in that sector. Although the specific provisions of each policy are important determinants of the eventual outcome, they are only important in the context of their influence on, and interaction with, the basic pay determination mechanisms which apply whether incomes policy is being pursued or not. Only when these mechanisms are explicitly and forcefully replaced or suspended (as in the case of the suspension of the PRU in the mid-1970s) do we see any real evidence of a pattern of settlements which differs from that which could be predicted *a priori*. Even in the cases where the government has taken steps (either explicitly or *de facto*) to hold the public sector to the terms of an incomes policy, and there is considerable circumstantial evidence to support the assertion that this has taken place in practice despite assertions to the contrary (Winchester, 1975), the evidence presented above and that provided in chapters 2 and 3 indicates that in the period following an incomes policy the reinstatement of the traditional mechanisms has led to the restoration of the original set of relativities and differentials via 'catch-up' settlements. The only significant instance of a shift in established differentials would seem to be the long-run decline in the relative position of non-manual workers, and even this phenomenon cannot be said to be peculiar to the public sector. Elsewhere (Elliott and Fallick, 1980) the present authors have argued that although this process was exacerbated by the incomes policies of the late 1960s and during the first half of the 1970s, it was not in essence the product of incomes policies. The impact of market forces, particularly the growth in the supply of university graduates during the 1960s, and the impact of inflation would seem to offer at least part of the wider explanation. Incomes policies only served to accelerate the trend, particularly when they specified flat money increases as opposed to percentage increases. If our proposition then is that incomes policies are less important in understanding the movement of relative pay in the public sector than are the mechanisms of pay determination it is appropriate to end this chapter with a brief restatement of the distinctive features of the mechanisms and their implications for the control of public sector pay in the future.

At the beginning of this chapter we highlighted the role of comparability in public sector pay determination. This principle was adopted in the public sector as a result of the unavailability of direct (or in some cases even indirect) measures of output and/or the marginal productivity of labour. This fact is a consequence of the nature of most public sector employment, and as the structure of that employment shifts progressively in favour of non-manual employment in service provision, and non-marketed services at that, the problem of unobservable marginal products becomes more, rather than less, important. Under this system of pay determination, when private sector pay advances, for whatever reasons, public sector pay will almost inevitably follow, although the length of the time-lag involved has tended to vary considerably across public sector sub-groups. This variable lag has been one of the main sources of short-term variations in differentials and relativities within the public sector, and it in turn can be seen as a function of the different types of pay determination mechanism employed by the various sub-groups. Its significance is considerably increased when governments opt for incomes policies. For example, if local authority manuals bargain annually, then direct comparisons with private sector earnings and rates can also be made annually, and the divergence can, potentially at least, be minimised. In the case of those workers covered by the PRU, however, the length of time required for a full-scale PRU assessment (usually two years) means that an interim settlement is usually reached. The divergence between public and private sector pay is both potentially and actually greater here and the mechanism itself introduces scope for discontent and industrial unrest as some groups of public sector employees feel that they are being 'left behind'.

The imposition of an incomes policy, by arbitrarily cutting across this process and restricting the size of settlements after a specific date, has inevitably generated severe short-term and long-term anomalies and as a result the initially complex and difficult process of determining pay in the public sector has been rendered more difficult and complex and consequently more unsettling to industrial relations. This argument applies with even greater force when one considers the myriad smaller bodies, such as the Top Salaries Review Body, the Review Body on Doctors' and Dentists' Pay and the arrangements governing the pay of those in HM Forces. Here the gap between successive awards may be up to five years, which in a period of rapid inflation will inevitably produce discontent and which moreover leads to infrequent awards which are extremely large. These very large settlements, when taken out of context, can have a considerable disruptive effect as in the case of the recent 40 per cent award to the police force. Other groups who are being actively held down by the government interpret these large awards as evidence of some form of favouritism on the part of the government, and in consequence increase their efforts to obtain a large settlement in turn. It would seem plausible to argue, on the basis of the historical evidence, that the Clegg commission has a high probability of engendering exactly this situation. By recommending awards which in some sense compensate a specific group for previous 'mistreatment' they will generate spillover effects, which although illegitimate may eventually cause the government to curtail or abandon the activities of the standing commission.

The impact of specific settlements within the public sector on the pay of other public sector groups is an important corollary of the basic comparability principle. Although only a few sets of formal linkages exist, as for example in the utilities (involving gas, water and electricity supply workers) it is clear that a much wider set of informal or notional relativities exist 'under the surface' of public sector agreements. The specific sets of linkages, and their strength, is practically impossible to determine, due in part to the flexibility of the arrangements and in part to the variations in the emphasis which negotiators place on these links. None the less, such relationships are important, as they may be used to justify large settlements within the public sector, when one of the informal groupings manages to obtain a large settlement as a result of a favourable external comparison or a productivity-linked award. Clearly, this process presents a considerable problem, as it is highly unlikely that productivity growth is uniform within the public sector and/or that this rate of productivity growth is equivalent to that which obtains in the best private sector organisations, with which the public sector employee representatives will doubtless wish to be compared. As a result of the mechanisms and processes by which pay is determined in the public sector, Baumol's unbalanced growth problem is made more acute.

If we now attempt to superimpose a series of incomes policies on this complex picture a further set of complications is almost certain to develop. The first of these is the simple problem of the timing of incomes policy. A specific date for the introduction of a policy has to be set. As the 'wage round' is a continuous rather than a discrete process, the policy will inevitably result in some groups settling as normal, or even advancing their settlement date in order to obtain their increase before the policy becomes effective, and some groups being held to the policy instead of reaching their negotiated solution. Anomalies will inevitably arise as a result, and in the case of the public sector, where a settlement may have been designed to compensate for pay movements over the previous two, three or even five years (as in the case of the Top Salaries Review Body) the extent of these anomalies may be considerable. Only two methods exist for removing the anomaly, namely an award based on the 'special case' principle or 'catch-up' awards after the period covered by the policy, which permit some form of compensation element. Historical evidence and simple common sense indicate that the 'special case' approach is almost unworkable; most groups of workers can find some arguments to support their special status, particularly where 'productivity' is introduced. Similarly the catch-up awards cannot be seen in isolation, due to the complexity of the comparability network, and in consequence any large award will almost certainly impart a general upward pressure.

The second principal problem produced by incomes policies is that pay claims tend to be based on the argument which is thought most likely to succeed. Accordingly, the long list of exception clauses (see the Appendix) have tended to undermine the overall effectiveness of the policies. This problem is obviously compounded by intra-public-sector comparisons, in the 'catch-up' period if not during the period of the policy itself. This *ad hoc* selection of the main justification for a pay claim led in the early and mid-1970s to the paradox of the public sector moving ahead of the private sector in terms of the size of settlements achieved. Had comparability been adhered to this could only have occurred to the extent that there was a divergence between the largest and smallest settlements in the private sector combined with the ability of the public sector to have its own settlements linked to the best settlements in the private sector. One can only conclude that the adherence of public sector employee representatives to the principle of comparability only extends as far as the usefulness of that principle. When superior arguments, or at least arguments likely to lead to superior pay awards, present themselves or are presented by the exception clauses of incomes policies, comparability is readily abandoned in the pursuit of the best results for those being represented. Finally, the influence of these particular considerations inevitably introduce a bias into public sector pay determination, in favour of manual workers. Because of the less frequent revision of non-manual pay (or at least the reduced frequency of thorough reviews) and because of the absence of productivity measures to support claims on that basis, manual employees are able to adjust their position more quickly, which in inflation will be of considerable importance; and one might even argue that the long-run narrowing of differentials between manual and non-manual workers referred to above has been given added impetus by the mechanism described.

At this point it would seem appropriate to raise the whole status of the current set of mechanisms for pay determination in the public sector. Clearly the mechanisms are distinctive and to a large degree they explain the ways in which successive incomes policies have actually affected the public sector. It would be difficult to argue that this influence has been either uniform, across policies or employee sub-groups, or particularly beneficial. The special cases problems, the impact of catch-up settlements and the diversity of bargaining strategies stem as much from the way in which pay is determined in the public sector as from the specific provisions of the various policies. In consequence, pay in the public sector can only be controlled when governments come to grips with the shortcomings of the present system; and it would seem that incomes policies have tended to increase rather than reduce these shortcomings.

Notes: Chapter 5

1 See chapter 2 of *Pay in the Public Sector* by R. F. Elliott and J. L. Fallick (Macmillan, 1980) for full details of the nature, size and timing of changes in the composition of the public sector labour force since 1950.
2 There are of course a few exceptions to this generalisation. However they are not a serious threat to the general validity of the argument presented.
3 For a detailed discussion of the machinery of collective bargaining in the public sector see Clegg (1976), Department of Employment and Productivity (1961), Levinson (1971), Loveridge (1971), and Thompson and Beaumont (1978).
4 However, it should be noted at this point that the PRU does not disclose the names of the organisations and occupations (grades, etc.) which are used in the comparison exercises. As a result one may only speculate as to the present make-up of the list of comparators.
5 A. Smith, *An Enquiry into the Nature and Causes of the Wealth of Nations*, Book 1, Chapter 10.
6 The equation which provided the best explanation of wage change over the period took the form:

$$W_t = -\cdot39 + \cdot01\ U_{t-2} + \cdot35 p_{t-2} - 2\cdot72\ F_1 - 1\cdot26\ F_2$$
$$(1\cdot17)\quad(\cdot00)\qquad(\cdot09\ )\qquad(1\cdot44)\qquad(1\cdot00)$$

$$+\ 2\cdot11\ F_3 - 1\cdot16\ F_4 - \ \cdot35\ F_5 + 6\cdot00\ F_6 - 2\cdot56\ F_7$$
$$(1\cdot84)\qquad(1\cdot51)\qquad(1\cdot40)\qquad(2\cdot10)\qquad(1\cdot97)$$

$$-3\cdot17 F_8$$

$$R^2 = \cdot58 \qquad D.W. = 1\cdot89$$

where W_t is the average size of wage settlement in the public sector, U_t is the unemployment rate, and p_t the rate of price change, both specified with a two quarter lag, and F_1 to F_8 are the incomes policy dummies as defined below. Taken in conjunction with the average size of settlement during periods of incomes policy, as reported in Table 5.1, these provide an insight into the impact of incomes policies on manual worker pay in the public sector.

The dummies were assigned the value of unity for the following periods and zero for all others: F_1, the freeze, 1950 I and II, 1961 III − 1962 I, 1966 III and IV, 1972 IV − 1973 I; F_2, the period of the National Incomes Commission, etc., 1962 II − 1966 II; F_3, the Macmillan wage and price plateau, 1956 I − IV; F_4, the period of severe restraint, 1967 I − 1968 II; F_5, incomes policies of 1968 to 1970,

1968 III – 1970 II; F_6, N–1, 1971 IV – 1972 III; F_7, Stages One and Two, 1973 II – 1974 II; F_8, £6 per week, 1975 III and IV.

7 Cmnd. 3150, which set out the details of the period of 'severe restraint'. See the Appendix for details.

8 We did not have sufficient information to be able to estimate the 'average pay bill over the twelve months prior to the settlement' as required under the legislation. None the less, some estimate of the percentage increase in basic rates which was compatible with the ceiling was achieved by calculating the percentage equivalent of £1 + 4 per cent of the gross weekly earnings of manual workers within each agreement in the period immediately prior to Phase II. The average bill is, of course, the sum of the gross weekly wages of each worker multiplied by the number of workers. We did not have information on the latter and therefore assumed this, rather unsatisfactorily, to be constant.

9 For a more detailed discussion of non-manual pay see Elliott and Fallick (1980) and Elliott and Fallick (1979).

10 The comparability exercises have been supplemented by 'factor analysis', so called. However, concerted attempts to discover what this means in practice, and how the various 'factors' are weighted, have produced no clear answers. It would appear that factor analysis may be no more than comparability with some set of unspecified weighting factors designed to allow for the fact that no two jobs are identical.

References: Chapter 5

Clegg, H. A., *How to Run an Incomes Policy* [etc.] (Heinemann, 1971)

Clegg, H. A., *Trade Unionism under Collective Bargaining* (Oxford: Blackwell, 1976)

Edwards, R., and Roberts, R. D. V., *Status, Productivity and Pay: A Major Experiment* (Macmillan, 1971)

Elliott, R. F., 'Public Sector Wage Movements: 1950–1973', *Scottish Journal of Political Economy*, vol. 24, no. 2, June 1977

Elliott, R. F., and Fallick, J. L., 'Pay Differentials in Perspective [etc.]', *Economic Journal*, vol. 89, June 1979

Elliott, R. F., and Fallick, J. L., *Pay in the Public Sector* (Macmillan, 1980)

Levinson, H. M., *Collective Bargaining by British Local Authority Employees*, ILIR, Ann Arbor, 1971

Loveridge, R., *Collective Bargaining by National Employees in the U.K.*, ILIR, Ann Arbor, 1971

Pay Board, *Anomalies*, Cmnd 5429 (HMSO, 1972)

Pay Board, *Relativities*, Cmnd 5535 (HMSO, 1974)

Pay Board, *The Relative Pay of Mineworkers*, Cmnd 5567 (HMSO, 1974)

Report of the Committee of Inquiry into the Pay of Non-University Teachers (The Houghton Report), Cmnd 5848 (HMSO, 1974)

Royal Commission on Doctors' and Dentists' Remuneration 1957–60 (Pilkington Commission), Cmnd 939 (HMSO, 1960)

Royal Commission on The Civil Service 1953–55 (Priestly Commission) (HMSO, 1955)

Smith, A., *An Enquiry into the Nature and Causes of the Wealth of Nations* (G. Bell & Sons, 1921)

Thompson, A. W. J., and Beaumont, P. B., *Public Sector Bargaining* [etc.] (Farnborough: Saxon House, 1978)

Winchester. D., 'Labour relations in the public sector in the United Kingdom', in Rhemus, C. M. (ed.), *Public Employment Labour Relations: An Overview of Eleven Nations*, ILIR, Ann Arbor, 1975

Chapter 6

Incomes Policies
and Low Pay

R. STEELE*

Introduction

Every formal incomes policy since 1965 has acknowledged the
problem of low pay. It is difficult to know, however, whether this
problem was seen as a general societal one, with incomes policies
simply affording the convenient possibility of redistribution, or
whether the incomes policies themselves were considered likely to have
particularly adverse effects on this specific group and as a result
special provisions were necessary as a counterbalance. In spite of the
admission in 1969 by Mr Harold Walker, the Under-Secretary of State
for Employment, that 'it is not a primary function of the
Government's prices and incomes policy to redistribute incomes', it is
probable that the former belief prevailed. Whichever sentiment
predominated, it was intended that the low-paid should *at least* fare
as well (or as badly) as other groups of workers under incomes
policies. In this chapter we assess the extent to which the various
policies managed to meet this objective.

Three broad types of policy have been tried in relation to the low-
paid: policies with low pay as a major exception to norms or
guidelines; policies allowing specific increases to *groups* of workers
but with some bias in favour of redistribution towards the lowest-
paid; and largely flat-rate policies on individual earnings, which *a
priori* will reduce percentage differentials and relativities. Of course,
the various policies and stages have differed in the degree of vigour
with which they have been applied by governments (and in the degree
to which they have been adhered to by employees and employers) as
well as in the form of their provisions. For instance, early policies

* The author would like to acknowledge the invaluable advice of Bob Elliott and
Ianthe Fordyce. Any remaining errors are his alone.

emphasised the existence of low-pay exception clauses in order to gain acceptance of policies by unions and the general public — 'packaging' as Moore and Bedoe (1976) called it. When it came to permitting increases under this criterion, however, their performance was less emphatic. During the lifetime of the National Board for Prices and Incomes (NBPI), it advocated special treatment on grounds of low pay on only two occasions (both for Agriculture).

For the purpose of the analyses presented in this chapter, the definition of low pay used is threefold, each aspect helping in different ways to analyse how different policies have affected 'those forming the bottom tenth of the relevant earnings league' (NBPI, 1971, p. 5):

(a) *Low-paid industries* are those which have a significant percentage of workers earning less than the lowest decile of the all industries and services earnings distribution for male manual employees.

(b) The *lowest-paid workers* are those who are earning less than or equal to the lowest decile of their industry's earnings distribution where the industry's lowest decile is less than the lowest decile of the all industries and services distribution for male manual workers. (These industries are invariably the same industries as those in (a).)

(c) Where the industry or service has been legally designated as low-paid through the presence of a Wages Council. (This definition is employed only when discussing rates, though some of the industries and services covered in (a) and (b) are covered by wages councils.)

Hourly earnings are used throughout and unless indicated are exclusive of the effects of overtime, which will vary with fluctuations in the business cycle. Moreover, data refer only to manual males. Little data exists for female earnings which exclude the effects of overtime, while legislation aimed at altering the position of female earnings in the labour market has existed contemporaneously with incomes policies at one time or another during the period under study — the Equal Pay Act and the Sex Discrimination Act (Hebden, 1978; Sloane and Chiplin, 1976). Since we are trying to focus on the effects of one specific labour market provision, incomes policies, rather than on the operation of the labour market as a whole, and since it is impossible to isolate the effects of the female-specific legislation it was decided not to include females in the analyses. In the case of non-manual workers the earnings distribution is greatly affected by the impact of the age distribution of lifetime earnings. The presence of occupations in the lowest decile whose earnings and earning changes are governed by professional institutions (chartered accountants, lawyers, and so on) and whose earnings in their early years in no way reflect that of average lifetime earnings, along with occupations normally accepted as being low-paid, leads to difficulties in interpretation and measurement of low pay for this group. Low wages are accepted in such occupations in return for considerably higher benefits and earnings in the future. This is rarely the case for full-time adult manual workers.

The exclusion of females and non-manual males, however, should not be taken as an indication of either the lack of a low-pay problem or a lack of concern at their problem. Rather it reflects the different nature of their problems and the inability of the existing data to isolate the differing effects from incomes policy effects.

This paper sets out to look at the experience of the low-paid under the different types of incomes policy operating in Britain since 1966. There are basically three central issues: how have low-paid industries fared under the different types of provision; how have the lowest-paid employees fared; and has there been any tendency *within* low-paid industries for redistribution in favour of the lowest-paid to occur? These questions are addressed by use of *New Earnings Survey* (*NES*) data. Earnings data are also used to examine the experiences of the low-paid within different bargaining sectors (the private, public and wages council sectors), before nationally negotiated basic wage rates are introduced to examine the effects of incomes policies on the operation of the legally defined low-paid sector, the wages council sector.

The paper finishes by highlighting certain implications of the results, then draws some conclusions on the operation of incomes policies for the low-paid.

The low-paid — who are they?

It would be repetitious and of little value, so soon after the *Lower Incomes Reference* by the Royal Commission on the Distribution of Income and Wealth (RCDIW, 1978), to go into any great detail on which occupations and industries form the lowest decile of the earnings distribution. That report adequately described the statistics on the incidence and distribution of low pay by occupation and industry. Moreover its findings differed little from those of earlier analyses by Marquand (1967) and Pond and Winyard (1976). Thus clerical and related, farming, selling, transport-operating and the catering and cleaning occupational groups contained over 56 per cent of low-paid men in 1977. The distributive trades and miscellaneous services alone accounted for over 31 per cent of low-paid men in all

Table 6.1 The industrial distribution and incidence of the low-paid and their relative earnings, 1979

	Percentage of low-earning men in the industry	Percentage in industry who were low-earning	Ratio of average hourly earnings*	Ratio of lowest deciles*
Agriculture and horticulture	7·1	36·0	72·8	88·0
Catering	8·2	52·6	74·4	66·5
Educational services	4·4	36·3	78·0	86·7
Dealing in coal, oil, etc.	1·0	19·2	84·2	92·4
National government services	2·1	30·5	84·6	90·4
Woollen and worsted	1·2	22·2	83·5	90·6
Retail distribution	13·6	25·5	85·1	85·2
Textile finishing	0·8	22·5	84·7	90·3
Local government services	4·4	14·7	87·7	94·6
Weaving of cotton, etc.	0·3	11·5	95·6	94·8
Motor repairers	3·9	16·6	88·8	90·6
Wholesale distribution	7·7	20·1	91·4	88·6
Clothing	1·0	24·1	85·0	83·8
Medical and dental services	4·3	24·5	85·0	89·8
Bacon curing	0·6	11·8	91·7	95·9
Bread and flour confectionery	0·7	13·6	83·9	93·0
Milk and milk products	0·3	8·3	89·0	95·5
Hosiery	0·7	17·7	96·5	94·7
Food	2·5	9·1	93·6	95·7
Road haulage contracting	1·7	5·9	93·5	96·2§

* Average hourly earnings (lowest decile) in each industry as a percentage of average earnings (lowest decile) in all industries and services.
§1978 figure.

industries and services (RCDIW, 1978). However, in order that the reader may be able to identify in slightly more detail the industrial location of the low-paid and lowest-paid, often referred to in this paper, Table 6.1 gives details of the proportionate distributions between and within the industries covered by the study as at 1979.[1] The purpose of this table is illustrative, it is only included to supply the reader with some background to the statistics rather than as an essential step in the analysis. Thus, it only gives approximations at one point in time of where the low-paid are to be found and in what quantities; the figures themselves can fluctuate from year to year for various reasons. In this fashion the table shows that agriculture in 1979 accounted for 7·1 per cent of all low-paid manual males and that about 36 per cent of agricultural workers were low-paid: catering accounted for 8·2 per cent with almost 53 per cent of catering workers low-paid; and so on. The Commission competently covered this aspect of low pay and concluded:

> There has generally been little change in the proportion of men manual workers having low earnings in manufacturing, apart from clothing and footwear where the proportion has increased. There have been falls in the proportion having low earnings in the public sector, and also in certain of the service industries. In many of the latter, however, the proportion is still above average and has been rising. (RCDIW, 1978, p. 55)

The study by Dean in Chapter 3 and later data presented in this paper support the Commission's finding of a relative improvement in the position of public sector workers.

Again for the reader's benefit, the table includes an illustrative example of the size of the ratios of average hourly earnings in each of the industries and services to the average for all male manual workers, and also the ratios of the lowest deciles: both measures are used extensively in the later analyses. These figures give some idea of the relative position of each industry to the average and of each low-paid industry's lowest-paid to the low-pay threshold (note that this threshold is taken merely for comparative purposes and does not indicate any opinion as to whether the threshold is in itself adequate). Thus average earnings in clothing are 85 per cent of average earnings elsewhere and its lowest-paid are paid some 83·8 per cent of the low-pay threshold (or 16·2 per cent beneath the lowest decile earnings for all workers).

The sample of industries covered in this study accounts for over 65 per cent of all low-paid manual male employees, with the remainder scattered over most of the remaining industries and services. (Pockets of low pay are to be found in nearly all industries.) Moreover the level of the lowest decile for all the industries and services in Table 6.1 can be seen to be below the low-pay threshold, that is, the lowest decile of the all industries and services earnings distribution. The industries covered in the rest of these analyses are therefore low-paid under both definitions (a) and (b) in the introduction – they contain significant proportions of individuals who are low-paid, and their lowest decile are, perhaps not surprisingly, earning less than the low-pay threshold.

Relative earnings of the low-paid under incomes policies

The aggregate picture
Between 1968 and 1979 the ratio of the lowest decile to the median of the male manual earnings distribution for all industries and services (excluding overtime effects) fell 0·4 percentage points, from 73 to 72·6 per cent (Table 6.2). This deterioration occurred in a period only rarely without some form of incomes policy operating. The series 'peaked' (if such a term is appropriate) in 1970 and 1977 at 74·3 per cent, and 'troughed' at 71·1 per cent in 1972. The period 1970 to 1972 saw a fall of 3·2 percentage points, and 1973 to 1977 a slow but gradual recovery, until in 1977 the ratio returned to its 1970 level. This aggregate picture of movements in the position of the 'low-paid' through the 1970s would appear to suggest that the incomes policies of the mid-1970s were improving the position of the low-paid (the lowest decile) relative to the median. However, annual movements in this ratio are normal and the 'improvement' may just as well have been a 'normal' recovery from the very low level reached in 1972 than from specific policy effects. Moreover, using movements in this ratio alone to assess the effects of policies assumes that all of the low-paid had similar experiences and that they were earning the decile wage. Neither of these assumptions is warranted. It is necessary to look beneath this level of aggregation to get closer to the true effects, if any, of policies.

The detailed picture
There will always be occasions when a change in the circumstances of one industry will alter its position relative to others for reasons other than the effects of incomes policies: for instance where an industrial dispute or some other factor leads to an alteration in the normal settlement date, and earnings levels at the time of the survey may not be representative of the usual relativities. However, in general, movements in the relationship between the average earnings of low-paid industries and all other industries and services should act as a good indicator of how policies have affected the overall standing of the low-paid.

During the 1970s, low-paid industries and services differed

Table 6.2 Changes in the relationship between lowest decile and median of male manual earnings

Gross hourly earnings excluding overtime

	1968/1970* %	1971* %	1972* %	1973 %	1974 %	1975 %	1976 %	1977 %	1978 %	1979 %
Manual men	+0·1	−1·8	−1·4	+0·9	+0·4	+0·3	+0·7	+0·9	−0·9	−0·8

* Including those affected by absence.
Source: NES, 1968–1979.

Table 6.3 Changes in average hourly earnings in low-paying industries *vis-à-vis* all industries

	1970 %	1971 %	1972 %	1973 %	1974 %	1975 %	1976 %	1977 %	1978 %	1979 %
Average ratio of low-paid earnings to all industries and services average*	85·4	85·4	84·9	84·4	84·9	85·0	85·2	85·3	84·7	85·3
Percentage number of low-paid industries improving their position		50§	22	38	50	50	53	53	37	63
Percentage of low-paid industries deteriorating		50	61	62	44	50	47	47	58	37
Percentage of low-paid industries showing no change			17		6				5	

* Unweighted average.
§ April 1970 to April 1971.

significantly in their experiences under policies. Certain of them improved their position – road haulage contracting, agriculture, medical and dental services, local government services and food manufacturing – while others showed distinct deterioration in their relative average wages, especially clothing, woollen and worsted, and retail distribution. Overall about 68 per cent of the industries and services in the low-paid group in the sample improved their position between 1970 and 1979, but the extent of relative decline by the remaining industries was sufficient to annul an overall improvement.

Between 1970 and 1973, the majority of low-paid industries saw their average earnings *fall* relative to those in other industries and it was not until 1976 that an improvement in the majority was recorded (Table 6.3). Improvement was sustained, however, only until 1978 when relative average wages significantly declined prior to picking up in 1979. This pattern reflects general deterioration during the 'N–1' policies; no particular pattern for the £1 + 4 per cent, £2.25 per week and the early Social Contract period; improvement during the £6 per week and £2.50–£4.00 per week policies; and, surprisingly perhaps, improvement at the end of the period, when the policy was regarded as being almost inoperative.

The only years in which low-paid manual occupations displayed any real improvement relative to other occupations were 1973 and 1976 (Table 6.4). Perversely perhaps, 1977 saw a slight deterioration in the position of a majority of low-paid occupations – perversely, because the 1977 pay policies were based on individual earnings and it might have been expected that individual occupations would display the discriminatory aspects of these policies more than they actually did.

Changes in relative average earnings will give an indication of whether particular incomes policy provisions have or have not in general helped low-paid industries. They will not necessarily indicate that there has been a change in the position of the low-paid *within* those industries, the mean of course being affected as much by changes at the top of the earnings distribution as at the bottom. Moreover it is perhaps the *lowest-paid* that are in mind when exceptions and help to the low-paid are discussed. Thus it is the *low-paid* agricultural worker and the *low-paid* catering worker rather than the average wage-earner in agriculture and catering who are often seen to constitute the problem group. Indeed this group has been the particular centre of attention in certain policy stages, most obviously those policies with a flat-rate element. But even the earlier policies tried to focus on this group – note the reluctance of the NBPI to grant exceptional increases because it felt that these increases might not be concentrated on the 'lowest-paid' (NBPI, 1967).

Rather than give a blow-by-blow descriptive account of the experience of the lowest-paid under different policies, the approach

Table 6.4 Changes in average hourly earnings of low-paying occupations *vis-à-vis* all occupations*

	1970 %	1971 %	1972 %	1973 %	1974 %	1975 %	1976 %	1977 %	1978 %	1979 %
Average ratio of low-paid earnings to all occupations' averages§	77·1	77·2	77·3	77·6	78·6	78·3	82·1	79·9	79·7	78·8
Percentage number of low-paid occupations improving their position		43+	38	75	50	50	63	22	40	70
Percentage of low-paid occupations deteriorating		57	62	25	50	50	37	78	60	30

* Occupational data are particularly weak, and the figures should be treated with caution.
§ Unweighted average.
+ April 1970 to April 1971.

adopted here is a statistical one utilising pooled time-series cross-sectional data for directional changes and predetermined hypotheses tested by Chi-square test.

Perhaps the first hypothesis that should be tested is the simple but important one of whether policies increased the chances of an improvement in an industry's lowest-paid employees relative to the low-pay threshold.

Hypothesis 1 $\displaystyle\sum_{i=1}^{20} \sum_{j=1}^{n} (A_{ij} > B_{ij})$ for 'policy-off' and 'policy-on'

periods and for flat-rate and group-norm policies[2]

where $A_{ij} = $ an increase in the ratio of the lowest-paid to the low-pay threshold (LD_i/LD_{all})

$B_{ij} = $ a decrease in the ratio of the lowest-paid to the low-pay threshold and

$i = $ industry

$j = $ years

The answer to this question is very much in the negative ($\chi^2 = 0.314: 0.05 < p > 0.10$) – there was as much chance of an improvement in the relative position of an industry's lowest-paid workers when policies were 'off' as when they were 'on', though two qualifications should be borne in mind. First, the definition of the 'policy-off' period is not as 'pure' as one might wish; and, secondly, we are talking about the *lowest*-paid employees *vis-à-vis* all other low-paid workers (or the level of earnings defined in general as being low-paid). The finding is just as true, however, regardless of the type of policy in operation – group or flat-rate increases. Occupational data support these findings.

Implicit in the rationale of allowing exceptional increases to low-paid industries or negotiating groups of workers was the belief that increasing the average wage in, for instance, agriculture or catering would lead to a general improvement in the position of the lowest-paid employees in those industries. However, it is not immediately obvious that such a policy would have the desired effect of lifting an industry's whole earnings structure. The second hypothesis tested then was: did improving relative average wages in a low-paid industry also lead to an improvement in the relative position of that industry's lowest paid?

Hypothesis 2 $\displaystyle\sum_{i=1}^{20} \sum_{j=1}^{n} (C_{ij} \text{ and } A_{ij}) > \sum_{i=1}^{20} \sum_{j=1}^{n} (C_{ij} \text{ and } B_{ij})$ for 'policy-on' and 'off' periods and different policy types

where C_{ij} = an increase in the ratio of relative average earnings between low-paid and other industries and services.

It would appear that an improvement in the general average of a low-paid industry did also have a beneficial effect on the lowest-paid within that industry relative to other industries ($\chi^2 = 4 \cdot 091:0 \cdot 01 < p < 0 \cdot 05$) though this was true regardless of whether incomes policies were operating or not (note that this does not require any compression in the distribution, only a 'leap-frogging' effect of the whole industry). Had the NBPI however made wider use of the low-paid exception clause to allow larger increases to low-paid industries then it is likely that this would have also had a beneficial effect on their lowest-paid workers (though the cost of such a policy might have been very high).

So far this section has assessed the patterns of change of average wages in low-paid industries relative to other wages and the effects of policies on the lowest-paid workers relative to the low-pay threshold. However there is one further provision which has been both explicitly expressed and implicitly available during many policies, the provision for internal redistribution through compression of wage differentials *within* industries. Certain policies, by their very nature, should have caused compression, that is, where the policies were stipulated as flat-rate increases and these increases were fully granted to each worker. Other policies were couched in terms of group norms or guidelines but were designed to permit additional increases to the lowest-paid (the 10 per cent policy for instance).

Between 1970 and 1979 slightly less than half of the sample of low-paid industries compressed their differential between lowest decile and median; moreover the size of compression was very small – on average about $2 \cdot 6$ percentage points per industry, whereas widening in this differential was on average about $3 \cdot 6$ percentage points per industry over the whole period. Three years in particular saw compression in the low-paid industries' distributions: 1974, 1976 and 1977, the periods including the £1 + 4 per cent, £2.25 or 7 per cent, and the £6 per week and £2.50–£4.00 policies – notably the flat-rate policies (Table 6.5). However, in keeping with the statistical approach adopted earlier, two hypotheses were tested as to the incidence of compression: was there more likely to be compression below the median when policies were 'on' rather than 'off'; and had there been some form of wage-charity effect (Mayhew, Chapter 4) with policies, i.e., was compression more likely to occur when average wages were relatively increasing (and trade unions and the average

Table 6.5 Performance of lowest-paid within low-paying industries

	1968* %	1970 %	1971 %	1972 %	1973 %	1974 %	1975 %	1976 %	1977 %	1978 %	1979 %
Average ratio of lowest decile to median within industries§	79·0	77·3	76·2	76·6	75·3	75·9	76·4	76·9	78·0	77·2	76·5
Percentage number of industries compressing this differential		54*	45	35	45	70	50	60	70	50	35
Percentage of industries widening this differential		46	55	65	55	30	45	35	25	50	65
Percentage of industries showing no change							5	5	5		

* On a smaller sample.
§ Unweighted average.

wage-earner were feeling more benevolent) than when they were relatively decreasing?

$$\text{Hypothesis 3} \quad \sum_{i=1}^{20} \sum_{j=1}^{n} (D_{ij} > E_{ij})$$

where D_{ij} = an increase in the ratio of the lowest decile to the median within low-paid industries (compression)

and E_{ij} = a decrease in the ratio (widening).

$$\text{Hypothesis 4} \quad \sum_{i=1}^{20} \sum_{j=1}^{n} (C_{ij} \text{ and } D_{ij}) > \sum_{i=1}^{20} \sum_{j=1}^{n} (F_{ij} \text{ and } D_{ij})$$

where F_{ij} = a decrease in the relative average wage of a low-paid industry.

The results showed there to be no greater tendency for compression to occur when policies were 'on' rather than 'off' ($\chi^2 = 0.83$) but there was a slightly greater tendency during the flat-rate policies ($\chi^2 = 2.82$: $0.05 < p < 0.10$). Group policies showed no effect. Similarly for the wage-charity effect there was not really any greater element of compression present when policies were 'on' rather than 'off' ($\chi^2 = 2.67$: $0.05 < p > 0.10$). Any element that was present was of the 'forced' statistical nature under the flat-rate policies ($\chi^2 = 3.19$: $0.05 < p < 0.10$). There was no indication of a greater wage-charity effect when group policies operated when compared to 'policy-off' periods.

Summary
The results of this section showed:

(a) The aggregate experience of the lowest decile of the all industries and services distribution cannot be regarded as being typical of all low-paid industries.
(b) The differing experiences of low-paid industries under incomes policies suggest that the flat-rate norms were not, as was often thought, regarded as entitlements to low-paid workers.
(c) Average earnings in a majority of low-paid industries fell relative to other industries between 1970 and 1973; displayed no particular pattern to 1975; improved 1976–7; fell 1978; and improved 1979.
(d) On balance the 'decade' of incomes policies has hardly even led to a maintenance, let alone an improvement, of the relative

position of low-paid industries; indeed in the aggregate it led to a
fall.

(e) Policies did not lead to an increase in the likelihood of an
improvement in the relative position of the lowest-paid within a
low-paid industry relative to the low-pay threshold.

(f) Policies were possibly more likely to cause compression *within* an
industry's earnings distribution – especially flat-rate policies –
but there was no evidence of any wage-charity effect.

Analysis by bargaining sector

Industrial and occupational earnings are of obvious interest in
identifying low pay in so far as economic production is structured
along these axes. However, wages are normally set by bargaining,
often through nationally negotiated agreements which may or may not
cover entire industries and services or occupations. Moreover it has
primarily been the purpose of incomes policies to affect *wage-bargains*
as such, and it is at the level of negotiated wage settlements that their
effects might be seen most clearly.

This section begins by looking briefly at the scant earnings data
available by agreement on low pay in the private and public sectors,
then concentrates on the sector already defined by legislation as being
low-paid – the wages council sector.[3]

Low-paid private and public agreements

Earnings data at agreement level of the type necessary for this study
are extremely poor. This is especially true of the private sector where
the number of agreements covered is small and yearly inclusions and
exclusions numerous. Results using these data, therefore, can only be
suggestive and conclusions drawn tentatively. (The definitions of low-
paid agreements and the lowest-paid are the same as specified for
industries in the introduction to this chapter.)

Between 1970 and 1979, average gross hourly earnings in a majority
of low-paid private agreements probably showed an overall
improvement compared to average wages elsewhere. In the public
sector, however, as many agreements deteriorated in their relative
position as improved but with the balance towards an improvement.
The agreements for food manufacturing, cotton spinning and
weaving, and textile finishing in the private sector showed significant
improvement, while baking, woollen and worsted and motor vehicle
repair relatively deteriorated. In the public sector the agreements for
nurses and midwives and local authority manual workers improved
most, while relative earnings for British Rail conciliation staff and
government industrial establishment employees deteriorated. Because
of the inadequacies of the private sector data little can be said as to
movements within the period, but for the public sector agreements

covered, there is a distinct pattern of deterioration between 1970 and 1974 (bearing out the suggestion, perhaps, that the 'N−1' policy bore largely on the public sector), significant improvement between 1974 and 1976 (the period of the Social Contract and the £6 per week policy) and deterioration again right through to the end of the period (Table 6.6). Again due to the deficiencies of data, the relatively small number of observations makes it impossible to statistically test the hypotheses presented in the previous section. (However, fuller analyses of the behaviour of the public and private sectors *in general* under incomes policies are available in Dean in Chapter 3 and Mayhew in Chapter 4).

One final observation of interest on the earnings position of low-paid private and public agreements has regard to the compression of differentials between the lowest decile and median. In the private sector, approximately 50 per cent of low-paid agreements compressed this differential, with most compression occurring between 1975 and 1977, and in 1979 − again mainly the flat-rate policy periods (Table 6.7). Only one (out of six) public sector agreements showed compression in its distribution over the whole period (British Rail conciliation staff), the remainder showing a significant widening in differentials between the lowest-paid and the median. Only 1972 and 1976−7 saw any form of compression in this differential.

Realistically the paucity of the earnings data given in the *NES* on low-paid private and public sector agreements preclude anything other than the most general statements being made on experiences under incomes policies for the low-paid covered by these different sectors. Not surprisingly, the results which do exist for the private sector tend to mirror those of the earlier analyses by industry. In the public sector the majority of low-paid agreements improved their position relative to average wages elsewhere and it could be argued that this reflects the improvement of the public sector in general (Dean, Chapter 3). Internal differentials between the lowest-paid and the median, however, widened over the period for almost all of the public sector agreements.

The wages council sector

As early as 1909, low pay was recognised by government to be a serious problem in certain industries and services; this recognition leading to the founding of a system of protection for the wages of these workers (Steele, 1978; Bayliss, 1962). Trade boards, as wages councils were originally called, were gradually set up to cover a considerable number of diverse industries and services such as agriculture (the Agricultural Wages Board), retailing, clothing, textiles, and some small metal and engineering industries − sixty-nine in all were established, though a significant number have been

Table 6.6 Performance of average hourly earnings in low-paying agreements

	1970 %	1971 %	1972 %	1973 %	1974 %	1975 %	1976 %	1977 %	1978 %	1979 %
Private sector										
Average ratio of low-paid earnings to all industries and services average*	85·2	77·8	86·5	85·9	83·8	id	id	id	id	86·2
Percentage number of low-paid agreements improving		0§	100	50	0	id	id	id	id	id
Percentage of low-paid agreements deteriorating		100	0	50	100	id	id	id	id	id
Public sector										
Average ratio of low-paid earnings to all earnings average*	81·7	78·7	86·8	84·3	82·8	86·3	91·1	90·7	87·1	84·0
Percentage of low-paid agreements improving		20§	100	33	33	100	60	33	0	0
Percentage of low-paid agreements deteriorating		80	0	67	67	0	40	50	83	100
Percentage of low-paid agreements showing no change								17	17	
Wages council sector										
Average ratio of low-paid earnings to all earnings average*	86·0	76·8	85·3	84·5	87·7	88·0	84·7	id	id	id
Ratio of 'all councils' average earnings to all earnings average (official index)			83·3	82·1	84·3	82·1	79·9	80·4	81·0	79·1
Percentage of low-paid councils improving		0	100	20	100	50	50	id	id	id
Percentage of low-paid councils deteriorating		100	0	80	0	50	50	id	id	id

Table 6.7 Performance of lowest-paid within low-paying agreements

	1970 %	1971 %	1972 %	1973 %	1974 %	1975 %	1976 %	1977 %	1978 %	1979 %
Private sector										
Average ratio of lowest decile to median within agreements*	77·4	75·9	76·1	76·0	75·3	75·8	76·7	78·0	78·0	76·7
Percentage number of agreements compressing this differential		63§	25	50	44	57	57	67	44	22
Percentage of agreements widening this differential		37	75	50	56	29	43	33	56	78
Percentage of agreements showing no change						14				
Public sector										
Average ratio of lowest decile to median within agreements*	83·1	79·4	80·7	79·2	79·3	77·0	78·9	79·5	78·6	78·0
Percentage of agreements compressing this differential		0§	60	33	67	17	50	67	17	33
Percentage of agreements widening this differential		100	40	67	33	83	50	33	66	67
Percentage of agreements showing no change									17	
Wages council sector										
Average ratio of lowest decile to median within agreements*	75·5	75·1	74·4	74·4	74·7	74·8	76·7	78·2	78·0	74·5
Percentage of councils compressing this differential		44§	22	56	38	62	71	71	29	17
Percentage of councils widening this differential		56	78	44	62	38	29	29	71	83

* Unweighted average.
§ April 1970 to April 1971.

abolished or amalgamated. The trades covered were chosen primarily because of a prevalence of extremely low wages and a lack of union organisation to protect the workers from exploitation. The councils have a tripartite forum for setting wages, with the usual sides of employer and employee representatives supplemented by independent members appointed by the Secretary of State for Employment in a conciliation/arbitration role (Bayliss, 1962). The peculiarly institutional format of their wage negotiations, and a noticeable lack of guidelines to members on which considerations should be taken into account in setting wages, contributed to extensive use of comparability (Steele, 1978). In practice wages councils sought basically to keep their rates 'in line' with the rates of other workers.

In assessing the performance of this low-paid sector under incomes policies, the main analyses are conducted using wage rates. In addition to the quite legitimate claim that wage rates set by national agreements are important in their own right to any analysis of wage movements (Elliott and Steele, 1975), the fundamental purpose of councils was and is the provision of Statutory Minimum Rates through the issue of Wages Regulation Orders. The performance of the system under incomes policies therefore should be judged through its direct actions on rates and not on its indirect results on earnings. However, for completeness, a very brief review of changes in the relative position of earnings for councils is first given.

Between 1970 and 1979, average gross hourly earnings in low-paid council agreements (in practice all of the councils covered by the *NES*) deteriorated significantly against average wages elsewhere. Only in 1972, 1974 and possibly 1976 was there any real improvement from the previous year in their earnings relative to other workers. In addition very little compression took place within the councils' earnings distributions, and when it did it was concentrated into the period 1974–7: normal experience however was for a widening of differentials to the detriment of the lowest paid (Table 6.7).

From 1972 the *New Earnings Survey* provided data at an aggregate level for 'all councils' and these data support the sample of individual councils' findings that 1974 was the only year when any real relative gain was made. All in all the data do not show incomes policies in a favourable light for improving or even supporting this sector's earnings during the 1970s.

It was stated earlier that the extensive use of comparability in wage determination by councils had led to an objective of keeping rates in the council sector in line with rates set under normal collective bargaining arrangements in nationally negotiated agreements. Figure 6.1, which is an up-dated and amended version of one used in an earlier study by this author (Steele, 1979), shows that this was almost achieved until the onset of policies in 1966. Throughout the

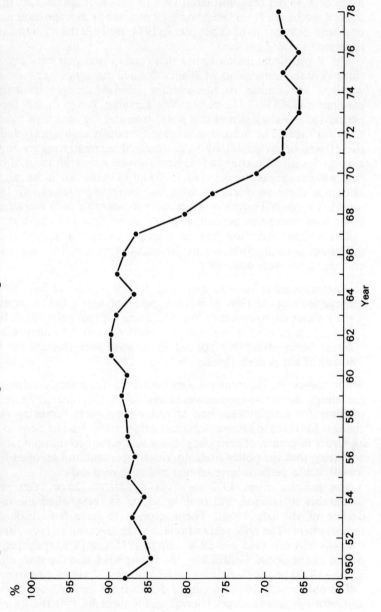

Figure 6.1 Ratio of mean wage rates in the wages council and non-wages council sectors

1950s and the first half of the 1960s, the ratio of average rates in the council sector to rates set elsewhere fluctuated little round the crude mean of 87·5 per cent. But from 1965 to 1974 average rates set in the council sector fell from being some 89 per cent of average rates in the non-council sector to 65·5 per cent in 1974. By 1979 the ratio had only recovered to 68·2 per cent.

The Royal Commission found that 'taking one year with another since 1970 the movements of Wages Council industry wage rates and earnings are similar to the average general changes in manual earnings' (RDCIW, 1978, p. 61). *New Earnings Survey* figures for the period 1972–9 suggest that this is not true and the data here belie its truth for rates. The ratio of average gross hourly earnings (excluding the effects of overtime) of wages council manual workers to the average for all industries and services showed a deterioration of over four percentage points. Between 1970 and 1978 the fall in the ratio of rates was three percentage points, but more importantly, by 1970, rates in the council sector *vis-à-vis* other comparable rates had already fallen some *seventeen* percentage points from their 1966 position.

The policies with low pay as a major exception to norms and guidelines proved expensive as far as rates in the low-paid wages council sector were concerned:

> What appears to have happened in the late 1960s was that, as the breakdown of the 1966/67 incomes policy occurred, the attempts of the Labour Government to maintain some form of policy until 1970 in the face of evasion and non-compliance led to the wages council sector being effectively policed as to wage rate changes for the whole of the period. (Steele, 1979, p. 229)

While non-council agreements were breaching this policy's norms and guidelines, the council sector was unable to. At this time the Secretary of State for Employment had to ratify the Orders decreeing wage changes for them to become legal and enforceable. Had he done so for an Order in breach of the policy this would have been tantamount to admitting that the policy itself no longer operated and an open free-for-all would perhaps have ensued earlier than it did.

The policies from 1973 onwards appear to have been more favourable to councils but only in so far as they halted the rapid decline of the late 1960s. There appears to have been little real improvement. The only years of relative improvement in rates for the councils between 1965 and 1978 were in 1975 and 1976, spanning the period of the Social Contract – the £6 per week and the start of the £2.50—£4.00 per week policies under the 'new' Labour government.

The only conclusion that can be drawn from the analyses of rates and earnings in the wages council sector must be that the incomes policies of the 1960s and early 1970s failed to protect the position of a large sector of low-paid workers designated by law to be within trades in need of protection, and the policies of the mid-1970s only halted a deteriorating trend but failed to make any significant improvement.

Conclusions

Incomes policies have done little to improve the position of the low-paid, and yet every policy during the late 1960s and 1970s stressed the specific problem of low pay. In the early policies the low-paid were catered for through the inclusion of clauses allowing for exceptional increases above the 'norms' or guidelines, while in the later policies the 'norms' themselves contained a flat-rate element specifically designed to improve their relative position. Undoubtedly, a powerful motive underlying this apparent concern for the welfare of the low-paid was the need to 'package' incomes policies in such a manner that they were attractive to the trade union movement. The flat-rate policies in particular were designed to ensure the co-operation of the powerful general unions, which represented the majority of the low-paid and whose agreement was considered vital to their success.

Given such concern over the issue of low pay when devising policies, it is perhaps more than a little surprising to find that their actual operation over a period of almost fourteen years led to no significant change in the position of the low-paid relative to that of other workers. Certainly, some policies did have an effect, but the evidence clearly shows that the policies up to 1970 containing exception clauses for low pay were singularly *unsuccessful* in helping the low-paid; indeed, in some cases they were even detrimental. In contrast, the policies of 1975–7 were in general the most successful. Parts of the Social Contract, the £6 per week and the £2·50–4·00 per week policies (both provided flat-rate increases on individual earnings), led to some improvement in the position of the low-paid, but the effects of these policies were short-lived, and other groups appear to have rapidly restored relativities and differentials. The temporary success of these policies was achieved by compressing differentials within industries rather than by improving the lot of the low-paying industries *vis-à-vis* the rest, and it is clear that in general they failed to install any real form of 'wage-charity' into the behaviour of bargainers.

The impact of incomes policies on the wages council sector was particularly deleterious. Throughout the 1950s and the early 1960s average wage rates in the trades covered by councils stood at some 85 per cent of the average level of wage rates in industries outside the council sector. In 1965 this ratio was 89 per cent, by 1971 it had plunged to 67 per cent. Increasingly, over the period of the late 1960s both the public and the private sectors evaded the 'norms' stipulated in the policies of this period. (Fallick and Elliott, Chapter 5.) In contrast, the council sector stuck closely to the guidelines. Principally, this was due to the institutional nature of wage determination in this sector. The wages councils consistently recommended increases that complied with the incomes policy norms of this period, for if they did not, the Secretary of State for Employment was able to exercise his authority and refuse to sanction such increases. This contrasted sharply with the inability of the government to police the policy in other areas of the economy.

In line with other low-paid workers, the low-paid in the council sector had their relative position improved by the flat-rate policies of the mid-1970s, but again this was only a small and a temporary improvement. Moreover, it is quite clear from the evidence presented here that even at such times the £6 per week and other flat-rate increases, which became entitlements in other areas of the economy, were by no means universally awarded to low-paid workers, and thus the relative position of some of them deteriorated.

Low pay is a relative concept. It follows therefore that it cannot be eradicated simply by increasing the total wealth of society through economic growth, although this is not to deny that the real income of the low-paid is increased with growth. Inequalities of earnings have not diminished greatly in Britain during periods of increasing wealth (Phelps-Brown, 1977). An improvement in the position of the low-paid necessitates the compression of certain differentials and relativities (though not all of them). It may be that all existing relativities and differentials serve important economic functions within the labour market for human-capital investment purposes, and there is widespread sympathy with the argument, but it is not a universal view. Talcott Parsons (1954), for example, argued that such an economic explanation of the hierarchy of occupations is insufficient and that the appropriate set of relativities and differentials is in part institutionally determined. On this view, therefore, incomes policies may have a role to play in altering and gaining acceptance of changes in certain existing relativities and differentials.

The general failure of incomes policies to mitigate the problem of low pay, and the rapid loss of any temporary gain in this area, may have been due to the economic circumstances under which policies have been asked to operate, but perhaps it was also due to their format. Policies have always been initiated in a situation of crisis in the general economy, and therefore their primary aim has been to ensure wage restraint in an effort to reduce labour costs. But short-term 'emergency' actions of the type that have operated in the past are unlikely to achieve any sustained improvement in the position of the low-paid, simply because they will have insufficient time to elicit the necessary psychological acceptance of the need to alter differentials. The building of 'stages' on to a 'freeze' and the emphasis on the short-term need for wage restraint by politicians will lead to an expectation by bargainers that any fall in their standard of living is only a temporary phenomenon to be made up once the policy eases. Thus, as the policy begins to ease, a free-for-all is initiated in which the strongest groups attempt to make up the lost ground. This results in the largest increases being achieved by the stronger more powerful groups of workers and inevitably these groups are not the low-paid. This being so, it would require an incomes policy of both structure and length to alter differentials and relativities in favour of the low-paid.

The low-pay problem has been an obdurate one. Incomes policies of the type seen so far in Britain have provided only a small and temporary alleviation of the problem, and therefore in this respect they have always failed. If the decision is made to substantially improve the position of the low-paid − and this has not been taken so far − then the policy options are few. The first appears to be a commitment on the part of the unions and the Trades Union Congress as a whole to operate a *policy on incomes* to the benefit of the low-paid. To be successful this would probably require a fundamental alteration in the structure of unions and collective bargaining. The present mixture of industry, craft and general unions makes it difficult to gain consensus on who the low-paid are (the argument of the 'low-paid' craftsman versus the 'high-paid' labourer), let alone a policy to improve their position. An agreed policy on differentials and relativities would need to be devised; discipline would need to percolate through from union officials to the shopfloor to stop earnings 'drift' from countering any 'national' attempts at compressing differentials, and there would need to be a considerable expansion of union coverage and collective bargaining into non-covered sectors. As the Royal Commission on the Distribution of Income and Wealth suggested, a significant number of the low-paid are not covered by collective agreements, and these perhaps are both the most vulnerable and most difficult to deal with under existing arrangements (RCDIW 1978). Most important of all, there would need to be an acceptance that low pay can only be improved at the cost of smaller increases to the higher paid. The only alternative policy to be considered appears to be that chosen by a number of other countries with varying success and with varying costs in terms of inflation and unemployment, namely, a statutory national minimum wage (DEP, 1969). It is clear that the results of this study add fuel to the debate for a national minimum wage, and it is to be hoped that this will soon be initiated.

Whichever option is chosen, a preliminary step can be taken by an acceptance of three facts:

(1) Incomes policies of the type employed in the UK have failed to

improve the position of the low-paid over the past fourteen years.

(2) No improvement can be achieved without co-operation on the part of other workers.

(3) This co-operation will 'cost' them in the form of reduced relativities and/or differentials.

Notes: Chapter 6

1   Similar occupational data are not presented for reasons of space. The occupations used are given in Appendix 6A; their choice was on similar grounds to the industry sample but was even more constrained by the adequacy of the data.
2   'Policy-off' periods were taken as 1971, 1972 and 1975. Group policies covered the years 1974 and 1978. Individual policies were 1976 and 1977. 'Policy-on' periods were 1974, 1976, 1977 and 1978.
3   See Appendix 6B for a list of the agreements used.

References: Chapter 6

Bayliss, F. J. (1962), *British Wages Councils* (Oxford: Blackwell)
Department of Employment and Productivity (DEP) (1969), *A National Minimum Wage: An Inquiry* (HMSO)
Elliott, R. F., and Steele R. (1976), 'The importance of national wage agreements', *British Journal of Industrial Relations*, Vol. XIV No. 1
Hebden, J. (1978), 'Men's and women's pay in Britain, 1968–1975', *Industrial Relations Journal*, Vol. 9 No. 2
Marquand, J. (1967), 'Which are the lower paid workers?', *British Journal of Industrial Relations*, Vol. 1 No. 5
Moore, R., and Beddoe, R. (1976), 'Low pay: the record since 1964' in *Are Low Wages Inevitable?*, ed. F. Field (Spokesman Books)
National Board for Prices and Incomes (1967), Report No. 27, *Pay of Workers in the retail drapery, outfitting and footwear trades*, Cmnd 3224 (HMSO)
National Board for Prices and Incomes (1971), Report No. 169, *General problems of low pay*, Cmnd 4646 (HMSO)
Parsons, T. (1954), *Essays in Sociological Theory* (London: Butterworth)
Phelps-Brown, H. (1977), *The Inequality of Pay* (Oxford University Press)
Pond, S., and Winyard, S. (1976), 'A profile of the low paid', in *Are Low Wages Inevitable?*, ed. F. Field (Spokesman Books)
Royal Commission on the Distribution of Income and Wealth (1978), *Lower Incomes Reference*, Cmnd 7175 (HMSO)
Sloane, P. J., and Chiplin, B. (1976), *Sex Discrimination in the Labour Market (Macmillan)*
Steele, R. (1978), *Wage Patterns in the Wages Council Sector*, unpublished M.Litt. thesis, Aberdeen
Steele, R. (1979), 'The relative performance of the wage council and non-wages council sectors and the impact of incomes policies', *British Journal of Industrial Relations*, Vol. XVII No. 2
Walker, H. (1969), *Hansard*, Vol. 780 No. 86 col. 1625 (26 March)

Appendix 6A   Low-paid manual occupations used in the analysis

Hospital porters
General farm workers
Stockmen
Gardeners/groundsmen
Goods porters
Packers, bottlers, etc.
Bakers and confectioners

Butchers, meat-cutters
Cleaners
Storekeepers
Other goods drivers
Caretakers
Agricultural machinery drivers
General labourers

Appendix 6B   Low-paid agreements used in the study

Private Sector

Baking
Food
Cotton, spinning, and weaving
Woollen and worsted
Textile finishing

Retail co-operative society
Retail multiple grocery
Motor vehicle repair
Pottery

Public Sector

Local authorities (manuals),
    England and Wales
Local authorities (manuals),
    Scotland
Government industrial employees

Nurses and midwives
National Health Service ancillary
    staff
British Railways conciliation staff

Wages Councils

Agriculture (England and Wales)
Agriculture (Scotland)
Licensed non-residential establish-
    ments
Licensed residential establishments

Retail drapery and outfitting trades
Retail food distribution
Retail furnishings
Road haulage
Milk distribution

Chapter 7

The American Experience with Incomes Policies

JOHN H. PENCAVEL*

Therefore we who are the protectors of the human race, are agreed, as we view the situation, that decisive legislation is necessary, so that the long-hoped-for solutions which mankind itself could not provide may, by the remedies provided by our foresight, be vouchsafed for the general betterment of all. . . . We hasten, therefore, to apply the remedies long demanded by the situation, satisfied that no one can complain that our intervention with regulations is untimely or unnecessary, trivial or unimportant . . . we have decided that maximum prices of articles for sale must be established. We have not set down fixed prices, for we do not deem it just to do this . . . when the pressure of high prices appears anywhere . . . avarice . . . will be checked by the limits fixed in our statute and by the restraining curbs of the law.

Diocletian's Edict on Maximum Prices, AD 301
(Lewis and Reinhold, 1955, p. 465)

1 Introduction

The purpose of this chapter is to present an analysis of the experience of the United States with incomes policies in the past thirty-five years. By the term 'incomes policy' I mean an attempt by the government to reduce the rate of price and wage inflation by methods that amount to establishing an administered ceiling on prices and wages. Occasionally, this ceiling has taken the form of permitting *no* increases in prices and wages for a stipulated period. More often, a

* I am indebted to Paul Evans for his comments on a preliminary draft and to Kathie Krumm for her resourceful and unstinting research assistance.

moving ceiling has been specified in the form of the government determining permissible rates of change of prices and of wages.

These policies represent attempts by the government to regulate prices and wages (or their rates of change) directly, and in many respects they resemble other government regulations on prices and wages such as farm price supports, minimum wage legislation, and rent controls. These latter regulations are directed at prices and wages in particular sectors of the economy whereas it is the aggregate price and wage level that constitutes the target of an incomes policy. Nevertheless, the attempt by the government to control aggregate prices inevitably involves it in price determination in particular markets. This becomes manifest when agencies are created to administer a maximum price or wage policy for particular industries. An example is provided by the Construction Industry Stabilization Committee that was established in March 1971 to restrain wages in the construction industry. Sometimes the incomes policy is administered by exhortation (frequently called 'jawboning') and by appeals to individuals to place the general interest above the interest of a particular group. On other occasions, formal controls have been imposed on prices and wages.

Since the form taken by particular incomes policies will be conditioned by the institutional arrangements and the climate of ideas in a society, some understanding of these arrangements and these ideas in the United States should precede an analysis of the policies. First, wage and price determination is more decentralised in the United States than is the case in the European economies. For instance, a considerably smaller fraction of the output of goods and services in the United States is produced by government-managed or government-regulated firms. With respect to the labour market, in the early 1970s approximately 45 per cent of production workers and 30 per cent of all workers in private employment were covered by collective bargaining agreements (Freeman and Medoff, 1979). By contrast, in Britain the coverage percentages in 1973 were 81 and 72 respectively (Thomson, Mulvey and Farbman, 1977). Not merely is collective bargaining less extensive in the United States, but even for these unionised workers much of their wage contract determination takes place at the local level. The leaders of the American Federation of Labor are little more than spokesmen for the unions and the Federation has no statutory authority to enforce on its member unions any incomes policy to which it agrees. There are, of course, conspicuous price leaders and powerful unions, but even if their price and wage decisions could be superseded by the government much of the larger part of the economy would be left unregulated. Therefore, it is important to remember that US incomes policies have operated in a context in which price and wage decisions are highly dispersed throughout the economy.

Secondly, in part because of the smaller role played by business and labour monopolies in the US economy, there has been considerable discussion on the question of whether the government should seek the participation of trade unions and management in the operation of an incomes policy or whether it should be administered by an all-public agency. There is some reason to believe that an all-government body may be more successful in maintaining the strict rules of an incomes policy, but for this reason may be less adept at tailoring the policy to particular circumstances (where such tinkering may be desirable on efficiency grounds) than would a tripartite body (Rees, 1975). For their part, the trade unions' attitude towards incomes policies has vacillated: at one time, they have been inclined towards joining the administration of an incomes policy while at another they have spurned any association; or one union may be found in support of the policy while, at the same time, others will be heard decrying it. The unions have been caught in a dilemma: if they eschew any involvement in an incomes policy, then they may be straitjacketed with a wage increase limitation much more confining than if they had been a party to its formation and implementation; if they do join in the administration of the policy, they risk disaffection among the rank-and-file that may result in the defeat of the incumbent leadership.

Thirdly, to a degree that is unknown in Britain, the conventional macroeconomic instruments of government policy in the United States are dispersed among different arms of government. The US executive shares the responsibility for fiscal policy with a sometimes stubborn and independent-minded Congress and the sort of budgetary changes that the structure of the political system permits a British government to implement are far more difficult to engineer in the United States. In addition, although the Governors of the Federal Reserve System are selected by the President and confirmed by the Senate, once appointed they do not act with the approval of either the executive or the legislature and they have been known to pursue a monetary policy that conflicts with the wishes of both. Under these circumstances, an incomes policy has sometimes had the appeal of being a weapon of macroeconomic policy that is more completely (though by no means entirely) under the direction of the executive.

Fourthly, the prevailing attitude of professional economists in the United States towards incomes policies has moved from one of mild scepticism about thirty years ago to one of outright opposition today.[1] Thus a recent survey of US professional economists (J. R. Kearl et al., 1979) reported that, in answer to the proposition 'Wage–price controls should be used to control inflation', only 6 per cent classified themselves as 'generally agreeing', 22 per cent 'agreed with provisions', and 72 per cent 'generally disagreed'. In part, these attitudes are a reflection of the resurgence of neoclassical economics within the profession, but they can also be traced to the disenchanting experience with wage–price controls in the early 1970s. Today, American professional economists are far less disposed towards the use of incomes policies to combat inflation in the United States than are British economists with respect to these policies in Britain. In part, this difference between American and British economists reflects institutional differences in the two countries and especially the greater importance in Britain of the government in the direct management of certain industries and the greater role of British trade unions in fixing wages in the labour market. In addition, this difference is also the product of an intellectual climate that for many years has displayed a greater scepticism towards the ability of government to achieve commonly-shared goals than has been the case in Britain. This is not to say, however, that this scepticism is shared by the American public at large. On the contrary, the Gallup Poll of American public opinion (as reproduced in Table 7.1) indicates only one instance in the last thirty years when the majority of respondents expressed an unfavourable opinion on the subject of wage–price controls. (This occurred in October 1966 when the Guideposts had been in effect for four years.) Since economists do not elect governments, it is not surprising that successive administrations have turned to an incomes policy to give the appearance of 'doing something' about inflation without incurring the electorate's disapproval. Therefore, the absence of a large and articulate body of professional opinion advancing the case for a government maximum wage–price policy certainly does not imply that incomes policies are a thing of the past. It does imply, however, that, if an incomes policy is introduced in this climate of opinion, it is likely to be less defiant than its British counterpart of underlying market forces that work against the success of the policy.

With these points in mind, section 2 briefly describes the main features of the four incomes policy episodes in the United States since the Second World War. Section 3 presents an economic analysis of these incomes policies with special attention to recent proposals for a tax-based incomes policy and to President Carter's real wage insurance incomes policy. Section 4 offers some simple evaluation of the effects of these incomes policies on the rate of wage inflation. Some concluding observations are presented in section 5. An appendix presents some rudimentary results examining whether any empirical regularities exist in determining when an administration will invoke an incomes policy.

Table 7.1 Public opinion on government wage−price controls as measured by the Gallup Poll

	Percentage expressing opinion on wage−price controls			
	Favourable	Unfavourable	Neutral	No opinion
Nov−Dec 1946	49	43	—	8
July−Aug 1950	55	27	9	9
Oct 1950	63	21	9	7
Jan 1951	62	22	9	7
June 1951	65	16	—	19
Oct 1951	53	31	8	8
Dec 1952	61	29	—	10
Aug 1958	47	43	—	10
May−June 1959	44	42	—	14
May 1962	40	46	—	14
Dec 1965−Jan 1966	45	42	—	13
Apr 1966	42	44	—	14
Oct 1966	33	51	—	16
Jan 1968	46	43	—	11
June 1969	47	41	—	12
May 1970	48	41	—	11
Feb 1971	49	38	—	13
June 1971	50	39	—	11
Aug 1971	68	11	—	12
Nov 1971	38	15	37	10
Jan 1972	48	11	29	12
Mar 1972	53	13	25	9
Aug 1972	45	15	29	11
Apr 1973	51	17	23	9
June 1973	52	32	—	16
Aug 1974	50	39	—	11
Dec 1976	44	41	—	15
Feb 1978	44	40	—	16
Apr 1978	52	37	—	11
May 1978	52	36	—	12
July 1978	54	34	—	13
May 1979	57	31	—	12

Notes: 'Favourable' responses include 'more strict', 'satisfied', 'approve', 'good idea', 'continued', 'strengthened', 'more important', and 'yes'. 'Unfavourable' responses include 'oppose', 'less strict', 'dissatisfied', 'disapprove', 'poor idea', 'done away with', 'less important', and 'no'. This table is taken from 'Whither Controls? A History of Public Attitudes toward Wage−Price Restraints', *The Gallup Opinion Index*, October 1978, Report No. 159, p. 4, and from *The Gallup Opinion Index*, June 1979, Report No. 167, p. 20.

2   A chronology

The Wage Stabilization Board, 1950–3

The Government's first attempt after the Second World War at direct controls on the upward movement of prices and wages came with the Korean War, which started in June 1950. Under the Defence Production Act of September 1950, President Truman established the Office of Price Stability (OPS) and the Wage Stabilization Board (WSB) whose purpose was to oversee wage movements in the economy. The OPS was a governmental agency while the membership of the WSB consisted of representatives from employers' organisations, from trade unions, and from the 'general public'. Initially there were nine members, but in the spring of 1951 it was reorganised into a board of eighteen members and, in response to trade union pressures, its potential powers were enlarged to include the investigation of management–union disputes.

At first, apart from appeals to business and unions to limit price and wage increases, the only mandatory aspect of the wage–price programme was the freezing of new automobile prices and of auto-workers' wages. This was generally felt to be inadequate, so that a general price and wage freeze was decreed in late January 1951. In particular, the OPS froze prices at the highest level at which deliveries had been made between mid-December 1950 and the end of January 1951 and some 65 per cent of the bundle of commodities entering the consumer price index were covered; correspondingly, the WSB froze wages and other compensation at their end-January 1951 levels. Within a month the wage freeze was replaced with a regulation permitting increases of up to 10 per cent of January 1950 straight-time wages and there were provisions for special cases above that 10 per cent. Criteria for raising the prices of manufactured goods and machinery were established in April 1951 while the effectiveness of the controls was further weakened in July 1951 by various Congressional measures. In November 1951 the price regulations permitted general passing-on of cost increases and from that date the controls were further relaxed.

The WSB's influence derived from its pronouncements of permissible wage increases, but when these were challenged by a coalition of the United Mine Workers and the coal employers it was the WSB that finally gave way. In this case in the autumn of 1952 the union and the employers negotiated a wage increase of $1.90 per day whereas the WSB approved no more than a $1.50 wage increase. The resulting strike was resolved by the intervention of President Truman who sanctioned the management–union negotiated increase and which induced mass resignations from the membership of the WSB. Wages and prices were formally decontrolled in February 1953.

The guideposts, 1962–6

In response to the economy's slow growth and comparatively high unemployment rates in the late 1950s, the new Kennedy administration embarked on an expansionary monetary policy. The effects of this policy on price and wage changes were of increasing concern to the administration and, in particular, the anticipated renegotiation of the steelworkers' contract in 1962 was believed to be of considerable importance in setting the pattern for other wage settlements. Consequently, the Economic Report of the President in January 1962 contained a section dealing with 'Guideposts for Noninflationary Wage and Price Behavior' and the core of the argument rested on the educational effect of a guidelines policy. It was argued that, when the economy occupies a position between heavy unemployment and rapid inflation, there is an important non-competitive sector in the economy where substantial discretionary powers of price or wage determination exist. The exercise of these discretionary powers are likely to be sensitive to public opinion so that inflation could be restrained by an informed public opinion. In general terms, the policy advocated was one of keeping wages from rising by more than increases in average labour productivity and of ensuring that prices could rise only to cover inescapable cost increases. Compliance with the guideposts was monitored by the Council of Economic Advisers, an agency with a professional staff of about twenty people and with responsibilities in many areas other than price and wage inflation. As a consequence, only the most conspicuous of wage and price decisions could be investigated and then not in detail. If the Council found a case of non-compliance with the guideposts, it attempted to persuade those involved to alter their decision. The guideposts were never enshrined in law nor were official penalties determined for non-compliance. Instead, in the few instances in which offenders were penalised, these penalties took the form of *ad hoc* measures taken by the executive branch of government. For instance, in the steel, copper, and aluminium industries, the Department of Defense was instructed to redirect its purchases away from the offending firms while threats were made to sell some government stocks of these commodities to apply downward pressure on market prices.

As in the case of the wage–price controls during the Korean War, a dramatic confrontation between the government's announced policy and bargains in the private sector led to the abandonment of the guidelines policy. In 1966, the employers and the union leaders agreed upon a wage increase for airline machinists of 4·3 per cent at a time when the wage guidepost was 3·2 per cent. President Johnson found a way to excuse this particular breach of his guidepost policy which sufficiently emboldened the union rank-and-file that they rejected the 4·3 per cent settlement negotiated by their leadership and eventually won a wage package estimated to be equivalent to a 4·9 per cent wage increase. Shortly thereafter, the wage–price guideposts were abandoned by the government.

The wage–price controls, 1971–4
The mid- to late-1960s witnessed an accelerating rate of inflation to which the new Nixon administration responded with half-hearted monetary and fiscal measures. The effect of these measures on real output and employment was more apparent than their effect on price and wage inflation. So the economy entered a recession in output while prices and wages continued to rise and in particular sectors the pace of inflation was especially marked. Thus the large wage settlements in the construction industry in 1969 led to the establishment of a special collective bargaining commission for this industry, whose task was loosely specified as one of outlining a plan to reduce the rate of increase of construction wages and prices. Meanwhile the economy's rate of growth of output picked up in the first half of 1971 and, in an attempt to reduce price and wage inflation without depressing output and employment, President Nixon invoked the authority granted to him by Congress in the Economic Stabilization Act of 1970 and declared a comprehensive ninety-day freeze on all wages, prices, and profits beginning on 15 August 1971. (The prices of unprocessed agricultural products and commodities involved in international trade were not covered by the freeze.) Thus the United States embarked on its most thorough peacetime experience with wage and price controls.

The wage–price freeze was part of a package of measures, the New Economic Policy (NEP), which included a 10 per cent temporary surcharge on imports, the ending of the convertibility between the dollar and gold, the devaluation of the dollar, and fiscal measures designed to increase employment and output. The ninety-day freeze came to be regarded as Phase I of a longer-term programme of wage–price controls to reduce inflation, and this ninety-day period was used to design the bureaucratic machinery for administering the programme in subsequent phases. Just as the Korean War experience with price and wage controls saw the establishment of one agency to oversee price movements and another to monitor wage movements, so the beginning of Phase II on 14 November 1971 saw the setting up of a Price Commission with responsibility for prices and rents and a Pay Board whose concern was with wages and salaries. Once again, paralleling the Korean War episode, members of the Pay Board were drawn from employers' organisations, from trade unions, and from the 'general public' – although the union members withdrew in March 1972, expressing their dissatisfaction with the Price Commission's performance.

The criteria governing price and wage movements in Phase II were similar to those designed in the guideposts: wage increases were related to changes in labour productivity while price changes were permitted only in so far as they were linked to changes in costs. Both the Price Commission and the Pay Board operated primarily as agencies specifying general regulations rather than monitoring individual cases. The Pay Board established a general standard of annual wage increases of 5·5 per cent with a further 0·7 per cent increase for fringe benefits. Underlying this 5·5 per cent was an assumed growth in productivity of 3·0 per cent and a cost-of-living adjustment of 2·5 per cent. Exceptions were made for workers whose wages had risen less than 7 per cent a year for the last three years and for those earning less than $2·75 per hour. The Price Commission's strategy was to divide firms into one of three categories according to the dollar volume of their sales: tier I firms had sales of $100 million or more and they required the Commission's sanction before their wages or prices could be altered; tier II firms had sales of $50–$100 million and were obliged to notify the Commission after making any wage or price adjustments; and tier III firms had sales of less than $50 million and had to abide by the same standards as larger firms, but were subject to spot checks by the Internal Revenue Service. This differential treatment of firms by volume of sales has been described by a member of the Price Commission as 'controls for the bigs and sermons for the smalls'![2]

Phase II lasted from 14 November 1971 to 11 January 1973, when Phase III came into operation. This was intended to be a transitory phase between controls and a period of voluntary restraint. The Price Commission and the Pay Board were merged into the new Cost-of-Living Council while controls on prices and wage increases were gradually relaxed. But led by increases in prices for food and energy, price inflation took a sharp upward turn in the first half of 1973, which induced the imposition of another freeze, this one for sixty days from 13 June 1973 to 12 August. After two years of controls, public opinion for this freeze was distinctly less enthusiastic than in the case of Phase I; and when Phase IV came into operation in August the clear intent was to phase out controls, and this began selectively in October. The Economic Stabilization Act expired in April 1974 and with it ended authority for price and wage controls. The years 1973 and 1974 had seen in food and energy prices the sharpest changes in *relative* prices since the Korean War and these were largely beyond the government's control.

The pay and price standards, 1978–
As a candidate for President in 1976, Jimmy Carter repudiated the use of wage–price controls as an anti-inflationary weapon of government

policy, but as President the pressure to invoke some sort of incomes policy as a response to the accelerating rate of price inflation proved irresistible. Thus in October 1978 a wage–price programme was unveiled that involved limitations on price and wage increases. As far as prices were concerned, price increases for each company were limited to the actual rate of price increase on the company's products over the 1976–7 period less one-half percentage point. Where current cost increases made adherence to this price deceleration standard impracticable or where the introduction of new products rendered any comparable price increases over the years 1976–7 meaningless, firms were asked to hold their profit margins over the following year to no more than the average profit margin in the best two of the company's last three fiscal years. In fact, in administering the standards the Council on Wage and Price Stability came to make increasing use of this profit margin criterion instead of the price deceleration rule. The programme exempted from these limitations those companies designated to be operating largely in 'competitive markets' (which meant those firms engaged in business in organised exchanges, in agricultural and raw material markets, and in export markets).

As for employee compensation, Carter's anti-inflation programme stipulated a maximum permissible increase of 7 per cent in earnings and private fringe benefits net of overtime pay. This standard was meant to apply not to every individual employee but to groups of employees in a firm where a 'group' was defined as the collective bargaining unit or as all management personnel or as non-management employees not covered by a collective bargaining contract. Pay increases that result from the operation of existing collective bargaining agreements and those that were the consequence of the workings of existing piece-rate schemes were exempted from these standards. Further exemptions were granted, such as those relating to employees earning no more than $4·00 per hour and those concerning workers for whom a case of 'acute labour shortage' could be demonstrated.

Although the government's publications[3] spelling out these standards provided details on how each firm could determine its permissible price and wage increases, no information on penalties for non-compliance was supplied. In announcing the programme, the President outlined a 'real wage insurance' scheme that offered tax rebates to those employees in groups who met the 7 per cent pay standard. (More detail on this insurance scheme is provided in section 3.) In fact, Congress refused to pass the legislation that would implement the scheme, so it came to nothing. The fact is that, as inflation inexorably increased, so these pay and price standards appeared far-fetched and they were modified piecemeal to accommodate several collective bargaining agreements, notably the Teamsters. Consequently, when the wage–price programme was revised in October 1979, President Carter promised union labour an important role in determining the new pay standards, an attempt to move the unions from a status of poacher to one of gamekeeper. A tripartite pay advisory committee was established with members drawn from the unions, from business and from the general public, and with Professor John Dunlop as chairman, a distinguished academic with demonstrable pro-union sympathies. The committee recommended in January 1980 that the pay standard be 8·5 per cent as the 'normal' increase for wages, but they refused to specify the circumstances that would entitle a group of workers to more than 8·5 per cent and they refused to assert that union workers with cost-of-living escalator clauses should settle for 8·5 per cent or less. In March 1980 (at the time of writing this chapter) a new anti-inflationary package was announced which involved small reductions in government expenditures, restrictions on credit, and a fee on imported crude oil for gasoline. Also measures were introduced to secure compliance with the pay and price standards in the form of doubling the number of monitors to 480 and of increasing the number of companies required to file quarterly reports. It is difficult to believe that such an incomes policy will have any appreciable impact on inflation.

3 Conceptual framework for understanding the effects of a maximum wage–price policy

The conventional analysis of price and wage controls is to be found in a number of the standard textbooks from which students learn their economic principles. This analysis runs as follows. If these price or wage controls are binding and effective (that is, if they are not cosmetic and they do affect the money prices at which commodities are exchanged), then the quantities of the commodities exchanged will also be affected. Price ceilings (or 'moving ceilings' specifying that prices may not rise by more than a stipulated amount) result in 'shortages' because the quantities being supplied to the market fall short of the quantities being demanded at that controlled price. The amount of the unsatisfied demand increases with (1) the degree to which prices diverge from their equilibrium values; and (2) the sum of the absolute values of the slopes of the demand and supply curves.[4] The frequently stated reluctance to extend price controls to agricultural products reflects, in part, the belief that the supply of such items is more price-elastic than manufactured products in all but the very short run and, therefore, that the amount of the shortage is likely to be substantial. In addition, since demand and supply elasticities tend to increase the longer any price change persists, this simple analysis also implies that the shortages will be greater the longer the price controls are in effect.

There is much to be said for this textbook analysis and it has prompted the search for the degree to which these controls on prices and wages produced shortages. There is, in fact, considerable evidence that after two years of wage–price controls, shortages were pervasive in the second half of 1973.[5] None the less, the analysis presumes that in the absence of the controls prices and wages would be at their competitive levels. If, in fact, non-controlled prices and wages are above their competitive levels, then a judiciously chosen price or wage ceiling may not lead to shortages. Indeed, elements of this reasoning can be found in some of the arguments in support of the guideposts in the 1960s; in particular, it was argued that monopolistic elements in price and wage determination would be restrained through an effective incomes policy.[6] In fact, there is some evidence to support the belief that the discretionary power of one important monopoly element, namely trade unions, was contained by the guideposts since the union–non-union wage differential narrowed during these years.[7] In addition, Darby (1976) asserts that trade unions were the primary casualties of the first two years of Nixon's wage–price controls, although this appears inconsistent with the fact that union–non-union wage differentials increased from 1967 to 1973 and then again from 1973 to 1975.[8] But if the argument is that a government incomes policy can reduce the welfare losses of monopolistic pricing, then it calls for government intervention in a world of constant prices no less than in a world of inflation. Expressed differently, this is really a familiar argument – the government should take steps to reduce the resource misallocation impact of monopolies in the economy – and has nothing to do with an incomes policy designed to reduce inflation.[9]

Although in the American context it may be appropriate to concentrate on a model of competitive markets to analyse the effects of an incomes policy, the simple textbook treatment sketched out above is inadequate in three respects. First, the coverage of an incomes policy is necessarily incomplete. This is not merely a consequence of the fact that some individuals evade the administration of an incomes policy (an issue that is addressed below), but because each of the four periods of government wage and price restraint described in the previous section has expressly excluded certain sectors from the controls. Thus the Korean War price freeze of January 1951 covered approximately 65 per cent of the items weighted in the consumer price index, the guidelines were explicitly designed for what was called non-competitive markets, and Carter's price standards excluded 'competitive' firms. Even the comprehensiveness

Table 7.2 Percentage of the consumer price index covered by price controls, 1971 – 4

Month	1971	1972	1973	1974
January	0	81·8	47·7	42·6
February	0	81·3	47·7	42·6
March	0	80·8	47·7	28·0
April	0	80·2	47·7	12·1
May	0	72·2	47·7	0
June	0	69·8	69·9	0
July	0	67·3	91·2	0
August	45·6	64·9	66·9	0
September	91·2	62·4	42·6	0
October	91·2	60·0	42·6	0
November	90·4	57·6	42·6	0
December	84·5	55·1	42·6	0

Note: The numbers in this table are taken from Blinder and Newton (1979) who construct them from (sometimes fragmentary) information provided by the publications of the US Cost of Living Council.

of Nixon's wage–price controls lasted only a few months, as is indicated by the data in Table 7.2 on the percentage of the consumer price index covered by the programme. Similarly, with respect to the labour market, relatively low-wage workers were excluded from the regulations specified by Phase II of Nixon's wage–price controls and by Carter's pay standards, while the Kennedy–Johnson guidelines concentrated on major union contracts. The fact that a sector of the economy is excluded from the regulations of an incomes policy does not mean, of course, that the unregulated sector is unaffected by the incomes policy. On the contrary, where the commodities exchanged on the unregulated markets are substitutes for those exchanged on the markets covered by an incomes policy, the prices of the commodities on the unregulated markets will increase faster than they would have done in the absence of an incomes policy. Therefore, a situation in which the economy-wide rate of change of prices exceeds the 'norm' or 'standard' set by the incomes policy does not necessarily imply widespread non-compliance with the policy. On the contrary, even where the regulated sector fully complies with the incomes policy, an inflation rate in excess of the 'norm' is to be expected whenever the coverage of the policy is incomplete.

A second reason for regarding the textbook presentation of price ceilings as inadequate is that it portrays commodities as possessing a unidimensional characteristic (such as pounds of potatoes or hours worked per employee). In fact, each transaction involves the exchange of a bundle of characteristics and each of these characteristics has an explicit or an implicit value (or shadow price).[10] These characteristics are sometimes lumped together and described as the 'quality' of the commodity although, of course, quality itself consists of a number of dimensions. Wage–price controls regulate the explicit money price of each commodity with the consequence that the forces that would otherwise operate in part through money prices are deflected to the implicit prices of the other dimensions of the exchange. For instance, the purchase of gasoline for one's car at a service station in the United States was at one time accompanied with cleaning of the windscreen, checking the oil and battery, and testing the air pressure in the tyres. Obviously, the price that one paid for the gasoline incorporated the implicit price for these other services. Put differently, the dollars spent on the purchase of gasoline represented the expenditure on a whole bundle of items. With the binding price controls in the 1970s, the price of gasoline now buys the gasoline and little else, since these other services have been drastically reduced or eliminated. The controls have affected the expenditure of dollars at a service station by obliging the consumer to purchase a smaller bundle of total services. Or, to provide an illustration from the labour market, if employers are constrained from raising wage rates to attract labour, then non-wage (including non-pecuniary) items in the job package will be improved to provide the necessary inducements.[11] That is, employees sell the services of their labour and simultaneously purchase utility-bearing characteristics of the firms in which they work while the employer purchases labour services and sells characteristics of his firm to workers. The wage rate is the price of the total package of labour services net of the value of the on-the-job non-pecuniary goods, so that binding controls on wages can be avoided by altering the bundle of non-wage items sold to employees. This avoidance is not achieved costlessly, however, since non-pecuniary items are not perfectly substitutable for money wages in the employee's total compensation. Of course, the administrators of the wage–price controls are well aware of this and try to specify all dimensions of the transaction, but of course this is impossible since it requires knowledge of 'the particular circumstances of time and place' (Hayek, 1946). Understood in this way, wage–price controls place a tax on using money signals to allocate resources; they impose costs on the use of the price mechanism as an information network.

A third reason for amending the textbook analysis of wage–price controls is to allow for the fact that the government's regulations are not enforceable at zero cost. The fact is that, in so far as the effectiveness of these controls requires individuals to behave in a manner that conflicts with their self-interest, then incentives are created for individuals not to abide by these regulations and at the same time resources have to be spent by the government to ensure compliance. Yet the guidelines of the 1960s and Carter's pay and price standards did not set down the punishments for non-compliance although, as mentioned in section 2 above, penalties were threatened in the guidelines period in the form of redirecting government contracts away from firms not following the stated limits. Instead, the government relied most on what was called 'voluntary compliance'. There is here, however, a necessary tension between the extent to which such voluntary measures can be relied upon and the effectiveness of wage–price controls: the more that controls cause wages and prices to diverge from their equilibrium values, the greater the incentive for individual parties not to comply voluntarily with them. This is why some observers would maintain that, if a post-mortem on controls declares voluntary compliance to have been a success, then this is *prima facie* evidence of the controls being essentially cosmetic and of their having no real effect on behaviour. In fact, primary emphasis was placed on enforcement by voluntary compliance even during the most comprehensive of the government's attempts in the last thirty-five years to control wages and prices, namely, the wage–price freeze of 1971. During this episode, 'The image cultivated was one of businessmen, landlords, and employees forthrightly denying themselves personal gain in the name of the national interest, as contrasted to one of cadres of accountants poring over ledger books and payroll stubs to bring malefactors to justice' (Weber, 1973, pp. 85–6). However, this exhortation and appeal to patriotism was supplemented by civil penalties and criminal fines for violations though the lengthy legal proceedings necessary to obtain a criminal conviction rendered the criminal charges unattractive as an enforcement technique. Under these circumstances, each firm and union forms its price and wage decisions in an environment of uncertainty since they are incompletely informed of the procedure by which the government's administrative agencies monitor compliance with the incomes policy. It is straightforward to show that the probability of non-compliance with the incomes policy increases with the absolute value of the own-price (or own-wage) elasticity of demand.[12] In fact, during the Nixon wage–price controls, when a firm was found to be violating the regulations, normally the government sought only to bring the firm into compliance. In this event, except for any possible loss in public goodwill, the firm's penalties for violation are zero.

These compliance problems in administering an incomes policy have concerned policy-makers, who have recognised that vague appeals to the national interest might conceivably offer some promise of success in economies where price and wage determination is highly centralised; but their effects are likely to be short-lived in an economy such as the United States where price and wage determination is more decentralised. Hence, in recent years, a number of proposals have been advanced to increase the effectiveness of an incomes policy by offering monetary incentives for compliance. The best known of these is the Wallich–Weintraub tax-based incomes policy (TIP) which involves levying 'a surcharge on the corporate profits tax for firms granting wage increases in excess of some guideposts figure. If the wage guidepost were $5 \cdot 5\%$ and a wage increase of 7% were granted, the corporate profits tax for the firm would rise above the present 48% [now 46%] by some multiple of the $1 \cdot 5\%$ excess.'[13] Thus the tax rate t for the ith firm is

$$t_i = b + \alpha(\Delta w_i - n)$$

where b is the base tax rate, $\alpha > 0$ the policy-determined TIP 'multiplier', Δw_i the average percentage wage increase of firm i, and n the stated wage guideline. The Wallich–Weintraub proposal was to apply TIP to all corporations paying income tax, which already implies a large uncovered sector, namely those corporations registering net losses or carrying forward tax credits in a given year, non-profit-making institutions, state and local governments, and partnerships and proprietorships. The case in favour of TIP rests critically on two propositions: first, that discretionary price and wage determination characterises an important segment of the private economy and that this segment has played an active part in the inflationary process;[14] and, secondly, that in this sector these tax incentives will induce greater resistance on the part of employers to union wage demands.[15]

The TIP proposal spawned a number of other tax-based schemes,[16] some involving tax reductions for compliance and others aimed directly at employees (rather than or in addition to employers). All these schemes possess the three characteristics described above with reference to conventional incomes policies: first, one sector of the economy is effectively untaxed, with consequent resource reallocation between the covered and uncovered sectors; secondly, these schemes explicitly tax the use of money prices and wages and encourage the substitution of non-price methods to allocate resources; and, thirdly, there remain questions of tax evasion and compliance. In addition to these issues, there is the issue of the incidence of these taxes: as Rees (1978) observes, where wage agreements effectively cover a whole industry, each firm suffers little, if any increased profits tax is passed on to consumers in the form of higher prices: here a tax designed to reduce inflation results in higher prices. Moreover, these tax-based incomes policies involve the establishment of an appropriate norm or guideline, something that turned into a real problem during the Kennedy–Johnson guidelines period.

Nevertheless, the appeal of these TIP proposals lies in the fact that they appear to offer an alternative to the unemployment-increasing effects of a strict monetary and fiscal policy without having to invoke the formal wage–price controls that produced widespread disillusionment by the time they were abandoned in April 1974. Presumably it was for this reason that a variant of TIP was enshrined in President Carter's anti-inflation programme in October 1978. He submitted to a sceptical Congress a 'real wage insurance' scheme, a form of tax credit designed to induce compliance with his pay standard. The proposal was directed to a resolution of the 'free rider' dilemma presented to an individual by the pay standards: an individual will suffer a decline in his real wage if he accepts the restraints of a pay standard at a time when others do not exercise similar restraint, so the fear of others failing to comply induces none to comply. The real wage insurance scheme was aimed at shifting this risk from individuals to the Federal government by promising each member of an employee unit[17] that complied with the pay standard a tax credit if the consumer price index increased by more than a specified threshold. In particular, the Carter proposal specified the tax rate faced by each individual eligible for the 'real wage insurance' to be

$$t = b - (\Delta p - z) \text{ for } z < \Delta p \le 10\%$$

where b is again the base tax on labour income, Δp is the actual rate of change of consumer prices, and z is the threshold rate of price increase which triggers a tax reimbursement. In fact, z was set at 7 per cent so that members of employee units complying with the 7 per cent pay increase limit would have received a tax credit if the consumer price index increased by more than 7 per cent during the year. However, price increases of more than 10 per cent would be computed at only 10 per cent. Thus, the 13·9 per cent increase in the consumer price index actually registered in 1979 would have been compensated through tax credits only up to the amount of 10 per cent. Eligibility for tax credits would depend upon the behaviour of the group while the actual tax credits would be paid out on an individual basis at the end of the year when the individual filed his annual income tax return. The Internal Revenue Service would monitor compliance with the scheme.

There is, of course, a real problem of adverse selection with this inflation insurance plan: individuals whose pay increases would have met the pay standard in the absence of the real wage insurance scheme would qualify for a tax rebate. Moreover, in the event of large numbers of employees complying with the pay standards and yet of rapid increases in the consumer price index attributable to, say, increases in the prices of energy and of food, the cost of the programme could be considerable. Without tax increases elsewhere in the economy, this would have only increased the Federal budget deficit further and provided more fuel for the inflation fire. It was reasons such as these that induced Congress not to act on the real wage insurance plan, so that it was never put into effect.[18]

4   The causes and consequences of incomes policies

In the previous section reasons were provided for an incomes policy to affect *relative* prices and wages: the prices in the effectively controlled sector will tend to rise relative to the prices in the unregulated sector and the implicit prices of non-pecuniary items will rise relative to money prices. However, the stated purpose of these incomes policies has not been to change relative prices, but to alter the rate of change of the aggregate price or wage level. Much research effort has been devoted to determining whether or not these incomes policies have succeeded in affecting inflation. The typical procedure consists of specifying some maintained hypothesis about the determinants of wage or price changes, of identifying a period during which government incomes policies were operative, and of contrasting the behaviour of wages or prices during this period with what is implied by the maintained hypothesis. This may be achieved by estimating separate wage or price change structures for the period when the incomes policy was in effect and for the period when the policy was not in effect. A special case of this procedure is when an incomes policy dummy variable is simply introduced into a wage change or price change equation fitted to the entire period.

Since there is far from universal agreement over the appropriate maintained hypothesis and since the power of aggregative data to discriminate between competing explanations of inflation is low, there exists a large number of different econometric studies. Among the best known of these is Gordon's (1975) analysis of a price index that excludes food and energy. He first estimated with quarterly data from 1954 to 1971 an equation accounting for the movement in the rate of change of this price index and then he compared the post-sample predictions from the fitted equation with the actual values of price changes. Gordon found that Phases I and II of the wage–price controls reduced the rate of price inflation by 2·0 per cent per annum and by the third quarter of 1973 the price level was some 3·5 per cent below what it would have been in the absence of controls. However, from this date prices rose faster than they would have done had controls not existed and by the first quarter of 1975 the price level was 1 per cent above what it would have been if controls had not been imposed.

Another study, McGuire's (1976), attributed to the wage–price controls a considerably smaller effect on price inflation although again after a while prices increased by a greater amount than they would have done had controls never been imposed. A more recent investigation by Blinder and Newton (1979) models explicitly the fact that one sector of the economy was unregulated by the wage–price controls. Their estimates also suggest that the controls reduced the rate of price inflation until the beginning of 1974, at which time price inflation exceeded the rate that would have prevailed in the absence of controls. Hence, as far as price changes are concerned, the wage–price controls appear to have affected the path of prices – reducing price inflation during one period and then leading to an acceleration in inflation subsequently.

Less analysis seems to have been performed on the effects of incomes policies on wage inflation, but what work exists is consistent with the results from the following model. Suppose the determinants of wage inflation may be described by the following stochastic equation:

$$\Delta w_t = \alpha_0 + \alpha_1 U_{t-1}^{-1} + \alpha_2 \Delta x_{t-1} + \alpha_3 \Delta p_{t-1} + \alpha_4 I_t + \alpha_5 (U_{t-1}^{-1} \cdot I_t)$$

$$+ \alpha_6 (\Delta x_{t-1} \cdot I_t) + \alpha_7 (\Delta p_{t-1} \cdot I_t) + \varepsilon_t \qquad (1)$$

where the subscript t relates to a particular quarter and ε_t is a stochastic disturbance term. The variables are defined as follows:

$$\Delta w_t \equiv (w_t - w_{t-1})/w_{t-1}$$

is the quarter-to-quarter rate of change of average hourly compensation in the private non-farm economy;

$$U_{t-1}^{-1}$$

is the inverse of the civilian unemployment rate in quarter $t-1$;

$$\Delta x_{t-1} \equiv (x_{t-1} - x_{t-5})/x_{t-5}$$

is the annual rate of change in the index of industrial production;

$$\Delta p_{t-1} \equiv (p_{t-1} - p_{t-5})/p_{t-5}$$

is the annual rate of change in the consumer price index; and

$$I_t$$

is a dichotomous variable taking the value of unity when an incomes policy is in effect and of zero otherwise.

There are serious measurement problems involved with each variable in this regression equation and it is somewhat heroic to treat the error term as distributed independently of the regressors. Nevertheless, it is by no means untypical of the sort of equations encountered in the literature on the determinants of wage inflation[19] and for this reason it is worth investigating. One feature of this equation bears emphasising, however, and this is that the left-hand-side variable has been defined as the one-quarter rate of wage change. A number of researchers employ a definition of wage changes over four quarters which introduces positive serial correlation in the residuals and which artificially inflates estimated 't-statistics'.[20]

The dichotomous variable, I_t, takes the value of unity in the following four periods: from 1950–III to 1952–IV; from 1962–I to 1966–III; from 1971–III to 1974–I; and from 1978–IV to 1979–II, which represents that last quarter in our time-series of observations. There is, of course, an element of arbitrariness in identifying I_t for some of these quarters. The consequences of fitting equation (1) to quarterly data for the thirty years from the second quarter of 1949 (1949–II) to the second quarter of 1979 (1979–II) are presented in line 1 of Table 7.3. These estimates imply that, evaluated at the sample mean values of U_{t-1}^{-1}, Δx_{t-1}, and Δp_{t-1}, the rate of change of wages when an incomes policy is in effect is $0 \cdot 225$ per cent per quarter (or $0 \cdot 9$ per cent per year) lower than when an incomes policy is not in effect. However, a test of the hypothesis that the relationship is no different during an incomes policy episode except for the intercept (that is, a test of the null hypothesis $\alpha_5 = \alpha_6 = \alpha_7 = 0$) results in our retaining that null hypothesis and this is maintained in the results reported in line 2 of Table 7.3. These results produce no evidence of a Phillips curve (that is, of a significant association between wage changes and unemployment) while the coefficient on price changes implies that an annual rate of change of prices of 10 per cent is associated after a short lag with a $6 \cdot 4$ per cent ($= 1 \cdot 6\% \times 4$) increase in the annual rate of change of wages. Correspondingly, a 10 per cent annual increase in the industrial production index is associated with a $0 \cdot 8$ per cent ($= 0 \cdot 21\% \times 4$) increase in annual wage inflation. The estimated coefficient on the incomes policy dummy variable implies that when an incomes policy is in effect, the annual rate of change of wages is a trivial $0 \cdot 5$ per cent ($= 0 \cdot 13\% \times 4$) lower than in the absence of the policy. Moreover, this coefficient is not estimated with precision and the effect of the incomes policy would not be judged significantly different from zero by conventional criteria. If the incomes policy dummy variable, I_t, is disaggregated into four separate variables for each of the four incomes policy episodes in the past thirty years, the estimated coefficients (and estimated standard errors) on these four variables are as follows:[21]

Table 7.3 Estimates of equation (1) determining the rate of change of money wages from 1949–II to 1979–II

Line	Period	Estimated coefficients (and estimated standard errors) on:								R^2	D–W	s
		Constant	U_{t-1}^{-1}	Δx_{t-1}	Δp_{t-1}	I_t	$U_{t-1}^{-1} \cdot I_t$	$\Delta x_{t-1} \cdot I_t$	$\Delta p_{t-1} \cdot I_t$			
1	1949–II to 1979–II	·0090* (·0024)	−·0018 (·0100)	·0142* (·0098)	·1636* (·0211)	−·0067 (·0042)	·0191 (·0171)	·0350 (·0188)	−·0340 (·0395)	·464	1·67	·0058
2	1949–II to 1979–II	·0086* (·0019)	−·0002 (·0077)	·0209* (·0081)	·1611* (·0174)	−·0013 (·0012)				·439	1·64	·0058
3	1949–II to 1959–IV	·0122* (·0032)	−·0089 (·0130)	·0202 (·0114)	·0330 (·0502)	·0075* (·0031)				·326	1·83	·0067
4	1960–I to 1969–IV	·0053 (·0056)	·0146 (·0380)	·0146 (·0380)	·1268 (·1379)	−·0015 (·0025)				·289	1·73	·0047
5	1970–I to 1979–II	·0028 (·0049)	·0118 (·0230)	·0459* (·0144)	·2205* (·0378)	−·0027 (·0019)				·556	2·46	·0047

Notes: For convenience of reading, an asterisk has been placed next to coefficients estimated to be more than twice their standard errors (in absolute value). D – W means the calculated Durbin-Watson statistic and s is the standard error of estimate for the regression equation. The mean values of variables with their associated standard deviations in parentheses over the entire estimating period are as follows:

$$\Delta w_t = ·015 \; (·0076); \; U_{t-1}^{-1} = 5·09 \; (1·47); \; \Delta x_{t-1} = ·045 \; (·0733); \; \Delta p_{t-1} = ·035 \; (·0309); \text{ and } I_t = ·355 \; (·481).$$

These data have been taken from the *Employment and Training Report of the President, 1978*, with more recent observations drawn from the issues of the *Monthly Labor Review*.

I_t for the Korean War $= \cdot 0037;$
$$(\cdot 0021)$$
I_t for the guideposts $= - \cdot 0038^*;$
$$(\cdot 0016)$$
I_t for the Nixon wage–price controls $= - \cdot 0016;$ and
$$(\cdot 0019)$$
I_t for the pay standards $= - \cdot 0004.$
$$(\cdot 0035)$$

Only the coefficient on the guideposts dummy variable would be judged as significantly less than zero by conventional standards and this implies a lower rate of wage inflation during the guideposts years of $1 \cdot 52$ per cent per year (or $0 \cdot 38$ per cent per quarter). This is consistent with the well-known results of Perry (1967, 1970) and of Eckstein and Brinner (1972) and with Sheahan's (1967) judgement that the guideposts reduced wage inflation by an amount that ranged between $0 \cdot 8$ and $1 \cdot 6$ per cent a year. However, competing interpretations of the behaviour of wage changes during the guideposts years have been offered (Black and Kelejian, 1972; Throop, 1968) and it is difficult with the available data to discriminate among these various explanations. Although negative, the estimated coefficient for Nixon's wage–price controls is less than its estimated standard error so that, if one believes that price increases were restrained during the first part of the controls programme (as was suggested earlier in this section) and that wages were not affected, then the controls must have squeezed profit margins.

All these equations have been fitted to the entire thirty-year period from 1949 to 1979, yet recent work in monetary economics has cast severe doubt on the structural stability of such wage change equations. Indeed, a formal test of the hypothesis that the structure whose results are reported in line 2 of Table 7.3 is the same in the three decades rejects the hypothesis of stability. Consequently, wage change equations were estimated for three separate periods that correspond to each of the three decades and these results are reported in lines 3, 4, and 5 of Table 7.3. In none of these sub-period equations is the estimated coefficient on the incomes policy dummy variable significantly less than zero. Therefore, these results are not very encouraging to those who believe that incomes policies have had a marked effect on reducing the pace of wage inflation.[22]

This procedure for evaluating the effects of incomes policies on wage inflation not only suffers from the fact that our knowledge of the determinants of wage changes in the absence of an incomes policy is lamentably deficient, but also it rests on the tacit assumption that the adoption of an incomes policy is an event independent of the course of inflation itself. That is, even though casual observation and the research on political business cycles[23] suggest the contrary, the appropriateness of treating the incomes policy dummy variable as exogenous in the estimating equations above seems not to have been questioned in this literature. While the role of 'political' factors in determining the actions of government with respect to the conduct of fiscal and monetary policy have been the subject of considerable research, no one seems to have investigated whether any empirical regularities exist as far as the determinants of an incomes policy is concerned. This issue is pursued in the appendix, where the estimates from some linear probability functions are discussed. The problem here is that, in essence, the last thirty-five years presents us with only four observations on incomes policies in the United States. Perhaps data from many countries over time can be pooled to analyse this question with more confidence.

Therefore, such as it is, the evidence suggests that aggregate wage changes were restrained by the guidelines and aggregate price changes were moderated during the earlier part of the wage–price control programme. The reduction in wage inflation during the guidelines episode appears to have been achieved by affecting union wage settlements so that the union–non-union wage differential narrowed during these years. It was restored by the early 1970s, however, and paradoxically the relatively large wage settlements towards the late 1960s that reflected the restoration of the pre-guidelines union–non-union wage differential contributed in part to the concern over inflation that resulted in the wage–price controls in 1971. Similarly, the effect of Nixon's wage–price controls on price changes was accomplished by reducing profit margins. When these profit margins were restored from 1974 onwards, price inflation ran ahead of what would have obtained in the absence of the wage–price controls. In each of these instances, therefore, the effect of the incomes policy on inflation was temporary and it was achieved by disturbing an equilibrium. The subsequent restoration of the equilibrium brought the economy back to a position that differed little from what would have occurred if an incomes policy had never been implemented. If this assessment is correct, then an incomes policy tends to substitute greater inflation a few years in the future for less inflation today, but the long-term course of price and wage inflation has not been affected appreciably by these policies.

5 Conclusion

In the United States as in other Western countries the government has assumed ostensibly the responsibility for maintaining a stable price level. Yet successive governments have been reluctant to implement the severe fiscal and monetary restraint that would achieve this stated goal because of the belief that these measures would compromise other goals of economic policy and because of the belief that the immediate unemployment-increasing effects of these measures would be more apparent to the electorate than the longer-term benefits. For these reasons, governments have experimented with income policies and, at least at first, these policies have been welcomed by the electorate who have discounted the longer-term implications of these extensions of government control over civil liberties.[24] It is manifest, however, that incomes policies are not *sufficient* to prevent inflation nor is it clear that they are *necessary* to a successful anti-inflationary package. Nevertheless, as is evident from the historical record dating at least from the Roman Emperor Diocletian (Michell, 1947), they have a persistent appeal to governments. There is no reason to believe that this appeal has worn off in the United States, so the future is likely to see further and perhaps more ingenious use of incomes policies.

Notes: Chapter 7

1   There are, of course, prominent exceptions to this generalisation, such as John Kenneth Galbraith, Robert Heilbroner, and Robert Lekachman. None the less, it is interesting to observe that even so ardent an advocate of price controls as Galbraith presents a case for controls that explicitly excludes markets 'approaching pure competition'. He writes:
> Thus there are markets where prices can be fixed, in face of a considerable excess of demand over supply, without formal rationing controls. There are some, however, where this cannot be done. One of the control tasks of price administration is to distinguish between the two. (Galbraith, 1952, p. 26)

2   See Lanzillotti, Hamilton and Roberts (1975, p. 29).

3   These are collected in *Pay and Price Standards: A Compendium*, Executive Office of the President, Council on Wage and Price Stability, June 1979.

4   Thus, if $x = S(p)$ is the supply function with $dS/dp > 0$ and if $x = D(p)$ is the demand function with $dD/dp < 0$, then the equilibrium price obtains (call this p_e) when $S(p_e) = D(p_e)$. Denote by p_c the price established by controls where $p_c < p_e$. Then taking second-order Taylor series expansions of the supply and demand functions around their price-controlled values and subtracting one from the other yields the following expression for the excess of the quantities demanded over the quantities supplied at p_c:

$$D(p_c) - S(p_c) = (\frac{dD}{dp} - \frac{dS}{dp})(p_c - p_e) + (\frac{d^2 D}{dp^2} - \frac{d^2 S}{dp^2})(p_c - p_e)^2$$

The first term on the right-hand side forms the basis for the statements in the text.

5   See, for instance, Kosters (1977), pp. 169–73.

6   See Solow (1966).

7   This result is contained in Ashenfelter, Johnson and Pencavel (1972) where the cumulative effect of the guideposts over the 1962–6 period is estimated to have reduced the union–non-union wage differential by approximately 12 percentage points. The robustness of this result is questioned, however, by Johnson (1977).

8   See Ashenfelter (1978).
9   It might be relevant if monopolistic elements were of increasing importance in the economy, but I know of no compelling evidence to suggest that this is the case in the United States.
10 The model implicitly referred to here is developed in a number of papers such as Tinbergen (1956) or Rosen (1974).
11 See Bureau of Labor Statistics (1977) for the large number of items specified in US collective bargaining contracts, each of which is, in part, substitutable for wages in the total utility package consumed by the employee. Further, non-union employment contracts are generally more flexible than the union contracts.
12 Thus define a firm's maximising profit function by $\pi(p, r)$ where p is the price of the firm's output and r a vector of prices paid for the firm's inputs. Let p_c be the price that satisfies the rules of the incomes policy $(p_c < p)$, let D be the fine imposed on the firm for not complying with the policy, and let θ be the probability of the firm being monitored by the government's agencies. Then the expected profit of the firm may be written as

$$E(\pi) = (1 - \theta)\pi(p, r) + \theta\pi(p_c, r) - \theta D.$$

The employer will not comply with the incomes policy if $E(\pi) > \pi(p_c, r)$ or if $(1 - \theta)[\pi(p, r) - \pi(p_c, r)] > \theta D$. Now replacing the term in square brackets with a second-order Taylor series expansion and using Hotelling's lemma $\partial\pi/\partial p = X$ and $\partial^2\pi/\partial p^2 = \partial X/\partial p$ enables the condition for non-compliance to be written

$$X(p - p_c)[1 + \tfrac{1}{2}(\tfrac{p - p_c}{p})e] > (\tfrac{\theta}{1 - \theta})D$$

where $e < 0$ is the own-price elasticity of demand. Clearly, the employer is more likely to comply with the incomes policy if either the fine (D) is high or if the odds of being detected, $\theta/(1 - \theta)$, are high. Similarly, an employer is the less likely to comply the larger the absolute value of the price elasticity of demand and the greater the gap between the controlled and uncontrolled price.
13 See Wallich and Weintraub (1971), p. 2.
14 According to Weintraub (1972), inflation since the Second World War has been predominantly of the 'cost-push' variety.
15 Would this greater employer resistance produce more and longer strikes? Wouldn't the unions push for the same wage increases, expecting these wages and the higher taxes to be paid out of the firm's profits? Wallich and Weintraub answer 'no' to both questions; Rees (1978) presents reasons for believing the opposite.
16 See, for instance, Okun (1977) and Seidman (1976) and for a French variant see Malinvaud (1978). A precursor of these plans is Scott's (1961). Abba Lerner's (1978) ingenious proposal involves the issue of 'wage increase permits' that would be freely tradeable. An excellent compendium of these proposals is contained in Fogarty (1973).
17 Recall from the description in section 2 above that Carter's pay standards applied to 'groups' of employees where these groups consisted of the collective bargaining unit or of all non-management employees in a firm or of all management personnel.
18 For further information on the real wage insurance scheme and a comparison with conventional TIP plans, see Flanagan (1979).
19 See, for instance, the models described in Oi (1976).
20 On this, see Black and Kelejian (1972) and Ashenfelter and Pencavel (1975).
21 The estimated coefficients on $U_i^1{}_{-1}$, Δx_{t-1}, and Δp_{t-1} are virtually the same as those reported in line 2 of Table 7.3.

22 A number of variations on these equations yielded this same conclusion. For instance, allowing for various lags on the price change variable did not alter any inferences in any meaningful sense. Also, replacing the hourly compensation series in the private non-farm economy with hourly earnings changes (either straight-time hourly earnings or gross hourly earnings) of production workers in manufacturing industry did not result in any different conclusions.

23 A business cycle is said to be 'political' if government attempts to influence aggregate economic activity in accordance with the timing of elections. References to this literature include Nordhaus (1975), Tufte (1978), and Carter (1979).

24 Most American and British observers tend to disregard the political implications of wage and price controls although there is ample recent and relevant evidence to indicate that these implications are very real. In this regard, Chile's recent experiences are most instructive. Here is a country that, at one time, could boast of a record of civil and political liberties of which most European countries would be envious. Yet, in explicit opposition to this historical tradition, the Marxist regime of Salvador Allende employed price controls to try to silence newspaper opinion opposed to its policies. For instance, with respect to *Papelera*, the only private source of newsprint in Chile, the Allende government refused.

> to allow the company to raise its prices while costs soared because of statutory wage increases and the higher tariffs charged by public sector service industries. By June 1972, the real price of the company's products had dropped to only half of their 1958 price and the business was losing about 3 million escudos *a day*. Persistent appeals for an increase in prices were ignored by DIRINCO, the government's price-fixing agency, although it was written in the agency's own statutes that it was required to take account of the 'legitimate profit margin' of the producer . . . It was only the resoluteness of its shareholders and employees, and the tremendous campaign on its behalf in the free press, that had enabled it to survive that long. (Moss, 1973, pp. 139–40)

References: Chapter 7

Ashenfelter, O. C., 'Union Relative Wage Effects: New Evidence and a Survey of Their Implications for Wage Inflation', in R. S. Stone and W. Petersen (eds), *Econometric Contributions to Public Policy* (New York, 1978, pp. 31–60)

Ashenfelter, O. C. and J. H. Pencavel, 'Wage Changes and the Frequency of Wage Settlements', *Economica*, Vol. 42, No. 166, May 1975, pp. 162–70

Ashenfelter, O. C., G. E. Johnson, and J. H. Pencavel, 'Trade Unions and the Rate of Change of Money Wages in United States Manufacturing Industry', *Review of Economic Studies*, Vol. 39, No. 1, January 1972, pp. 27–54

Black, S. W., and H. H. Kelejian, 'A Macro Model of the U.S. Labor Market', *Econometrica*, Vol. 38, No. 5, September 1970, pp. 712–41

Black, S. W., and H. H. Kelejian, 'The Formulation of the Dependent Variable in the Wage Equation', *Review of Economic Studies*, Vol. 39, No. 117, January 1972, pp. 55–9

Blinder, A. S., and W. J. Newton, 'The 1971–1974 Controls Program and the Price Level: An Econometric Post Mortem' (Princeton University mimeo, October 1979)

Bureau of Labor Statistics, *Characteristics of Major Collective Bargaining Agreements: July 1, 1975*, Bulletin 1957 (1977)

Carter, Michael, 'Political Business Cycles in the United States: Theory and Evidence', unpublished Ph.D. dissertation, Department of Economics, Stanford Unversity (December 1979)

Darby, M. R., 'Price and Wage Controls: the First Two Years', *Journal of Monetary Economics: The Economics of Price and Wage Controls*, Vol. 2, 1976, pp. 235–63

Galbraith, J. K., *A Theory of Price Control* (Harvard University Press, 1952)

Gordon, R. J., 'The Impact of Aggregate Demand on Prices', *Brookings Papers on Economic Activity*, 3, 1975, pp. 613–62

Flanagan, Robert J., 'Real Wage Insurance as a Compliance Incentive', Stanford University Graduate School of Business, Research Paper Series, No. 510, August 1979

Fogarty, Michael P., 'Fiscal Measures and Wage Settlements', *British Journal of Industrial Relations*, Vol. XI, No. 1, March 1973, pp. 29–65

Freeman, R. B., and J. L. Medoff, 'New Estimates of Private Sector Unionism in the United States', *Industrial and Labor Relations Review*, Vol. 32, No. 2, January 1979, pp. 143–74

Hayek, F. A., 'The Use of Knowledge in Society', *American Economic Review*, Vol. 35, No. 4, September 1945, pp. 519–30

Heckman, James J., 'Some Statistical Models for Discrete Panel Data Developed and Applied to Test the Hypothesis of True State Dependence Against the Hypothesis of Spurious State Dependence', *Annales de l'insée*, 30–31, April-September 1978, pp. 227–70

Johnson, G. E., 'The Determination of Wages in the Union and Non-Union Sectors', *British Journal of Industrial Relations*, Vol. 15, No. 2, July 1977, pp. 211–25

Kearl, J. R., C. L. Pope, G. C. Whiting, and L. T. Wimmer, 'What Economists Think: A Confusion of Economists?', *American Economic Review, Papers and Proceedings*, Vol. 69, No. 2, May 1979, pp. 28–37

Kosters, Marvin H., 'Controls and Inflation: An Overview', in Joel Popkin (ed.), *Analysis of Inflation: 1965–74*, National Bureau of Economic Research, Analysis in Income and Wealth, Vol. 42 (Ballinger Publishing Company, 1977) pp. 121–89.

Lanzillotti, R. F., M. T. Hamilton, and R. B. Roberts, *Phase II in Review: The Price Commission Experience*, Brookings Institution Studies in Wage–Price Policy, 1975

Lerner, Abba P., 'A Wage-Increase Permit Plan to Stop Inflation', *Brookings Papers in Economic Activity*, 2, 1978, pp. 491–505

Lewis, N., and M. Reinhold (eds), *Roman Civilization: Selected Readings*: Volume II *The Empire* (Columbia University Press, 1955)

Malinvaud, Edmond, 'Some Problems of Prices and Incomes Policy in France', in Richard Stone and William Peterson (eds), *Econometric Contributions to Public Policy* (International Economic Association, 1978) pp. 13–26

McGuire, Timothy W., 'On Estimating the Effects of Controls', in *The Economics of Price and Wage Controls* (North-Holland Publishing Company, 1976) pp. 115–56

Michell, H., 'The Edict of Diocletian: A Study of Price Fixing in the Roman Empire', *Canadian Journal of Economics and Political Science*, Vol. 13, No. 1, February 1947, pp. 1–12

Moss, Robert, *Chile's Marxist Experiment* (John Wiley & Sons, 1973)

Nordhaus, W. D., 'The Political Business Cycle', *Review of Economic Studies*, Vol. 42, April 1975, pp. 169–89

Oi, Walter Y., 'On Measuring the Impact of Wage Price Controls: A Critical Appraisal', *The Economics of Price and Wage Controls* (North-Holland Publishing Company, 1976) pp. 7–64

Okun, Arthur M., 'The Great Stagflation Swamp', *Challenge*, Vol. 20, November/December 1977

Perry, G. L., 'Wages and the Guideposts', *American Economic Review*, Vol. 57, No. 4, September 1967, pp. 897–904

Perry, G. L., 'Changing Labor Markets and Inflation', *Brookings Papers on Economic Activity*, 1970, pp. 411–48

Rees, Albert, 'Tripartite Wage Stabilizing in the Food Industry', *Industrial Relations*, Vol. 14, No. 2, May 1975, pp. 250–8

Rosen, S., 'Hedonic Prices and Implicit Markets: Product Differentiation in Pure Competition', *Journal of Political Economy*, Vol. 82, No. 1, January/February 1974, pp. 34–55

Scott, M. F. G., 'A Tax on Price Increases?', *Economic Journal*, Vol. 71, June 1961, pp. 350–66

Seidman, Lawrence S., 'A Payroll Tax Credit to Restrain Inflation', *National Tax Journal*, Vol. 29, December 1976, pp. 398–412

Sheahan, J., *The Wage–Price Guideposts* (Washington, D.C.: Brookings Institution, 1967)

Solow, R. M., 'The Case Against the Case Against the Guideposts', in G. P. Schultz and R. Z. Aliber (eds), *Guidelines, Informed Controls, and the Market Place* (University of Chicago Press, 1966)

Thomson, A. W. J., C. Mulvey, and M. Farbman, 'Bargaining Structure and Relative Earnings in Great Britain', *British Journal of Industrial Relations*, Vol. 15, No. 2, July 1977, pp. 176–91

Throop, A. W., 'The Union–NonUnion Wage Differential and Cost-Push Inflation', *American Economic Review*, Vol. 58, No. 1, March 1968, pp. 79–99

Tinbergen, Jan, 'On the Theory of Income Distribution', *Weltwirtschaftliches Archiv*, Band 77, 1956 II, pp. 155–75

Tufte, Edward R., *Political Control of the Economy* (Princeton University Press, 1978)

Wallich, Henry C., and Sidney Weintraub, 'A Tax-Based Incomes Policy', *Journal of Economic Issues*, Vol. 5, June 1971, pp. 1–19

Weber, Arnold R., *In Pursuit of Price Stability: The Wage–Price Freeze of 1971*, Brookings Studies in Wage–Price Policy (Washington, D.C., 1973)

Weintraub, Sidney, 'Incomes Policy: Completing the Stabilization Triangle', *Journal of Economic Issues*, Vol. 6, December 1972

Appendix 7A   Determinants of the probability that an incomes policy will be in effect

The purpose of this appendix is to present some exploratory results concerning the determinants of whether an incomes policy will be in effect in any given quarter. Equivalently, the work here may be thought of as a search for instrumental variables so that the endogeneity of incomes policy dummy variables in price change and wage change equations may be addressed through a consistent estimating technique. Of course, because of the fixed costs involved in establishing and implementing an incomes policy, the determinants of the adoption of an incomes policy have to cross some threshold value before an incomes policy is actually invoked. And once adopted, it is less costly for the policy-makers to continue the policy than it is to set it up in the first place. This state dependence (see Heckman, 1978) is not modelled in the results that follow, so they should clearly be treated as provisional and tentative. None the less, they are suggestive and, in fact, tell a story that is consistent with casual observation.

Consider the following multiple regression equation where the left-hand-side variable is dichotomous:

$$I_t = \beta_0 + \beta_1 G_{t-1} + \beta_2 U_{t-1} + \beta_3 \Delta U_{t-1} + \beta_4 \Delta x_{t-1}$$
$$+ \beta_5 \sum_i \lambda_i \Delta^2 p_{t-i} + \beta_6 \sum_i \mu_i \Delta^2 w_{t-i} + u_t$$

where the subscript t identifies quarterly observations and u_t is a stochastic disturbance term. The incomes policy dummy variable, I_t, and U_{t-1} and Δx_{t-1} have been defined in the text. The other variables are defined as follows:

$$G_{t-1}$$

the fraction of people either expressing approval or expressing no opinion of the President's performance in quarter t-1 as measured by the Gallup Opinion Poll;

$$\Delta U_{t-1} \equiv (U_{t-1} - U_{t-5})$$

is the annual change of the unemployment rate lagged one quarter;

$$\Delta^2 p_{t-j} \equiv \Delta p_{t-j} - \Delta p_{t-j-4} \text{ (where } \Delta p_{t-j} = (p_{t-j} - p_{t-j-4})/p_{t-j-4})$$

or the change in the annual rate of change of the consumer price index; and

Table 7.4 Determinants of the probability of an incomes policy being in effect, 1949–II – 1979–II

Estimated coefficients (with estimated standard errors in parentheses)

Line	Constant	G_{t-1}	U_{t-1}	ΔU_{t-1}	Δx_{t-1}	$\Sigma\Delta^2 p_{t-i}$	$\Sigma\Delta^2 w_{t-i}$	$\Sigma\Delta^2 r_{t-i}$
1	·347	−·559	·049	−·368	3·650	13·173	−14·166	
	(·270)	(·308)	(·032)	(·155)	(·723)	(5·317)	(6·695)	
2		−·078	·072	−·116	·267	·050	−·049	
3	·406	−·577	·045	−·295	3·069			−8·871
	(·258)	(·296)	(·032)	(·142)	(·628)			(4·680)
4		−·080	·066	−·093	·224			−·022

Notes: The entries in lines 1 and 3 correspond to point estimates (with standard errors in parentheses) of a linear probability function. The entries in line 2 are the point estimates of each coefficient in line 1 multiplied by the sample standard deviation of that variable; this provides the effect of a 'typical' increase in each right-hand-side variable on the probability of an incomes policy being in operation. For the entries under $\Sigma\Delta^2 p_{t-i}$ and $\Sigma\Delta^2 w_{t-i}$, line 2 consists of the coefficients in line 1 divided by eight (the number of lags on each variable) and then multiplied by the standard deviation of each variable. A corresponding interpretation holds for the entries in line 4 which are derived from the estimates in line 3.

Table 7.5 Estimated lag coefficients on the acceleration in prices, money wages, and real wages

Lag	Corresponding to the estimates in line 1 of Table 7.4		Corresponding to the estimates in line 3 of Table 7.4
	$\Delta^2 p_{t-j}$	$\Delta^2 w_{t-j}$	$\Delta^2 r_{t-j}$
1	·622 (1·249)	−2·130 (1·395)	−·852 (1·186)
2	1·408 (·870)	−2·246 (1·096)	−1·165 (·849)
3	1·948 (·811)	−2·252 (1·042)	−1·358 (·737)
4	2·241 (·906)	−2·149 (1·087)	−1·432 (·760)
5	2·287 (·973)	−1·937 (1·103)	−1·385 (·787)
6	2·086 (·936)	−1·617 (1·022)	−1·219 (·747)
7	1·638 (·767)	−1·187 (·820)	−·933 (·610)
8	·942 (·457)	−·648 (·481)	−·526 (·363)
mean lag	3·646 (1·524)	2·872 (1·665)	3·280 (1·916)

Notes: Estimated standard errors are in parentheses.

$$\Delta^2 w_{t-j} \equiv \Delta w_{t-j} - \Delta w_{t-j-4} \text{ (where } \Delta w_{t-j} = (w_{t-j} - w_{t-j-4})/w_{t-j-4})$$

or the change in the annual rate of change of hourly compensation in the private non-farm economy.

The variables $\Delta^2 p_{t-j}$ and $\Delta^2 w_{t-j}$ measure the change in the price and wage inflation rate and each is highly correlated with deviations of the rate of inflation from its trend. The conjecture here is that it is not inflation *per se* that induces governments to invoke an incomes policy, but rather surprises or deviations of price and wage inflation from their trends. The lag coefficients on the price and wage acceleration variables are estimated by Almon's procedure. (A second-degree polynomial is used lagged over eight quarters with the restriction that the estimated coefficients taper off to zero at a finite lag.) The problems with applying ordinary least squares (the linear probability function) to an equation with a limited dependent variable are well known: although the estimator is unbiased, the error variances are heteroskedastic and, in addition, there is no guarantee that the predicted values of the dependent variable will lie between zero and one. Nevertheless, naive least squares has demonstrated its reliability in these circumstances on very many occasions and for the exploratory results that I present here, this procedure is sufficient.

Tables 7.4 and 5 present the results from fitting the above equation by ordinary least squares. Line 1 of Table 7.4 gives the regression estimates while line 2 multiples each coefficient by the observed standard deviation of the variable to derive a measure of the effect of a 'typical' increase in each variable on the probability of an incomes policy being in effect. Thus, a decrease in the fraction of the public expressing approval of the President's performance (that is, an increase in G_{t-1}) increases the probability of an incomes policy being invoked. Moreover, the estimated coefficient on U_{t-1} suggests that an incomes policy is more likely to be employed when the unemployment rate is relatively high although the estimated coefficients on ΔU_{t-1} and Δx_{t-1} imply that an incomes policy is more likely to be in effect during the expansionary phase of a business cycle when industrial production is rising and unemployment falling. An acceleration in prices encourages the use of an incomes policy while an acceleration in money wages discourages the use of an incomes policy. The estimates in line 3 impose the constraint that it is the behaviour of real wages that matters – that the coefficients on $\Delta^2 p_{t-i}$ are the same in absolute magnitude as those on $\Delta^2 w_{t-i}$. Thus, the variable $\Delta^2 r_{t-j}$ is defined as $\Delta^2 w_{t-j} - \Delta^2 p_{t-j}$. Put simply, governments have been inclined to turn to an incomes policy when the popularity of the government is low, when the economy is moving from a recession and into an expansion, and when the growth in real wages is falling below its trend. The story told by these results is a plausible one: relatively high unemployment and a decelerating growth in real wages induces dissatisfaction with the President's performance and he responds with incomes policy measures that give the appearance of 'doing something' about inflation; in addition, an incomes policy has been seen (incorrectly) as a policy instrument that affects price and wage inflation without affecting output, so has a particular appeal *vis-à-vis* fiscal and monetary restraint at a time when the economy is coming out of a recession.

These results should be regarded as a point of departure for a more thorough and careful study that does not treat each quarterly observation as independent of the preceding observation and that makes use of more reliable estimating techniques. None the less, these results indicate that empirical regularities exist as far as the determinants of whether or not the authorities will invoke an incomes policy are concerned, and this should be taken into account when measuring the effects of incomes policies.

Chapter 8

Incomes Policy: the Recent European Experience

JOHN T. ADDISON

1 Introduction

In this chapter we review developments in European prices and incomes policy over the difficult decade of the 1970s, in which the task of controlling inflation has been complicated by discrete upward movements in the price of oil and recurring recessionary tendencies. Our analysis focuses in the main on the experiences of eight countries, namely Austria, Finland, France, Germany, Ireland, the Netherlands, Norway and Sweden. The sample is at once representative of the generality of West European experience and fully inclusive of the more ambitious approaches to the problem of reconciling competing *ex ante* claims. Moreover, supplementary information on other European countries is provided in the text as appropriate.

The plan of the chapter is as follows. First, we identify the basic ingredients of policy in the continuum ranging from information provision through persuasion/promises to the development of a more fully comprehensive consensus. Second, we investigate the constraints on policy as these have emerged in the sample. Third, we provide an assessment of incomes policy, placing especial emphasis on appropriate policies of economic management in the post-1971 regime of fluctuating exchange rates. A detailed commentary on prices and incomes policy in each of the eight countries is provided in Appendix 8A, to provide the necessary backdrop to the more thematic material considered in the main body of the text.

2 The ingredients of policy

Before outlining the basic ingredients of European incomes policy measures as these emerged in the sample over the decade of the 1970s, it is important to point out that such policies and related labour market measures have been introduced as elements in complex mixes of aggregate demand management. Incomes policies have to be viewed in the light of each country's general economic position and exchange rate strategy over the period as a whole. The sample of countries employing incomes policies faced basically different problems and constraints over the 1970s. Thus, some countries were more vulnerable to the oil price hike in 1973 because of their balance of payments position, the prevalence of wage indexation and the vulnerability of their tax structures to distortion by inflation. The countries in the sample had different priorities and reacted differently to the inflationary shock, some giving priority to bringing down the rate of price and wage inflation by restrictive demand management and others providing temporary stimuli to support economic activity until recessionary tendencies eased. This background is necessary to understand both the form that incomes policies took and the results achieved.

Despite their differences, incomes policies were viewed in all countries as methods to promote a better social consensus and serve as a complement to, rather than a substitute for, demand management policies. The aim in each case was to alter the way the participants reacted in a given economic situation.

With these introductory comments in mind, let us proceed with an outline of the evolving elements of policy.

Information

The most basic ingredient of incomes policy is the provision of information. This information may aim at ensuring that the parties base themselves on identical assumptions as regards the economic situation and the effects on the trend of real incomes of alternative wage increases, possibly coupled with measures on the part of the authorities. Information may also refer to an exchange of views regarding plans and intentions so as to remove misconceptions with regard to the future course of action of the other participants.

In Norway, for example, the former type of information has been prepared by the Technical Expert Committee, a tripartite body whose task it is to provide an analysis of the economic situation and to provide information for the real economic basis of wage negotiations. To achieve these purposes it was necessary for that body to establish an 'economic framework', within which the important issues could be distinguished and the facts relating to them set out. In this economic framework a fundamental distinction is made between the 'exposed' sector, comprising the export and import-competing industries, and a 'sheltered' or non-trading sector. In the former, selling prices are determined in the world market and cannot be raised in response to an increase in costs; these have to be absorbed via a reduction in profits. The sheltered sector is in a different position: because it does not risk losing markets to foreign competition, it tends to compensate for cost increases by raising output prices. However, the productivity of the exposed sector is (assumed to be) higher and so this sector is better able to absorb wage increases without affecting prices and profits than the sheltered sector.

Based on these characteristic properties of sheltered and exposed sectors, a simple two-sector model may be advanced to describe the mechanisms determining the long-run movement of wages and prices in a small open economy. As noted above, world market prices (coupled with the exchange rate) determine the output prices of the exposed sector. These prices and the 'existing technology' (that is, the productivity of the exposed sector) determine its profitability. Wages in the exposed sector are directly related to sectoral profitability, such that wages adjust to leave actual profits close to a 'normal' level. In turn, wages in this sector spill over, via a mix of 'solidaristic' collective bargaining and market forces, into the sheltered sector so as to maintain wages in the two sectors in normal relation to each other. The wage level within the sheltered sector together with that sector's existing technology (its productivity) determine sectoral output prices; it being assumed that mechanisms such as cost-plus pricing exist, causing the sheltered sector to adjust output prices so that a normal relation between wages and prices is maintained. And output prices for the two sectors, together with world prices for goods not produced domestically, appropriately weighted, determine the national price level.

In this way the model explains national wage and price trends in terms of price trends in the world economy, existing foreign exchange rates, and productivity trends within the two sectors.

Further insights into the mechanisms that determine price and income trends within the economy may be gained by disaggregating the two-sector model, and this is in fact the basis of the analysis provided by the Technical Expert Committee. Originally, this analysis proceeded on the basis of a multi-sector price-income model known as PRIM – a short-term, cost-push, input-output type of model (Aukrust, 1970). Over time, the model has been refined and today the sector-sector model has given way to a fourth-generation sector activity model, although the main ideas of PRIM are built into its price sub-model.

The reports of the Technical Expert Committee have contained particulars of national output, wage, profit and price developments in preceding years, and of real disposable income, after tax and social insurance payments, and including children's allowances and pensions, for families of various sizes and levels of earnings. They have also included an account of international developments likely to affect Norway's economic position and statistics of relative labour costs to indicate Norway's competitive strength. On the forecasting side, the first report in each negotiating year contains estimates of the effects on consumer prices, real and money wages and agricultural income, and profits in the sheltered and exposed sectors of a variety of possible wage and agricultural price settlements. The second report gives post-settlement forecasts of the effects of negotiated wage and price outcomes in terms of real disposable income for earners with various levels of income and size of family.

The Technical Expert Committee was established to facilitate the work of the Contact Committee, which brings us to the second type of information referred to in our opening comments. The purpose of the Contact Committee when it was set up in 1962 was mainly to provide a preparatory forum for discussion on wage and price developments and on maintaining reasonable inter-sectoral incomes parity.[1] It thus provided the interest groups with an opportunity to discuss basic assumptions before strategies were fixed for wage and income negotiations. The government for its part often sought to inform the parties on the major features of economic policy. Economic conditions for wage and price settlements were likely to be discussed in the Contact Committee both before and during the biennial bargaining round.

However, over the course of time, important changes have taken place in the Committee's work. While the exchange of information between the interest groups was its original remit, the Contact Committee gradually became a body in which *decisions* of central importance were arrived at in connection with integrated, combined and co-ordinated wage settlements – see below.

Returning to the former type of information, a tripartite body resembling the Norwegian Technical Expert Committee also exists in Finland – the Incomes Policy Reporting Committee. This body prepares the basic economic information required in the bargaining process, and employs a model similar in structure to the Norwegian PRIM (Halttunen and Molander, 1972). A derivative form of the Norwegian model, the so-called EFO model (Edgren, Faxén and Odhner, 1969, 1973) is also used in Sweden and has had a considerable influence on collective bargaining. Interestingly, this model was generated by the principal labour market organisations themselves in an attempt to exercise bipartisan self-restraint, so obviating the need to take the government into explicit partnership. However, informal discussions are also initiated by the Swedish government on the nature of the trade-offs with the union federation and the employers' confederation. Procedures are somewhat more explicit in Finland because of the more direct nature of government participation in the bargaining process.

Outside the Nordic countries (and Austria), there cannot really be said to exist joint (bipartite/tripartite) economic analysis of the economic framework. Instead, the parties prepare to a greater or lesser extent their own analyses and forecasts. Having said this, governmental bodies (such as the Central Planning Bureau in the Netherlands) or independent agencies (such as the Council of Economic Experts in Germany) have had a major impact on collective bargaining in their analysis of the economic framework and the perceived scope for wage increases. And in all such countries, with the exception of France, there exists a structure to promote a dialogue between unions, employers and governments in respect of the second type of information.

Persuasion/promises – the trade-off approach

Persuasion goes a step further than information provision, although the line of demarcation is necessarily imprecise since the aim of 'education' is to influence behaviour. There is, in turn, only a short step between simple persuasion and *promises* on the part of the authorities to take specific measures provided wage increases are kept within a further specified limit. The trade-off approach is perhaps the most notable feature of incomes policy developments within the sample, except in Germany and France. Where the trade-off approach has been attempted and *not* implemented, one often observes the imposition of statutory wage and price control as in the Netherlands.

There is of course a further development of trade-off into a more comprehensive *consensus* whereby the parties and the authorities agree on a target for the real economy and for incomes policy; a target attempted to be reached by way of incomes, prices, taxes and subsidies. The package deals arrived at in Norway during 1975–7 belong to this category. And, for a number of years now, such consensus has been arrived at in Austria, although with less reliance on the use of specific measures. We shall return to the question of consensus subsequently. Meanwhile, let us consider the elements in the developing trade-off framework.

Indexation. The case for indexation is that it takes expectations out of the bargaining process and offers the prospect of an effective and fairly speedy reduction of inflation expectations, given an appropriate set of other policies. The disadvantage of indexation is that it permits little or no downward adjustment in real wages when this is required by, say, a depreciation of the exchange rate or a sudden deterioration in the terms of trade. Thus, in 1973, the indexation of a large proportion of nominal incomes was inappropriate to the then situation of a sudden worsening in the terms of trade and the need to adjust the balance of payments by an increased transfer of resources. Efforts to mitigate the effects of indexation were an important constituent of policy measures in all countries where explicit or implicit indexation was most pervasive, namely the Netherlands, France, Ireland and to a lesser extent Norway within the sample, and Belgium, Denmark and Italy outside the sample. Because of their comparative absence of indexation provisions, Austria, Germany and Sweden (and of course Finland, where indexation had been abolished in 1969 — see Appendix 8A) were somewhat better placed in theory to restrain the rise in nominal incomes.

Table 8.1 gives some indication of the size of the initial problem posed by higher energy prices and the subsequent adjustment process in various countries by comparing the 'norm' GNP (corrected for terms-of-trade changes and divided by total employment) with the development in wage costs and earnings deflated by, respectively, output prices and consumer prices. Only in Germany was the rise in real wages held below the norm. In Austria, the Netherlands, Finland and Sweden real earnings by 1976 were largely in line with the norm, but in each case real total labour costs exceeded productivity by some margin. In almost all other countries, real earnings exceeded the norm by 5 per cent and more.

One response, and that practised in the Netherlands,[2] was to retain indexation and to make price stability the principal policy objective, to be achieved by restrictive demand management, price controls and statutory wages policy. Elsewhere within the sample, the attempt was made to postpone the real transfer of resources corresponding to the terms-of-trade loss. Governments sought to match the change in the foreign balance and 'absorb' part of the decline in real incomes by allowing a deterioration in the budget balance and simultaneously to introduce measures to reduce the risk of an acceleration in the rate of inflation. In the latter context, incomes policies in Norway and Ireland sought a modification and gradual abolition of existing wage indexation or escalator clauses.

Tax remission. *Ad hoc* tax concessions have formed important components of the trade-off approach. Of the countries within the sample, only in the Netherlands was there semi-automatic indexation of tax rates and brackets on the cost of living over the decade of the 1970s, although Sweden introduced automatic indexation of tax scales in 1978. (Outside the sample, taxation has been subject to semi-automatic indexation in Denmark since 1969, and in Belgium since 1978.)

The rationale for tax concessions is that the growing severity of fiscal drag tends to lead to an escalation of nominal wage claims. Again, the backdrop is a situation of a powerful exogenous price shock. To limit the inflationary effect of, say, an oil price rise it is

Table 8.1 Developments in real income, productivity and costs, selected countries, 1972–6 (Indices, 1972 = 100)

Country	'Norm'*	Real wages	Real disposable income	GDP per employee	Real total labour costs	Real wage costs	Nominal wages
Austria	115·3	115·5	119·7	115·4	115·1	114·0	164·7
Germany	113·4	112·6	105·2	115·2	117·4	114·3	140·5
Finland	111·7	113·3	105·8	110·6	112·8	109·0	199·2
France	110·0	116·3	108·2	112·8	121·4	118·0	183·8
Netherlands	111·5	112·2	106·0	115·1	118·0	114·3	163·8
Norway	105·8	112·0	117·0	110·8	111·5	111·5	182·0
Sweden	103·7	104·8	104·3	104·2	111·5	100·8	163·0
Denmark	103·8	117·1	116·0	106·3	114·3	115·0	192·3
Italy	102·4	112·8	106·4	109·4	115·8	113·0	233·4
Switzerland	106·5	110·2	110·3	104·7	113·4	113·4	132·2
Belgium	111·6	118·2	108·4	114·5	121·8	117·6	187·5

* GDP in constant prices, corrected for changes in the terms of trade and divided by total employment.
Source: Schelde-Andersen, P. (1979), 'Recent Wage Trends and Medium-Term Adjustment Problems', in *Collective Bargaining and Government Policies* (Paris: OECD) Table 1, p. 195.

necessary to prevent wages from rising in response. Any attempt to regain the lost purchasing power is self-defeating. Since payment in real resources for most of the cost of higher oil prices was being postponed a tax reduction could maintain after-tax real incomes without raising wage costs and simultaneously offset the demand-depressing effects of the oil price increase. The argument here is that to be effective in moderating inflation such a policy requires some kind of explicit arrangement between government and union leaderships to count the tax reduction as equivalent to a wage increase. In other words, the purpose of such an agreement is in effect to remove the rise in oil prices from the cost of living index, in so far as changes in that index form the basis for wage bargaining. Again we note that, while such actions might ease the internal adjustment process, additional measures will be needed to achieve an improvement in the external position as this policy response will not be conducive to a transfer of resources to the open sector. Indeed, since domestic demand is not reduced relative to output and real national income there is an obvious risk that the internal deficit will widen further. And the policy itself presupposes a high degree of social consensus regarding the distribution of factor incomes.

Before looking at the question of tax-push inflation, let us briefly consider some of the other repercussions of progressive taxes under rapid inflation as these emerged in the sample following 1973. First, in countries relying on progressive systems of taxation, notably the Nordic countries and the Netherlands, the rapid increase in wages under the impetus of sharply rising consumer prices led to unplanned increases in tax liability at given levels of real income. Countries such as Denmark, which had already implemented some form of indexation of tax brackets and allowances, did not escape this effect because adjustments for the effect of inflation were made with a time lag of fifteen months or thereabouts. Secondly, the unplanned rise in existing high rates of direct taxation intensified industrial and political conflict, undermined fiscal control, and made budgetary policy more erratic and less predictable. Thirdly, the unforeseen rise in direct tax liability intensified cost pressures, making it more difficult to bring down the rate of inflation and in some cases increased the difficulty of maintaining employment and investment in the exposed sector. Fourthly, the effect of progressive tax scales in reducing differentials between skilled and unskilled, and blue- and white-collar workers and, indeed, between recipients of untaxed unemployment and welfare benefits became divisive issues in industrial relations and national politics. We note here that the level of direct taxes figured prominently in the political crises in the Netherlands (and Denmark).

Let us now return to the highly controversial area of tax-push inflation. Table 8.1 indicates that in Germany, Finland, France and the Netherlands (together with Belgium and to some extent Italy) fiscal drag and discretionary policy changes strongly reduced the rate of growth of after-tax earnings in relation to pre-tax wages.[3] This is not to say that tax-push inflation operated in these countries. Here the evidence is rather unsatisfactory. There is some indication of tax push in Sweden and Finland (plus Denmark and Belgium). On the other hand, no evidence of tax push is discernible in Germany and the Netherlands. The results in question are based on a tax-push model emphasising a catch-up variable: it is assumed that there is some target for real after-tax incomes and that the tendency to bargain in terms of real disposable incomes will be particularly pronounced when the rate of growth of that variable falls significantly below the rate traditionally expected by wage-earners. Interestingly, results obtained for France and Italy, where deviations from the target have been quite large, do not point to any significant impact of taxes, casting doubt on this particular tax-push interpretation (Schelde-Andersen, 1979).

On balance, it cannot be concluded that tax increases are inflationary but this is a notoriously difficult area and the empirical literature is unsatisfactory. Countries within the sample employing tax reductions as part of a trade-off approach to incomes policy evidently believed that tax concessions induced wage moderation and were anyway concerned to postpone part of the decline in real incomes by absorbing them in the budget balance.

Equity and differentials. All incomes policies, whether voluntary or statutory in form, have sought to improve/protect the position of the low-paid. Thus, wage controls in the Netherlands in 1976 exempted minimum-wage earners from the freeze on incomes, and subsidies were granted to enterprises employing large numbers of minimum-wage earners to reduce the cost of wage increases. Similarly, in France the policy has been to raise low wages by adjusting the minimum wage in industry (SMIC) by more than the upward movement in the consumer price index at a time when most wage-earners have faced a freeze on purchasing power.

Under voluntaristic approaches, the low-paid have again figured prominently, and a variety of measures have been employed to effect a redistribution in their favour. This is perhaps most obviously the case in the Nordic countries, reflecting the 'solidaristic' wage policies of trade unions in that region; but it is no less true in Ireland, where all seven national pay agreements have incorporated an implicit or explicit bias toward the lower-paid in the terms governing basic pay increases. In Ireland this has been operated by one of the following means:

(i) full flat rate wage increases;
(ii) partial flat rate wage increases;

(iii) preferential percentage wage increases;
(iv) minimum increases;
 (v) minimum and maximum increases.

The precise method followed in each national pay agreement can be seen from the material on Ireland given in Appendix 8A.

The bias toward the low-paid is in itself less than surprising since in a centralised bargaining framework the larger industrial groups and the lower-paid workers tend to predominate.

Other forms of 'compensation'. Perhaps the most obvious facet of the trade-off framework has been a pronounced widening, and in some cases mushrooming, of the bargaining agenda; that is, of the issues tied to incomes policy. Important elements in the trade-off have been changes in social benefits through such elements as increases in social security benefits, the availability and quality of housing, education and welfare services. As an example, one might point to the package of measures agreed to and introduced by the Dutch Government in 1973 following the negotiation of the first, and as it was to prove only, centralised agreement between the unions and the employers in December 1972, though the government itself was not a party to that agreement. The measures in question related to employment and investment policies in the framework of an integrated regional policy. Measures were also foreseen to improve vocational schooling and lower the size of classes in primary schools. The government also agreed to renounce certain measures that it had earlier proposed, such as the introduction of an own-risk element into sickness insurance and an increase in VAT. In this particular instance, the contribution of the government was mainly conceived as an improvement of public services rather than a reduction in taxation.

To some extent, then, there has developed the concept of a social wage: a trade-off between benefits in the form of public as contrasted with private consumption.

Prices policy. Policies aimed directly at restraining price behaviour have been adopted in all countries, with the exception of Germany. The policies in question have comprised on-going price surveillance and the application of freezes. The broad rationale for prices policy has been to persuade unions to restrain their wage demands by reassuring their members that other economic interests in the community would not profit from their restraint, although this interpretation is perhaps somewhat overstated in those countries where a more comprehensive consensus prevails. Also, of course, price controls and, in particular, the application of freezes have been designed to dampen inflation expectations. Price subsidies have also figured prominently in this context. Nor should one neglect to mention that price controls have also operated on the other side of the market. Thus in the Netherlands, for example, price controls have stipulated that only a set proportion of wage costs can be passed on, the balance to be met from enhanced productivity (see Appendix 8A).

Price controls have formed the major plank in French efforts to restrain wages and prices, or so it was until 1978. Here, the system of price monitoring and control and the choice of the implementing mechanisms has varied widely, ranging from a freeze on all consumer prices, as in the fourth quarter of 1976, to the setting of a maximum rate of increase for certain categories of goods and services (6·5 per cent for public utility charges and rents in 1977). Price restraint or trade pricing agreements have also been concluded between the authorities and manufacturers or representatives of certain service activities: the purpose being to set an agreed percentage increase for a given period in the light of various factors − such as the trend of import prices and productivity. Another innovative price policy introduced in France in 1974 and 1976, though not applied, was the so-called *prélèvement conjoncturel* whereby firms were subject to a provisional levy computed as a percentage of their profit margins. This measure effectively comprised a combined profit and wage guideline − the details are given in Appendix 8A.

The added rationale sometimes provided for price policy in France, where the lack of social consensus has limited the scope for incomes policy, is that the highly oligopolistic organisation of important product markets and the existence of an important sector of nationalised industry have made recourse to price controls almost inevitable. On the other hand, it is acknowledged that price agreements themselves may have served to reduce competition. A similar objection may be entered in respect of Austrian price controls: there is the suggestion that they have hindered the subsequent deceleration of price increases because the implementation of controls by the employers' associations may have served to restrain competition.

Interestingly, price policy has recently undergone considerable change in France, with the decontrol of producer prices of manufactured goods in 1978. At the same time, and at the distribution stage, the former system of mark-up control was relaxed for industrial goods and food products, although service prices remained bound by a complex system of negotiation between representatives of the trade concerned and the price authorities. However, since 1979 there has been a progressive derestriction of mark-ups and service prices in return for measures to increase competition. In France, at least, the wheel appears to have turned full circle, and it is now accepted that the controls have tended to spread out price increases rather than prevent them. Elsewhere, controls are maintained for their (questionable) psychological impact, although their continuation is inevitable in regimes of statutory incomes policy.

Consensus

We referred in the introduction to this section to the ultimate development of the trade-off approach being a more comprehensive *consensus*, and pointed to the Austrian and Norwegian experiences in this respect. To give some idea of a truly consensual framework, we now describe the 1976 wage and income settlement in Norway. It is more difficult to identify the concrete expression of the unique Austrian *sozialpartnerschaft* experiment, though its achievements are no less real for that. The reader can, however, acquaint himself with the bare bones of *sozialpartnerschaft* by referring to Appendix 8A. We also refer the reader at this point to the report of the Skånland Committee (Appendix 8B) which much influenced the tenor of official policy in Norway.

The background to the combined and co-ordinated wage and incomes settlement in 1976 was a sharp deterioration in the competitiveness of Norwegian industry. Early in September 1975, in a meeting of the Contact Committee (see above), the government formally informed the other members of the committee that economic policies and income settlements in the following year ought to aim at:

(i)   moderating price and cost inflation;
(ii) safeguarding employment in the exposed sector;
(iii) securing an average increase in real disposable income for wage-earners of some 3 per cent, with a somewhat larger increase in the real disposable income for pensioners and a considerably larger increase in real disposable income for farmers;
(iv) reducing direct taxation.

The government made it clear that tax reduction could only be implemented as a *quid pro quo* for wage and income moderation. The parties in the Contact Committee expressed their willingness to participate and to contribute to a solution along these lines.

The negotiations proceeded partly in the traditional bilateral manner at centralised levels, and partly in the form of tripartite negotiations. Thus, as usual in centralised settlements, there were direct negotiations between the Norwegian Federation of Trade Unions (LO) and the Norwegian Employers' Confederation (NAF). There were also union-by-union negotiations to adapt the contracts to local demands within fixed limits. Similarly, there were direct negotiations between the government and its employees and between the government and the farmers' organisations. The tripartite negotiations focused on the combination of government measures and nominal increases of wages and incomes.

A number of alternative scenarios of different combinations of wage and income rises and tax changes were computed so as to enable the parties to study the different consistent combinations of increases in real disposable income, tax reductions and rates of inflation.

At a certain stage in the proceedings, the government presented a proposal for a co-ordinated solution to the parties involved. This proved to be the basis for the final negotiations and the agreements between the parties within the different areas of the settlement. The contract between LO and NAF was concluded with the help of the State Mediator who proposed, in close consultation with the Minister for Finance, a set of measures which were recommended for adoption by the two federations.

By April 1976 all negotiations had been concluded and the agreed contracts were ready for approval by referenda among employees, employers and farmers. By clear margins they were accepted by the members of the organisations and in mid-May Parliament approved the government's proposals and the budgetary implications.

As its contribution to the combined settlement, the Government proposed the following measures to be passed by Parliament:

 (i) a reduction in personal income taxes, amounting to some 2 per cent of wages;
 (ii) a reduction in the employers' contribution to social security by some 1·2 per cent of the wage bill (from an average of 16·7 to 15·5 per cent), which reduced the costs of the higher wages from 3·7 to 2·5 per cent;
 (iii) an increase in child allowances of some 8 per cent;
 (iv) a prolongation of the temporary increase in food subsidies instituted in the autumn of 1975;
 (v) a 5 to 7 per cent increase in the real value of pensions.

The direct wage component of the package, beyond full compensation for a reduction in the working week from 42½ to 40 hours, was a nominal wage increase of some 3·7 per cent to workers in manufacturing industries and slightly less than 7 per cent for central government employees (to reflect the virtual absence of wage drift in this sector).

Of the 3·7 per cent increase, some 2·2 per cent was granted in the form of a general wage increase, equal for all workers. Approximately 1 per cent was granted as a wage increase varying from branch to branch − higher for the low-wage groups and declining in the higher-wage groups. The residual was disposable by the separate branches and unions.

To achieve the desired growth in real disposable incomes of 3 per cent in the absence of the settlement, it would have been necessary to have had a direct wage increase of approximately 13–14 per cent as compared with the settlement increase of less than 4 per cent, and prices would have been raised by 12–13 per cent as against 9·5 per cent. It is widely accepted that traditional bargaining would have resulted in a settlement somewhere between these two sets of figures.

The contracts in question covered a two-year period and, interestingly, did not contain any escalator or indexation provisions. However, before the end of the first year of the contract period, the agreements were to be negotiated in the light of the general economic situation, and take account of the actual development in real disposable income from 1976 to 1977. A new integrated settlement was negotiated in the spring of 1977 – see Appendix 8A.

The 1976 settlement was perhaps the first of its kind in the world, seeking as it did to ensure that important financial policy decisions and wage settlements were made simultaneously and also made dependent on each other. This approach reflected the important finding of the Skånland Committee (see Appendix 8B) that a serious defect in the traditional system was that the public and private sectors were pursuing conflicting policies in their struggle for the use in each sector of as much as possible of national economic resources. The price resolution of this conflict was only possible as long as prices remained competitive. The fact that competitiveness did not actually improve under the 1976 (and 1977) settlements – that improvement came later – is perhaps less important than the emphasis that should be placed on the underlying degree of consensus necessary to permit such an approach to be attempted in the first place.

The failure of the 1976 settlement may be said to reflect the basic contraints operating on any form of incomes policy, and it is to a discussion of these that we now turn.

3 The constraints on policy

We shall discuss in section 4 perhaps the most basic constraint on incomes policy, namely the consistency of the mix of other policies pursued. In the present section, accepting for the moment the proposition that incomes policy may have a positive role to play in moderating wage demands/expectations by means other than monetary restraint, we consider a number of other potential and actual constraints that confront that policy. We will take it as read that incomes policy cannot operate as substitute for demand management and will not discuss the latter as a constraint except in so far as the particular constraint we identify has a distinct bearing on demand management.

The set of potential or actual constraints considered below is by no means exhaustive of the array of constraints facing incomes policy. Thus one might point to a number of constraints of a technical nature. For example, the commitment of governments to ensure via fiscal measures a certain rise in real disposable income, as in the 1976 and 1977 settlements in Norway, reduces the scope for timely adjustments of budgetary policy. If tripartite negotiations lead to or are followed by the emergence of excess demand pressure, the possibility of tightening fiscal policy is effectively constrained, since taxes, transfers and subsidies are tied to the guaranteed income development – public spending on goods and services being difficult to change in the short run.[4] Again, due to the fact that publication of data on actual earnings lags considerably behind that of price data, there is a built-in tendency during the upturn for income guarantees to lead to higher real wages than envisaged at the time of a settlement. Stronger than anticipated price rises tend to prompt the authorities to increase subsidies. Subsequent data on wage drift, however, may reveal that total real wage earnings have been rising at a faster rate than is consistent with general stabilisation aims. Then there are problems of co-ordinating policy measures because of the non-synchronisation of the timing of negotiations and fiscal budgets. One could lengthen this list of 'technical' constraints considerably by focusing on the meagre theoretical content of the underlying wage determination models employed in forecasting before turning to various other constraints such as the reconciliation of the functions of mediation/arbitration with the requirements of policy. Indeed, the catalogue of constraints is almost endless, because their character is dynamic. Hopefully, we have covered the principal issues in the following.

The structure of bargaining

It is often claimed that a policy seeking to influence the outcomes of the wage determination process is fundamentally constrained by the structure of collective bargaining itself. Thus it is conventional to regard the effectiveness of incomes policy as varying directly with the degree of centralisation of bargaining structures and the structures of trade unions and employers' associations. In addition to the advantages to a government of dealing with fewer and larger centres of authority there is the fact that the effectiveness of changing expectations is possibly greater the more centrally located is the target of persuasion.

However, the experience of the sample appears to suggest that a high degree of centralisation is neither a necessary nor a sufficient condition for the effectiveness of incomes policy. Thus industry-wide bargaining in the case of Germany can furnish the basis of central tripartite arrangements – if not in this case incomes policy *per se* – which include the government and some independent agent. Indeed, the effective functioning of such institutions could conceivably result in the accrual of influence or authority within the central union federation and perhaps the employers' organisation too. Here, the early Dutch experience points to a not altogether unsuccessful (at that time) approach even though workers were organised into three (now two) separate union movements along political and sectarian lines and collective bargaining was formally decentralised. At this stage in its development, then, incomes policy in the Netherlands helped to generate *de facto* central bargaining despite 'unpromising' initial structural conditions.

By the same token, where incomes policy is not effective in reducing union bargaining pressure there is likely to be a deflection of that pressure from the central institutions to the local level and thus a decentralisation of the bargaining system in the process.

The point to be made is that the success or failure of incomes policy is unlikely to be ultimately determined by the structure of collective bargaining *per se*, subject to the caveat that the form of incomes policy cannot be transposed from one collective bargaining structure in which it has evolved to another where it is alien. In this context it should be recalled that the origins of centralised bargaining do not lie in incomes policy considerations as usually understood. It was not so much the desire to moderate wage increases as a whole as a desire by the trade unions to obtain a redistribution of income between classes of employees that provided much of the initial impetus toward centralisation in the Nordic countries. The attempts by governments in such countries to introduce an incomes policy or to influence the development of wages naturally worked through the existing institutions.

Leadership-membership relations
The capability of union leaderships to implement a trade-off type of wage policy is primarily constrained by the attitudes and expectations of the membership.

A number of overt conflicts between union membership and its leadership may be identified. In the Netherlands, for example, a dramatic schism occurred after the years of tightly controlled incomes policy. An actual decline in the membership of blue-collar unions occurred and the leadership was vigorously accused of being in collaboration with the government to the detriment of workers' interests. Thus from 1974, and in response to rank-and-file pressure, Dutch unions have turned from a substantial interest in public services such as better education and housing to a renewed interest in maintaining and increasing the real private consumption of the workforce. Again, in Germany in 1973 membership pressure for increased wages led to the reopening of contracts before their expiry because of the prosperity and profits of German industry and under the impact of rising prices. This particular example points to the problems that arise in tying wage settlements under concerted action explicitly to economic forecasts – see Appendix 8A.

It is now conventional to attribute decentralising forces to pressures for the democratisation of unions and the prevalence of anti-authoritarian attitudes (Ulman and Flanagan, 1971). It is extremely difficult to isolate the particular 'negative' contribution of incomes policy or that of recession itself (which has frequently affected industries in a very uneven manner) to decentralising tendencies that are in fact observed in, say, the Nordic countries. Moreover, some tendencies toward centralisation can also be observed both within and outside the sample. Here one observes that in Germany and Austria machinery has been introduced for concerted action at the highest level, and even in France various national inter-industry agreements have been concluded dealing with security of employment, supplementary waiting allowance, improvement of working conditions, adult education and *mensualisation*. And, of course, there is the significant case of Ireland with the emergence of National Pay Agreements over the decade of the 1970s. Outside the sample, one can point to the 1977 inter-confederal agreement in Italy designed to hold down labour costs and recent national agreements on social planning in Belgium dealing with working hours, annual leave, minimum income and pensions. Simultaneously, there is evidence of other, decentralising trends in these countries.

What one can say with little fear of contradiction is that in countries with highly centralised bargaining the increasingly detailed national agreements have left little room for manoeuvre at lower bargaining levels and have been resisted at these levels. It has also proved increasingly difficult for union leaderships to sell the trade-off concept to union memberships. Very often the measures/components of the package deal are only partly relevant to the rank and file. The problem of the social wage approach in a nutshell is that it is difficult to ensure that those who are moderating their wage claims are satisfied with the distribution of benefits of government spending. Those who are currently not working may receive a substantial share of the transfer benefits of the package deal – via welfare and unemployment compensation – and may often be the beneficiaries of associated job-creation schemes. Thus the success of this element of the *quid pro quo* relies on either the social spirit (and perhaps, more cynically, the voting status of unemployed workers within unions) of those currently in work or their willingness to trade wage gains for those benefits in kind which may flow their way.

Major difficulties have also arisen in the context of the more 'direct' remunerative elements of package deals. Belief in the efficacy of price controls and subsidies appears to be waning among the rank and file, particularly in circumstances where indexation has been phased out. The focus on tax concessions is often interpreted as being more in the interests of white-collar workers and higher-paid groups. Incomes policies are regarded as having brought decreasingly tangible results. It is tempting to conclude that the central organisations have failed in their 'educative' role but this inference ignores the fact that in a number of countries (such as Finland) those groups which have opted out of framework agreements have generally obtained more favourable terms and conditions. There is the related point that when some groups are expected to alter their behaviour because of actions in the incomes policy field, they are apt to demand that the same restraints shall be required of all other groups. Yet a number of groups typically fall outside incomes policy or appear to obtain preferential treatment when their income formation does fall within the ambit of policy. Here one would point to the case of the farmers in Ireland and Norway respectively.

Finally, we note that the development of white-collar unionism has been rapid in recent years as a response to the economic pressures generated by inflation and the success of blue-collar unions in increasing their money incomes and real wages relative to those in white-collar occupations. Fiscal drag and the progressivity of the tax structure have further eroded the after-tax relationships of white-collar to blue-collar earnings. In the Netherlands, for example, the development of white-collar unions outside the main labour confederations has been a means of resisting the pressures for income redistribution developed by blue-collar unions. And in Finland it has become increasingly difficult for the predominant manual worker Central Organisation of Finnish Trade Unions to exercise a monopoly influence in deciding the terms of collective agreements and earnings policy. Similarly, in Sweden, white-collar unions have found it increasingly difficult to hold their members within a centralised bargaining framework because of the differing interests of various segments of the white-collar labour force, although here, as in Norway, there has been progress in accommodating the interests of white-collar workers by compensating them for their differential wage drift experience.

Wage differentials

We noted in section 2 that centrally negotiated trade-off policies have been associated with a narrowing of wage differentials. Yet in all countries there has been pressure to restore differentials eroded by egalitarian wage policies. The problem has always been one of reconciling the principle of a common increase with the recognition of a need for flexibility. The two principles are in conflict with one another. To be acceptable to the unions the level of the overall settlement often needs to be relatively high – particularly in circumstances where there has been a transfer of authority in collective bargaining toward the centre to meet the perceived needs of policy – but it is then likely that less can be afforded for local settlements. Internal conflict between the two principles may become acute and threaten the very existence of centralised bargaining, although economic recession might conceivably in certain circumstances mask heightening conflicts of this nature.

In Ireland over the nine years covered by the seven National Pay Agreements (NPAs) only the third and fourth phases of the 1975 NPA and the second phase of the 1978 NPA failed to incorporate an implicit or explicit bias toward the lower-paid (see Appendix 8A). This should have contributed to a marked compression of the wage structure. In fact, as Table 8.2 indicates, the intended compression did not occur to any significant extent, at least across industries. Among males there has been virtually no change in the distribution of hourly earnings among workers in low-paying, middle-paying and high-paying industries. In terms of weekly earnings, the workers in lower and middle-paying industries were paid even less in relation to those in high-paying industries, and the deterioration in the relative position of the workers in lower-paying industries over the period is slightly more significant. Among females, the workers in lower- and middle-paying industries gained somewhat relative to the hourly and weekly earnings of those in higher-paying industries over the period, and by 1977 the compression of the three earnings levels is greater than among the males – reflecting the extent of the implementation of equal pay legislation and provisions relating to equal pay in the more recent NPAs.

The major cause of the lack of compression of the wage structure in Ireland would appear to have been supplementary increases in pay in the higher-wage industries over and above the basic increases laid down under (Clause 3 of) the various NPAs, rather than from any frequent invocation by employers in low-paying industries of the special 'inability to pay' clauses of the Agreements.[5] These were allowable on grounds of improved productivity or distorted relativities, whether or not in agreement with the NPA guidelines in these areas. In fact, the estimated average increases in male hourly earnings in low-, middle- and high-paying industries all exceed by 50–75 per cent the respective increases in male average hourly earnings that would have occurred if Clause 3 of the first six NPAs

Table 8.2 Changes in average hourly and weekly earnings in low-, middle-, and high-paying industries,* Ireland, 1970–7

	Earnings Level (£)				Percentage Change		National Pay Agreement Increases(%)†
	QIV	1970	QII	1977			
HOURLY EARNINGS							
Male							
Low-paying	·476	(76·3)‡	1·404	(75·6)	195	212§	163
Middle-paying	·539	(86·4)	1·575	(84·8)	192	210	152
High-paying	·624	(100)	1·858	(100)	198	216	142
Female							
Low-paying	·274	(79·4)	·950	(82·9)	247	268	263
Middle-paying	·299	(86·7)	1·010	(88·1)	258	258	249
High-paying	·345	(100)	1·146	(100)	232	252	222
WEEKLY EARNINGS							
Male							
Low-paying	21·03	(72·3)	59·28	(68·9)	182	199	
Middle-paying	24·00	(82·5)	72·20	(81·6)	193	211	
High-paying	29·09	(100)	86·00	(100)	196	214	
Female							
Low-paying	10·02	(73·8)	32·84	(86·5)	228	258	
Middle-paying	11·53	(84·9)	39·68	(92·4)	244	265	
High-paying	13·58	(100)	42·95	(100)	216	235	

* 48 industries (43 for females) are separated into the three groups according to the rankings of the respective industrial earnings levels in December 1970.

† The increases in basic pay resulting from Clause 3 of the six National Pay Agreements, 1970–7.

‡ Figures in parentheses represent the ratios of the earnings level in each particular category to the earnings level in the high-paying industries for each sex group.

§ Estimated values for the percentage change QIV 1970–QIV 1977.

Source: CSO Quarterly Industrial Production Inquiries, 1970 and 1977.

had been strictly applied. The suggestion is, then, that workers in higher-paying industries have proved more adept at negotiating supplementary agreements which not only offset but in certain cases more than offset the intended bias toward the lower paid.

The exception to this general finding is the public sector. The relative earnings position of public sector employees in general service grades does not differ markedly from what would have obtained if the trends in basic pay in the NPAs had been followed exactly. In part, this outcome reflects the strict embargo by the Irish government on special increases in the public sector, which policy has of course its attendant industrial relations difficulties.

As in Ireland, wage settlements in Norway have typically had an egalitarian profile, achieved via flat-rate increases and low-pay supplements (see Appendix 8A), but again there is little evidence to suggest that this has been reflected in earnings.[6] Wage drift has largely counteracted the equalising effect of the flat-rate increases and supplements, and in recent years has either equalled or exceeded contractual hourly earnings advance.

In fact, the Norwegian experience suggests that egalitarian wage settlements have not only pushed up wage drift but also contractual increases themselves. This can be seen from the following wage rate and wage drift equations for the period 1954–74:

$$WC = \begin{array}{c} 0\cdot40 \\ (0\cdot67) \end{array} + \begin{array}{c} 0\cdot43P_{-1} \\ (0\cdot13) \end{array} - \begin{array}{c} 0\cdot15 \text{ DIFF } (S) \\ (0\cdot06) \end{array} + \begin{array}{c} 0\cdot028TM \\ (0\cdot015) \end{array} \tag{1}$$

$$R^2 = 0\cdot68$$
$$DW = 2\cdot24$$

$$WD = \begin{array}{c} 1\cdot21 \\ (0\cdot45) \end{array} + \begin{array}{c} 0\cdot09P_{-1} \\ (0\cdot05) \end{array} - \begin{array}{c} 0\cdot03 \text{ DIFF} (S) \\ (0\cdot02) \end{array} + \begin{array}{c} 0\cdot13 \text{ DIFF} (N) \\ (0\cdot04) \end{array} + \begin{array}{c} 0\cdot09X \\ (0\cdot03) \end{array}$$

$$+ \begin{array}{c} 4\cdot11U^{-1} \\ (1\cdot15) \end{array} \qquad\qquad \begin{array}{c} R^2 = 0\cdot83 \\ DW = 2\cdot27 \end{array} \tag{2}$$

where
 WC is the change in contractual hourly earnings measured from first quarter to first quarter (to include automatic or semi-automatic indexation and wage drift guarantees);
 WD is wage drift, measured from first quarter to first quarter as the residual increase in average hourly earnings;
 DIFF (S) is the change in wage differentials (ratio of hourly wage rate for male workers in engineering industries to hourly wage rate for female workers in canned food industries) in settlement years. (The general settlements usually take effect from the second or third quarter and the unlagged DIFF (S), therefore, indicates the change from a first quarter, preceding a settlement increase, to the next first quarter.)
 DIFF (N) is the change in wage differentials in non-settlement years. (Changes in non-settlement years refer to changes during the four quarters preceding the first quarter of the settlement year.)
 P is the change in consumer prices;
 TM is the marginal income tax rate;
 U is the rate of unemployment, first quarter; and
 X is the change in export prices, first quarter to first quarter.

Over the period in question egalitarian wage policies in Norway pushed up both contractual increases and wage drift, contributing more than 10 per cent to the total rise in wages. If we consider the 1970 settlement, for example, this reduced wage differentials by some 9 per cent. According to equation (1) this reduction led to a contractual extra increase of 1·4 per cent. From equation (2), this is turn led to a rise in wage drift of 0·3 per cent during the first four quarters after the settlement.

If the change in wage differentials over the next four quarters can also be ascribed to the settlement, an extra 1·2 per cent is added to drift. There apparently the process stops: the widening of differentials in non-settlement years does not seem to have any significant impact on subsequent wage claims and settlements.

There is evidence of a similar process at work in Finland. However, one must be wary of generalising beyond the Nordic countries,[7] not least because of the difficulties surrounding the measurement of drift. Thus in the Netherlands, for example, although wage drift has persisted – generally adding between 1½ and 2 per cent to average earnings over and above centrally negotiated increases – it has been shown that the changing professional and age composition of the employed labour force may have produced a statistical effect equivalent to wage drift.[8]

In Sweden, the reduction in income differentials has long formed a central component of economic policy, pursued via the fiscal system and through the operation of solidaristic wage policies on the part of organised labour. The wage spread in Sweden has narrowed through time, and only in the last few years has this process been halted. The narrowing process observable up to the early 1970s is potentially explicable in terms of the acceleration of inflation in the latter part of the 1960s and the relative slack of the labour market in the early 1970s. By the same token, the subsequent tightening of labour market conditions and increased importance of wage drift largely explain why this process came to an end.[9]

It is extremely difficult to assess the inflationary impact of changes in differentials. There has of course been much discussion in the literature of the interaction between changes in wage dispersion and the rate of nominal wage change (Metcalf, 1977). In Table 8.3 we present very basic wage relationships with and without a measure of wages dispersion. It can be seen that the presence of the wage dispersion variable raises the R^2s of the wage relation for Austria, Sweden, Denmark and Norway, although not for Germany, France, Italy, Belgium and Finland. With respect to the sign of the estimated impact of changes in the wage structure, a widening of wage dispersions is in most countries accompanied by a subsequent acceleration of inflation. Only in Sweden and Denmark do smaller wage differentials seem to induce a subsequently higher rate of inflation.

The problem is that the degree of wage dispersion need not be an independent cause of inflation, since both dispersion and wage inflation depend on the level of unemployment (Wachter, 1974). On this view, the wage–wage spiral is a result rather than a cause of inflation. On the other hand, we have noted that changes in wage structure have been induced by policies *inter alia* and to this extent could add to overall inflationary pressures. Yet if this argument is advanced it is clear from our earlier discussion of Norway that a more carefully specified model of wage change is required. Thus in a country where the authorities pursue an egalitarian wage policy, but subsequently higher wage drift tends to eradicate the squeeze on differentials, wage dispersion will be negatively correlated with contractual increases, while the correlation between wage drift and

Table 8.3 Estimated wage relationships, selected countries (dependent variable: the percentage rate of change of wage rates)

Country	Explanatory Variable				R^2	DW
	Constant	$1/U$	CP1	CV_{-1}		
Austria	0·04*	0·01	1·06§		0·59	2·20
	−0·18*	−0·001	0·19	1·94§	0·78	2·49
Germany	−0·01	0·02§	1·34§		0·83	1·53
	0·03	0·02§	1·37§	0·09	0·85	1·78
Finland	0·05§	0·06	0·80§		0·87	0·83
	−0·21	0·03	0·88§	1·91	0·90	0·63
France	0·04§	0·05§	0·90§		0·96	2·53
	0·04§	0·04*	0·90§	0·05	0·97	2·42
Norway	0·07§	−0·03	1·09§		0·73	1·47
	−0·22	−0·02	0·62	2·89	0·78	1·29
Sweden	0·03	0·04	0·83§		0·65	1·75
	0·24	0·08	0·58	−2·20	0·73	1·80
Belgium	−0·03	0·15§	1·25§		0·93	1·53
	−0·03	0·14§	1·17§	0·08	0·94	1·74
Denmark	0·05	0·01	1·08§		0·72	2·09
	0·38§	−0·001	0·65*	−2·52	0·84	2·38
Italy	−0·24	1·06*	0·57		0·75	2·05
	−0·27	1·02	0·64	0·18	0·75	1·95

Notes:
U is the rate of unemployment.
CP1   is the percentage rate of change in the consumer price index.
CV_{-1} is the lagged coefficient of variation for inter-industry wage structure.
  * denotes statistical significance at the 5 per cent level.
  § denotes statistical significance at the 1 per cent level.
Source: Schelde-Andersen, P. (1979), 'Recent Trends and Medium-Term Adjustment Problems', in *Collective Bargaining and Government Policies* (Paris: OECD), Table 5, p. 220.

dispersion is positive, and the sign of the aggregate dispersion measures in an equation determining total wage increases is *a priori* undetermined.

Endogenous politicians

Thus far, our discussion – if not the material of Appendix 8A – has implicitly assumed a benign, unitary nature of government policy, short-term and long-term, and an unexpressed view of the government as a single, predictable source of decision-making. This is to fail to recognise the political motivation of elected governments, which frequently constitutes an important impediment to the development and implementation of economically sound and balanced pro-grammes.

Government is not a distinct element clearly separate from the many interests that comprise it, and is unlikely to come to the bargaining table as a pure 'third man'. It is an unworkable assumption, then, to view representative government as a simple, consistent, rational prescriptive third party. Recognition of this fact may be said to provide an infertile setting for superimposing upon it governmental intrusion into the collective bargaining process on the lines discussed in this chapter.

It is interesting, to say the least, that incomes policies have often been advocated because of the alleged inefficiencies of the market system. Non-symmetrically, politicians have conventionally been treated as well-informed guardians of the public good.

The above comments are particularly relevant in the context of minority or coalition governments, and it is noticeable that the decade of the 1970s has been characterised by unstable and shifting coalitions and minority governments both within and outside the sample. Also, in several countries parties which had not held office for many years came to power and inexperienced policy-makers were faced with formulating a new set of policies in exceptionally difficult circum-stances.

Minority governments may easily be confronted with a situation in which group interests or party interests in Parliament are strong enough to force through measures which have incomes policy effects that are incompatible with the government's policy aims. Clearly, an incomes policy is scarcely tenable if the party responsible for drawing up the plans is not itself able to act in accordance with them.

Coalition governments also provide clear examples of situations in which a government is forced to accept an incomes policy that is not sufficiently conducive to balanced growth. Thus in Norway, for example, there has been a tendency for large awards to be made to politically influential groups in pre-election years. And, at the time of writing, there is a political crisis in Finland because the four-party, left-of-centre coalition is divided over the demands for price increases and supports put forward by the agricultural producers' union. The Social Democrats and the Communists in the coalition government maintain that the farmers' demands are too high and will generate earnings increases of 20 per cent in this sector. Meantime, the trade unions have settled for a rise of approximately 9·5 per cent.

Another problem of a political nature is that if the government has embarked on an incomes policy but is unable to gather support for the party line chosen it cannot very easily call a halt to the process and tell the parties to straighten up as best they can. This would be interpreted as a political defeat which a government, naturally enough, seeks to avoid. The danger thereby arises that the government can be forced to accept an incomes policy that is not sufficiently conducive to balanced growth and rather try to solve its problems by means of measures resulting in an over-expansionary fiscal policy.

It is no accident that the Skånland Committee recommended the partial depoliticisation of incomes policy – see Appendix 8B. And it is no accident that many observers point wistfully to the German system in which the government has been able to limit inflationary increases by announcing before wage bargaining that aggregate demand in money terms will only be allowed to increase by a certain amount.

Finally, there has been much discussion of the implications for the sovereignty of Parliament of the politicisation of industrial relations. Interestingly, in the light of the British experience, there has been altogether less discussion of the possibility that unions will use their heightened political power under incomes policy to buttress their economic power in the market-place. The implicit assumption here has been that restrictions are simultaneously placed on the autonomy of collective bargaining.

4   Assessment

It is difficult to draw general conclusions on the European experience with incomes policies in the decade of the 1970s, not least because the results achieved would seem to have depended far more on the appropriateness and consistency of the mix of monetary and fiscal policies and the exchange rate regimes adopted than on the efficacy of the incomes policy measures themselves.

The most outstanding example of a successful incomes policy is provided by the *Sozialpartnerschaft* experiment in Austria. The main thrust of policy in that country has been to limit lay-offs and unemployment, relying on the hard currency option and price surveillance to restrain price increases and upon trade union co-

Figure 8.1 A 'Phillips curve' for Austria

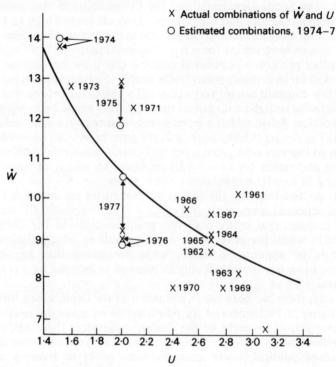

Notes:

Basic estimating equation was

$$\dot{W} = 0\cdot9 + 13\cdot39\,I/U + 0\cdot42\,G\dot{N}P_{-1} + 0\cdot26\,\dot{P}C_{-1}$$
$$\quad\quad\quad\;(4\cdot2)\quad\quad\quad(3\cdot7)\quad\quad\quad(1\cdot2)$$

$$R^2 = 0\cdot76, DW = 1\cdot99$$

where $\dot{W}$ is the rate of change in nominal earnings;

U is the rate of unemployment;

$G\dot{N}P$ is the rate of change in gross national product at constant prices;

$\dot{P}C$ is the rate of change in the implicit deflator for private consumption; and

t-values are given in parentheses.

The curve in the figure is obtained by inserting average annual values of $G\dot{N}P$ and $\dot{P}C$ into the above equation, which thus transforms to a two-dimensional function as follows:

$$\dot{W} = 4\cdot0 + 13\cdot4\,I/U$$

operation to secure deceleration of wage claims in return for minimising unemployment. These stabilising forces would seem to have positively influenced the quantitative trade-off between increases in wages and unemployment. The 'Phillips curve'[10] for Austria, shown in Figure 8.1, suggests that the 1976 and projected 1977 outcomes compare favourably with both the high-inflation years of the early 1970s, and the interval of lower wage rises − but higher unemployment − in the 1960s.

Needless to say, the Austrian experiment has had associated costs in the form of a very large deficit on current account, profits squeeze and a relatively unfavourable climate for private investment.

By the same token, it might also be pointed out that countries achieving price stability and a marked moderation of wage increases over the difficult 1973−6 period suffered from under-utilised capacity and rising unemployment − though in the cases of Germany and Switzerland this largely occurred beyond their national boundaries. Moreover, reliance on restrictive demand management in Belgium failed to secure a similar moderation of wage increases and that country suffered a marked deterioration of the current account *and* high unemployment.[11]

The fact remains that incomes policy cannot be used as a substitute for demand management. Now a number of countries over the difficult 1973−6 period chose as their primary goal the maintenance of high levels of employment. The policy of maintaining employment with a pegged exchange rate was not inappropriate for Austria, Norway and Sweden.[12] Austria possessed an initially favourable competitive position and had been successful in limiting cost inflation. Norway could afford to incur large current account deficits owing to the favourable balance-of-payments prospects from oil production. The policy mix was not necessarily inappropriate for Sweden either, given its initially strong current account position. What made the policy mix unsuccessful in Norway and Sweden was the disproportionately rapid expansion of domestic demand in these countries.

Again, in all these countries (and Finland) the reversal of an expansionary demand phase of policy has led to a marked reduction in the rate of inflation. It is difficult if not impossible to calculate the independent contribution of incomes policy to this development, though we have commented favourably on the Austrian case. Thus the marked improvement in the Swedish inflationary experience (up to 1978/79) has been achieved without recourse to comprehensive incomes policy, and the recent, favourable, Norwegian experience may owe its success primarily to wages and prices 'freeze' rather than incomes policy *per se*. Again, the success achieved by Finland has occurred against the backdrop of steadily increasing unemployment.

In comparative terms, however, the post-1976/77 record is not favourable in these countries and it seems that incomes policy has exerted some moderating influence on cost developments. It is no accident that relatively ambitious incomes policies have achieved modest successes in the smaller industrialised economies. Because of their 'openness' these countries are exposed to much stronger and more competitive forces than are the larger economies. At the same time, smaller countries are often better placed to try to reach a consensus on economic policy through discussion and negotiation simply because of their smaller size – less diversity, fewer actors, easier communication – and, in a number of cases, their traditions of social and political cohesion. The latter factor is of crucial importance. Both economic management and co-ordinated incomes policy are impeded by an unstable balance of political power, as is evidenced by the experience of Denmark. Social and political cohesion, then, seem to provide the best possible basis for relatively ambitious prices and incomes policy.

Having said this, the temptation to extrapolate from this experience to other countries where these conditions are absent should be resisted.[13] Nevertheless, some of the instruments found necessary in such countries can be very worthwhile in themselves. We refer in particular to arrangements for the regular collection and dissemination of information on price developments together with an analysis of how far they conform to norms for anti-inflationary behaviour. There is an equally good case for improved information and analysis of trends in both wage and non-wage incomes before and after taxes. One can thus support unequivocally those elements in incomes policy which are designed to build up a consensus on the main aims of economic policy and contribute to the *ex ante* reconciliation of competing claims through the provision of information and analysis, and regular discussions with the various interest groups concerned.

Finally, we turn our attention to the important question of exchange rate policy. During most of the 1970s most continental European countries attempted to maintain the exchange rate (pegged to the Deutschemark), impelled by a desire to curb the rate of inflation and by the fear of spiralling inflation stemming from devaluation.[14] By opting for this strategy, despite the tendency for domestic wage and production costs to continue rising faster than in the stronger economies, the authorities exposed the open sector of their economies to strong deflationary pressures. It became increasingly difficult in such circumstances to maintain output levels, employment and invest-ment because of foreign penetration of home producers' domestic and export markets. Thus the authorities severely limited the feasibility of expansionary fiscal policies aimed at maintaining the level of employment and 'bridging the gap' until foreign demand strengthened in the wake of the mid-1970s recession.

For the governments that undertook to maintain a pegged rate within the snake and yet wished to implement expansionary budget deficits to support employment and further social objectives, the combination of objectives required the enforcement of tight monetary policy, giving rise to public or private borrowing that served to support the exchange rate by offsetting the current account deficit. Pegging of the rate on a strong currency, in a context where several major currencies were floating, imposed a stiffer constraint on monetary expansion than would have been required under a rigid par value system. More importantly, it exposed producers in the open sector to additional pressure as their competitiveness was reduced by the appreciation of the Deutschemark versus non-snake currencies. Thus there was less possibility of maintaining employment by deficit spending than under the par value system.

For those countries which did not undertake to peg the exchange rate but were concerned to limit the rise in unemployment (such as France, and latterly Sweden) the adoption of a floating exchange rate regime intensified the need for co-ordination of budgetary and fiscal policy because the exchange rate was now highly responsive to monetary policy.

Tight monetary policy aimed at reducing price inflation will achieve its goal by reducing profits, employment and investment in the open sector. This outcome may be inconsistent with the employment target, in which case there is the temptation to try for both price stability and high employment by the combination of strict monetary policy tending to maintain the exchange rate and a relatively large budget deficit financed by borrowing abroad. This policy mix may secure a greater degree of price stability than a less stringent monetary policy that accommodates the rise in domestic costs more fully and causes the exchange rate to depreciate. The initial effect of the stricter monetary policy in braking price increases may be all that is required to moderate price expectations and curb rapid cost inflation. To succeed, such a policy must bring the rate of cost inflation quickly into line with that in more stable countries before any marked worsening of the relative level of domestic costs at the going exchange rate has occurred. If rapid cost increases continue despite the breaking of price inflation via the stiffening international price constraint, the effect will presumably be to create growing expectations of a depreciation and renewed acceleration of price increases. If cost increases are checked and price stability is restored, but at an unfavourably high level of domestic costs at the going exchange rate, the result will be to subject the economy to protracted problems of unemployment in the open sector.

This combination of policies involves inherent contradictions. The results are achieved by importing unemployment in the open sector and then subsidising enterprises in one way or another to maintain employment there and/or expanding employment in the public sector as employment in the open sector declines. While price increases in the open sector are constrained via the exchange rate, expenditure rises in the sheltered sector where prices and costs are inherently less subject to constraint. The effect of greater price constraint in the open sector in slowing down the movement of domestic factor costs is liable to be weakened if rising public expenditure causes the movement of wages and salaries in the public sector, or of social security transfers and premiums, to be comparatively unconstrained. Moreover, efforts to mitigate the decline in employment in the open sector may serve to weaken the constraint on cost increases there in a number of ways.[15]

In general, then, a policy mix of strict monetary policy to maintain the exchange rate with expansionary budget measures is likely to be appropriate only in cases where the rate of domestic cost increase is not much greater than in the most stable economies and there is no pre-existing lack of competitiveness or serious current account imbalance. In other cases, depreciation of the exchange rate would seem to be required and here monetary policy will need to accommodate the relatively rapid rise in costs to some considerable extent. The accommodation of public sector deficits by the monetary authority will be appropriate in these circumstances. The aim should be to bring down the rate of monetary growth and of deficit spending gradually over time to exercise a consistent pressure in moderating cost and price inflation. Here, incomes policies might possibly be viewed as an important third element in such a policy, subject to the caveats entered above.

Notes: Chapter 8

1   The Contact Committee is presided over by the Prime Minister and includes also the Ministers of Finance and of Consumer Affairs and Administration (formerly the Minister of Wages and Prices) together with representatives of the trade unions, employers, farmers and fishermen.
2   Similar demand-restricting policies were resorted to in Germany, Switzerland and Belgium.
3   The same is true of Ireland, where tax thresholds changed as follows over the period 1970–7:

Category	Nominal Terms (%)	Real Terms (%)
Single	78	− 28
Married	69	− 32
Married + two children	69	− 32

4   In consequence, the task of preventing excess demand will fall upon monetary policy, which may be insufficiently flexible. In Norway, for example, monetary policy operated by reducing the availability of liquidity, at least until the more flexible interest rate policy adopted in 1978. This tended to create imbalances between supply and demand and to impair efficient allocation of credits and resources.
5   The 'inability to pay' clause dates from 1972.

6 Thus the standardised ratio of unskilled:skilled manual worker earnings rose by only two percentage points between 1971 and 1978, namely from 92 to 94 per cent. Here, as in other countries, the most visible change has taken place in the female:male earnings ratio, which improved from 78 to 84 per cent over the same period.

7 In France, for example, it has been calculated that a 2 per cent rise in SMIC increases total wages by between $0 \cdot 1$ and $0 \cdot 3$ per cent.

8 See OECD Economic Surveys, *Netherlands*, March 1979, p. 9.

9 See OECD Economic Surveys, *Sweden*, April 1978, pp. 27–32.

10 Certain aspects of the wage bargaining strategy of Austrian unions suggest that wage claims are typically influenced by expected output growth and price developments. In Figure 8.1 the growth of GNP and consumer prices in the previous year serve as proxies for these expectations.

11 Although Belgium was more vulnerable owing to the prevalence of wage indexation, the main problem is to be sought elsewhere. Specifically, economic management was impeded by political crises and the implementation of anti-inflationary measures repeatedly delayed.

12 It was a less successful policy mix for other countries such as Denmark whose competitive position was already unfavourable.

13 One must also recognise the limitations of incomes policies in regimes commonly thought most conducive to relatively ambitious experimentation. Here a tart reminder is provided by the Norwegian economist, Hermod Skånland:

> I believe that if anyone living under a system different from the one actually existing in our (Nordic) countries had suggested that prices and incomes should be determined by interest groups enjoying a more or less monopolistic position in the market, while the authorities should be responsible for maintaining full employment, the proposal would have been rejected as inconsistent, inflationary, and completely devoid of any promise of optimal use of productive resources. Nevertheless, such is the system under which we live. (Skånland, 1978)

14 Ireland until 1979 had monetary union with the UK.

15 For example, if the authorities in effect underwrite relatively high wage costs by subsidising employment so as to bring wage costs to the employer more into line with those abroad; or if the government finances production for inventory.

References: Chapter 8

Addison, J. T. (1979), *Wage Policies and Collective Bargaining Developments in Finland, Ireland and Norway* (Paris: OECD, August)

Aukrust, O. (1970), 'Prim I: A Model of the Price and Income Distribution Mechanisms of an Open Economy', *Review of Income and Wealth*, 16, pp. 51–78 [See also, by the same author, 'Inflation in the Open Economy: A Norwegian Model', in Krause, L. B., and Salant, W. S. (eds), *Worldwide Inflation: Theory and Recent Experience* (Washington, D.C.: The Brookings Institution) pp. 109–66]

Bjerkholt, O., and Longva, S. (1974), 'The Integration of Fiscal Budgeting and Income Policy in MODIS IV', *Working Paper 10 74/18*, (Oslo: Central Bureau of Statistics, March)

Edgren, G., Faxén, K. O., and Odhner, C. E. (1969), 'Wages, Growth, and the Distribution of Income', *Swedish Journal of Economics*, 71, pp. 133–60

Edgren, G., Faxén, K. O., and Odhner, C. E. (1973), *Wage Formation and the Economy* (Allen & Unwin)

Ferunes, N. J. (1975), 'The Environment of MODIS IV', *Working Paper 10 75/3*, (Oslo: Central Bureau of Statistics, March)

Halttunen, H., and Molander, A. (1972), 'The Input-Output Framework as Part of a Macroeconomic Model: Production–Price–Income–Block in the Bank of Finland Quarterly Model,' *Finnish Economic Journal*, 68, pp. 219–39

Metcalf, D. (1977), 'Unions, Incomes Policy and Relative Wages in Britain', *British Journal of Industrial Relations*, 15, pp. 157–75

Robinson, D. (1974), *Solidaristic Wage Policy in Sweden* (Paris: OECD)

Schelde-Andersen, P. (1979), 'Recent Wage Trends and Medium-Term Adjustment Problems', in *Collective Bargaining and Government Policies* (Paris: OECD) pp. 187–240

Skånland, H. (1978), 'Incomes Policy: Possibilities and Limitations', speech by Hermod Skånland, Deputy Director of Norges Bank, at the 1978 Meeting of Nordic Economists

Suppanz, H., and Robinson, D. (1972), *Prices and Incomes Policy: The Austrian Experience* (Paris: OECD)

Ulman, L., and Flanagan, R. J. (1971), *Wage Restraint: A Study of Incomes Policies in Western Europe* (Berkeley, Los Angeles: University of California Press)

Wachter, M. L. (1974), 'The Wage Process: An Analysis of the Early 1970s', *Brookings Papers on Economic Activity*, 2, pp. 507–24

Appendix 8A   A Survey of Incomes Policies in Selected European Countries

1   Austria

Austria provides an interesting example of formal tripartism in its approach to prices and incomes policies. While the Austrian experience can be seen as an extension and modification of certain aspects of centralised bargaining (see, for example, Sweden), the actual wage settlements are not negotiated centrally.

The principal instrument of incomes policy is the Joint Wages and Prices Board. The Board was set up in 1957 at the suggestion of the Austrian Confederation of Trade Unions (ÖGB). It is composed of four Government representatives, including the Federal Chancellor, and eight representatives of the interest organisations (two each from the Chamber of Commerce and Industry, the Chamber of Workers and Salaried Employees, the Chamber of Agriculture and Forestry and the ÖGB).[1] The decisions taken by the Board must be unanimous. Despite the presence of members of the government – who, incidentally, have not exercised their right to vote since 1966 – the Board represents an instrument for voluntary co-operation between the social partners on questions of wage and price determination. Since 1968 there has been an 'exchange of views' on economic policy every three months, following publication of the revised economic forecasts, at which the Head of the Economic Research Institute, the President of the National Bank and the Minister of Finance report on the economic situation.

The Joint Board was set up to control price and wage trends and is therefore a typical instrument of incomes policy. In addition, given its tripartite structure, it has become an instrument which gives the employers' and workers' organisations a voice in government policy in general and by the same token enables the government to ensure co-operation from the social partners on its economic policy measures.

Three sub-committees of the Joint Board function in respect of wages, prices and economic policy. The wages sub-committee includes representatives of workers and employers alone. Decisions have to be unanimous. Unions submit applications for wage and salary increase to the ÖGB which passes on the claim to the wages sub-committee. The fact that applications to negotiate are submitted to the wages sub-committee through the ÖGB means that claims have been co-ordinated in advance within the trade union machinery. The wages sub-committee takes no decision on the size of the claim but, rather, examines in each case whether the time is appropriate for a new collective agreement to be concluded. If a decision cannot be decided within six weeks the matter is referred to the Joint Board which has a further five weeks to reach a decision. The final outcome of negotiations has also to be submitted to the wages sub-committee for approval and the same procedural rules apply as in authorising the opening of negotiations.

The sub-committee on prices, a tripartite body, likewise considers applications by individual firms or branches for price increases – either directly or through the Chamber of Commerce. The sub-committee can accept an application unanimously (in its entirety or in part), hold it over, or refer it to the Joint Board.

Thus by virtue of their position as intermediaries, the central organisations of trade unions and employers can exert considerable influence on the form, content and timing of applications and in effect enforce co-ordinated wage or price behaviour.

Originally, the prices sub-committee's terms of reference covered all commodities, dealing with some two hundred standard items. Officially regulated prices and tariffs are free from control by the Joint Board, and in 1974 it was agreed to place a wider range of prices under the control of the Minister of the Interior. Today, the Joint Board's controls are confined to proprietary goods, staple commodities and standard services and cover less than one-fifth of articles in the CPI shopping basket; a slightly higher proportion being covered by official controls.

The creation of the third joint committee in part reflected a growing conviction that a broader scientific basis was required for economic policy measures designed to solve the 'structural' problems of falling growth rates and rising inflation in the first half of the 1960s. The Economic and Social Advisory Board, as the sub-committee is known, was given the task of studying economic and social policy questions in the context of the economy as a whole, and its findings serve as a basis for recommendations to be made by the Joint Board to the Federal Government. The sub-committee basically comprises three advisers from each of the four main employers' and workers' organisations. Its pattern of membership ensures that in the pursuit of its technical negotiations it tries to reconcile differences between the bodies concerned. Minority votes are possible but rare.

The main thrust of Austrian economic policy has been to limit unemployment and to rely on a hard currency policy (*Hartwährungspolitik*) plus price controls to restrain inflationary pressures. The remarkable feature of the Austrian economy has been the simultaneous achievement of a progressive reduction of inflation and a continued growth of employment. A necessary condition for the success of this policy mix has been the willingness of the two sides of industry to accept a gradual reduction in nominal wage claims and profit margins without having to be subjected to a prolonged period of slack. This is a tangible effect of the 'social partnership' (*Sozialpartnerschaft*). However, the maintenance of high levels of domestic demand and employment has necessarily entailed public and external sector deficits considered unsustainable by the authorities.

2   Finland

Finland, in common with Norway, passed through a period of tight economic regulation after the Second World War, although in her case the controls programme lasted longer, namely into the mid-1950s. Following the liberalisation of the economy, Finland was exposed to a number of currency crises. Inflationary pressure was often strong, unemployment relatively high, and strikes endemic. The political background was one of weak and unstable governments. Though various governments attempted to obtain 'stabilisation agreements' in 1963 and again in 1966, their efforts were rejected by the central labour market organisations[2] partly because they had weak political backing.

The political parameters changed substantially in the spring of 1966 with the formation of the first 'popular front' government. After seven years of rapidly shifting centre coalitions, Finland now had a relatively strong (leftist) government that was able to hold office for an unusually long period of time.

Organised co-operation between the new government and the labour market organisations began under the difficult conditions following the large (33 per cent) devaluation of the Markka in 1967.[3] The aim was to preserve the competitive export advantage gained from devaluation and to improve employment. To attain these targets a stabilisation agreement was concluded in March 1968, and in the autumn of the following year it was extended to end-1970.

The basis of the stabilisation agreements was a productivity criterion secured by means of a flat rate increase. Automatic cost-of-living adjustments that had been essential ingredients of many earlier collective agreements were abolished as, indeed, were all other index links within the economy. Prices were subject to fairly strict official controls.

The stabilisation agreement of September 1969 and the legislation giving the Government powers to regulate wages, prices and rents were to expire at the end of the year. From the early autumn attempts were made to find common ground for a continuation of some co-ordination of income settlements.

Four major difficulties presented themselves. First, sectors not benefiting from wage drift were pressing for some form of compensation for their relatively low rates of wage increase. Secondly, pressures had grown up among the white-collar confederation and skilled sections of the Central Organisation of Finnish Trade Unions (SAK) to resist too rapid a reduction of wage differentials. Thirdly, unions were concerned with the coverage of policy. It was felt that all incomes, and in particular profits, should be brought within the ambit of the stabilisation agreement. Finally, while there was scope for wage increases within the competitive sector without endangering its overall profitability, parallel increases within the sheltered sector would run foul of the existing price regulation guidelines.

Faced by a general breakdown in labour relations at the beginning of the year (major strikes were planned in the important building and metal sectors) the President of Finland intervened. In December 1970 he presented a mediation proposal of his own, which contained a limited wage increase, a continuation of the price freeze, a retroactive tax on forestry exports and a modest package of social reforms. These proposals were accepted by the central labour market organisations.

The agreement was on the face of it quite unsuccessful. Normal earnings rose by no less than 18·4 per cent over the period covered by the compromise proposal. There was a sharp fall in profits and productivity growth was weak. But any evaluation of the agreement has to take account of the political crisis that was imminent when the President's compromise was produced, together with a marked overheating of the economy during the preceding boom and the slower expansion of world trade.

One of the lessons of this period was that the employer side was only interested in wage contracts at the central level on condition that the agreed framework would be adhered to in negotiations at branch level. Had they not received reasonable guarantees of union adherence there would have been no centralised agreement in 1972. Its terms were similar to the earlier stabilisation agreements and again the emergency law was prolonged.

In the winter of 1972 unexpected complications arose during the preparations for new contracts that were to be valid from April 1972. Yet another political crisis intervened – the details are given in Addison (1979) – to effectively pre-empt stabilisation moves.

Despite these difficulties a new stabilisation agreement was eventually hammered out in the spring of 1974, covering the period April 1974–September 1976. This was considerably wider in scope than earlier settlements and proved to be the forerunner of subsequent incomes policy developments. To achieve a general settlement, the government announced a wide set of measures dealing with personal income taxation, social policy and prices. Wages and salaries were to be raised in four stages over the life of the agreement, again with emphasis on flat sum payments.

The agreement included a reopener clause: the parties were again to meet in 1975 to decide upon supplementary measures which might need to be undertaken in the light of economic developments. In the event, wages rose, via the reopener clause, by some two percentage points more than anticipated under the original agreement.

Negotiations for a new centralised agreement began in September 1975. Parliamentary elections were held in the same month, resulting in the formation of a caretaker government. It soon became clear that the government would not be strong enough either to carry through its budget proposals or to bring about the desired comprehensive incomes policy settlement. Presidential intervention resulted in the formation of a five-party majority government in November of that year which expressed employment promotion as its primary goal. Problems of financing the government's employment programme added to the delay, but eventually the central organisations once more agreed on an overall incomes policy settlement, effective end-January 1977. Wage increases were again specified in absolute values although, as in the 1974 settlement, there was a modest discretionary element for individual branch bargaining. A five-month price freeze was declared with retroactive effect to the January 1976 price levels. Price controls were to be continued after the freeze. And as part of the comprehensive incomes policy agreement the government undertook to modify tax scales and allowances in the light of price rises during the contract interval. Soon after the collective agreement was signed, nine of the member unions of SAK opted out of the framework agreement and secured better terms and conditions. There followed a large number of disputes in the white-collar sector.

Overheating of the Finnish economy in 1973–4 led to inflationary pressures, erosion of international competitiveness and growing external imbalance. Following a shift to a very tight policy stance made necessary by the current external deficit in the wake of the 1975 world recession, the Finnish economy experienced very sluggish growth in the three years to early 1978.

These economic developments provide a background to the more moderate stabilisation agreements of 1977 and 1978, which, together with the exchange rate adjustments of 1977–8,[4] secured a very favourable turn around by 1979.

Early in 1977, the government suggested that nominal pay rises over the next round should be limited to between 2 and 4 per cent. It soon became clear that there was going to be little scope for traditional-style centralised negotiations on the basis of this proposal. Wage negotiations were remitted to federation level but soon became deadlocked. The eventual settlement followed the proposals of the incomes policy official. The main features of this proposal were standard wage increases, additional improvements for the low-paid, earnings development guarantees,[5] special tax adjustments, and a price policy designed to guarantee the purchasing power of income. It was recommended that the agreement should last from March 1977 to end-February, the termination date subsequently being brought forward one month by agreement.

The proposals envisaged two 'inflation cuts' in tax to be introduced in April 1977 and March 1978. The former was designed to reduce income tax by some 3·5 per cent for the majority of tax brackets. The latter was geared to the actual inflation rate experienced during 1977.

The actual collective agreements negotiated sector by sector in 1977 followed closely on the mediation proposals presented to the unions by the incomes policy official, despite considerable unrest within the labour market. The settlement doubtless reflected the poor profitability and employment outlook.

The staged increases under the 1977 agreements for March and October 1978 were subsequently postponed by six months and four months respectively under a stabilisation programme passed by Parliament in December 1977. Other elements in the stabilisation programme comprised a price freeze (until September 1978), a standstill on indirect taxes and other charges, a reduction in the employers' pension contributions (down from 12 to 10 per cent of wages), extra income tax reductions for low income earners and the introduction of a maximum total tax rate.

A new centralised thirteen-month incomes agreement was reached in January 1979. Wages and salaries were to be raised, as of February, in such a way that the total cost effect of the rises would be 2·25 per cent of the wages bill of the industry concerned.[6] In addition, a sum corresponding to 0·5 per cent of the wages bill was set aside for discretionary payments at the union level. A wage drift guarantee formed at most an additional 1·5 per cent of the relevant wage or salary. In the private sector, it was agreed that part of the wage drift guarantee be used at plant level to correct for local distortions. Unusually, the agreement also included an indexation clause. Should the common index have exceeded 233 (1972 = 100) by October 1979 (that is, risen by 7 per cent from its January level) a flat 17 pennies per hour wage increase would have been paid from 1 December. Moreover, had the index exceeded the ceiling by more than 1 per cent full compensation would have been paid. In the event, the index clause was not activated, since the index was approximately 0·5 per cent below the ceiling by October.[7]

3 France

The incomes policy concept first attracted substantive interest in France during 1963/64. The debate was opened by a Conference on Incomes which was chaired by the General Commissioner of the Plan, Pierre Massé. An interesting facet of the difficulties confronting incomes policy in France is provided by the fact that Massé published, on his own authority, not the report of the Conference but rather a report 'drawn up following the Conference on Incomes'. This document defined an incomes policy as follows:

Deliberate action on the formation of income which has two closely linked purposes: first, to contribute towards rapid and balanced expansion, while maintaining full employment and preventing excessive or inadequate payments of income, in an outward-looking economy based on a system of competition; and, second, to contribute towards the enrichment of the purposes of development, as a result in particular of a fairer distribution of the fruits of expansion in a society which has, moreover, set itself important collective tasks (national defence, foreign aid, productive and social investment).

The document made it clear that incomes policy was (a) an extension of traditional economic and social measures, (b) designed to intervene at an early stage in the business cycle, (c) to be inclusive of all types of incomes, (d) to aim to create agreement on the distribution of incomes, and (e) to be voluntary.

But the Conference itself failed in its central objective to produce mutual agreement (*concertation*) among the interest groups on the distribution of personal income within the context of long-term planning. It thus became known as 'a dialogue of mutes'. The only groups willing to proceed with incomes policy were the farmers and family associations, namely those organisations which saw in incomes policy the prospect of sectional gain.

Despite the failure of *concertation*, the Fifth Plan (1967–70) included specific income guidelines for achieving stability of unit labour costs, as shown in Table 8.4.

Table 8.4 Income guidelines in the Fifth Plan, France, 1967–70

Income group	Maximum annual percentage rate of growth in income
Farmers	4·8
Entrepreneurs	3·3
Upgraded workers	3·3
Others	2·8

In practice, the publication of these indicative norms or 'guidelines' had several disadvantages. First, they were interpreted by the bargaining parties as minimum levels, not least because of the general lack of credibility of official forecasts of prices changes. Secondly, the guidelines were taken as guarantees by the government in discussions relating to civil servants' salaries. And with the May events of 1968 the guidelines fell into disuse. The practice of establishing guidelines was discontinued in the Sixth and Seventh Plans (1970–5, 1975–80).

One positive aspect of the Conference, however, was the setting up of the Centre for the Study of Incomes and Prices (CERC), albeit a watered-down version of Massé's proposal for a College for the Study and Evaluation of Incomes which would have been empowered to calculate and publicly criticise excessive increases in wages and other incomes.

Following this 'dialogue of mutes' episode, the government deployed direct and coercive measures, namely controls over prices, and over wages and salaries in the public sector. Price controls were the principal instrument of policy. Under planning contracts – the so-called *contrats de programme*[8] – prices were indirectly controlled in the private sector. More direct price restraint was practised in the public sector.

As intimated above, the indicative norms for the growth of incomes were abandoned following the May events of 1968. The explosion of social and cultural demands at this time was to set a different course for social policy and the development of costs and prices in the following year. Thus in 1969 President Pompidou undertook to make the system of monthly payment of manual workers' wages (*mensualisation*) more widespread. And the Chaban-Delmas government gave a strong impetus to collective bargaining by expanding the scope of collective agreements (improvement of working conditions, vocational training, and so on) and by making it easier to extend these agreements.

Such reforms grafted on to a system of free collective bargaining and a rapid improvement in minimum wages (SMIC) came up against the familiar stumbling-block of inflation. The authorities sought, as before, to contain prices by measures such as planning agreements and other undertakings by employers. But the prices policy had little success, particularly in view of the requirement to introduce realism into the pricing policies of the nationalised industries. Inflation accelerated and was accompanied by moves to safeguard and restore purchasing power in wage claims.[9] Real wages continued to rise at rates much the same as in preceding years although production and productivity fell.

Or so it was until the set of anti-inflation measures introduced in September 1976 – the so-called *Plan Barre*. The first stage consisted of a price freeze for nearly all manufactured goods and services until the end of the year. With effect from January 1977 the standard rate of VAT was cut from 20 to 17·6 per cent, which, it was estimated, would reduce the overall CPI by some 0·6 per cent. Public sector tariffs were frozen for six months, coupled with an announcement that the increase in the remainder of 1977 would be held down to 6·5 per cent. Rent increases during 1977 were also to be limited to 6·5 per cent. The government requested Parliament to reintroduce the conjunctural levy (*prélèvement conjuncturel*). This had been instituted under the Act of 30 December 1974 and was meant to apply from 1975 onwards. In fact because of the weak demand conditions and the associated strains on enterprises the first two quarterly instalments of the levy were not called in. The scheme was not reactivated subsequently but as we have seen formed part of the 1977 budget, albeit with a revised norm. Again the levy was not applied, but its rationale is worth pursuing. The levy sought to oblige enterprises to comply, in their wage and price policies, with the broad parameters set by the government, which foresaw a 14 per cent nominal increase in GNP and an equivalent rise in public expenditure and revenue. It was also meant to oblige enterprises to pass on below-average rises in input prices and above-average increases in productivity. The scheme was designed in such a way as to curb inflationary expectations without penalising exports, investment and employment. It was confined to some 15,000 enterprises accounting for approximately one half of the value added in industry and trade and was based on the increment of the value added (net of taxes and interest paid) of each enterprise above that recorded in the base year (1974) plus 14·3 per cent to account for the anticipated average rise in productivity and the overall price level. The increment was to be adjusted for the change in factor inputs, measured by the weighted average of changes in hours worked and in the capital stock subject to depreciation. That is to say, the norm effectively combined a wage and a profit guideline. A levy of 33⅓ per cent was to be paid in progressive quarterly instalments on the *adjusted* increment (net of export sales). The sums were to be paid into blocked accounts and refunded when the scheme was definitely suppressed (it was to be suspended when during a quarter the actual increase in manufactured prices did not exceed 1·5 per cent). The refund was to be used for investment within two years.

Under the system of voluntary price agreements, manufacturing industries agreed to maximum increases in prices for 1977, and a timetable for prices changes – which were not to exceed the level of 6·5 per cent during 1977 (8 per cent from 1976 to 1977). Where no such agreement was reached or in breach of an agreement, firms were placed under the tighter regulations applying to the services sector, requiring prior approval for each price increase.

Wage guidelines were announced, calling for wages to increase in line with the target increase in the cost of living (by 6·5 per cent in 1977, or some 10 per cent from 1976–77). The government forced this standard on the public sector and attempted to obtain compliance from the private sector. No increase was allowed for salaries in excess of 24,000 francs per month and those ranging between 18,000 and 24,000 francs were restricted in growth to one half the rate of increase in prices. Only those wages at the bottom of the scale and those covered by minimum wage legislation were to achieve (modest) increases in real wages over 1977.

For 1978 the wage policy for the public and semi-public sectors followed the lines laid down at the beginning of 1977, namely one of strictly maintaining the purchasing power of wages by keeping changes in the total wage bill in line with increases in the average price index.

In summary, the main thrust or anti-inflationary constituent of incomes policy in France has been direct intervention in pricing policy, especially with respect to larger enterprises. Lack of sufficient consensus among the various social groups has created conditions limiting the scope for incomes policy in that country. Reflecting this lack of consensus, all attempts under the Seventh Plan to reintroduce the idea of an incomes policy ended in failure.

4 Germany

It is often asserted that in Germany there is no incomes policy. To be sure the Federal government has repeatedly underlined the priority of influencing factor incomes by demand management. Equally, there has never been an application by the government of statutory incomes policy. Having said this, some forms of indirect measures have been applied with varying degrees of discretionary impact. Thus in 1960/61 there was a guideline approach linking the desirable development of wages to the average increase in productivity.

Partly as a result of the failure of this guideline approach an independent Council of Economic Experts (*Sachverständigenrat*) was set up in 1963. The Council's mandate was to report to the government at least once a year to review – not to recommend[10] – adequate policies to reconcile economic growth, price stability, full employment and balance-of-payments equilibrium in the context of a market economy.

Since 1967, a discussion forum described as 'concerted action' (*konzertierte aktion*) between the government, the Central Bank, the unions and employers and the Council of Economic Experts, takes place at regular intervals. The concerted action provision forms part of an Act on the Promotion of Economic Stability and Growth, which sets out the basic macroeconomic policy provisions regarded as compatible with the principles of a market economy. The Act does not provide any specific institutional framework. The function of concerted action is to reach a consensus on the future prospects of the economy based on orientation figures which the Federal government is legally bound to supply. The ultimate objective is concerned with wage and price developments in the immediate future as seen by the social partners; there is, however, no attempt by the authorities directly to influence this behaviour but rather to reach the highest possible degree of understanding about the general framework in which collective bargaining should take place. The intention of concerted action is, then, to provide an opportunity for the co-ordination of private decisions and official policy. On occasion, the government has quite explicitly given its view of the consequences of alternative actions.

The German experience provides interesting examples of the problems of linking settlements explicitly with forecasts. But before turning to these, it is worth while to note that controversy has often surrounded the causal relationships between major economic variables – if not priorities. The major controversy concerns employment-conducive wage behaviour, namely the extent to which wages have to be 'adjusted' to reach a level compatible with full employment. The disagreement stems from the dual role of wages as a source of income and demand on the one hand and as a major cost component on the other. Advocates of the purchasing power proposition argue that cyclical productivity gains associated with wage-induced demand and output growth would more or less offset the impact of higher wages on unit labour costs, while the accompanying increase in capacity utilisation rates and profits would stimulate investment. Advocates of the wage restraint proposition, however, contend that wage restraint will lower inflation and hence raise real non-wage income. The improved profitability would at the same time boost investment propensities and total aggregate demand.

In qualitative terms, the assumed relationships underpinning the opposing views are not inconsistent with each other. It is different assumptions about the quantitative importance and existing lag structures characterising these relationships that lead to different conclusions as regards the appropriate wage policy. The Council of Economic Experts has clearly come down on the side of the wage-restraint argument. In its central forecast for 1978, for example, the Council computed that two percentage points lower average wage contracts (here 3·5 per cent rather than a 5·5 per cent annual increase) would lead to 1 per cent higher GNP growth, due to higher consumption of non-wage income recipients, increased employment, higher real public expenditure and enhanced business investment.

Trade union economists have countered this line of argument on technical grounds, but the stance of the union movement is of course conditioned by the fact that the two hypotheses have very different implications for the functional distribution of income.

Returning to the problems of tying wage settlements explicitly to forecasts, it should be noted that in 1969 and again in 1973 agreements were made on the premises of official forecasts that proved to have underestimated the strength of economic expansion. In 1969 there was a marked increase in profits which exceeded expectations coupled with a moderate wage policy. There occurred a rash of wildcat strikes. In 1973, following successful operation of the concerted action machinery, union leaders made generally moderate claims. An unexpected acceleration of inflation led to a revival of rank-and-file militancy and wildcat strikes disrupted sections of the important metal industry. Unlike the 1969 episode, however, prompt reaction from union leaderships (and management, it is also to be noted) avoided an escalation of industrial conflict, and a large number of enterprise agreements were made to compensate for the rise in the cost of living. Trade unions here made adjustments in their organisational and institutional arrangements and allowed some pressures to express themselves without losing effective control of their members. One of the marked features of the German trade unions has continued to be the extent to which national organisations exercise strong leadership over the membership.

Problems also arose in 1974 when a non-accommodating monetary norm was adopted but not publicised. Since that time the German Bundesbank has periodically announced an annual target growth for the central bank money stock. The target is derived from projections of growth rates in potential output, 'unavoidable' price increases, and the expected increase in capacity utilisation. This policy approach has been consistent with a continuous reduction in inflation rates despite repeated overshooting of the target. It is often considered that incomes policy in Germany is a veil for monetary policy. This is perhaps to underestimate the success of the concerted action programme and to underplay responsible trade attitudes. The latter has undoubtedly been a decisive factor in the achievement of better economic performance as the deceleration of inflation has enabled more expansionary demand management. It should be added that the process of reducing inflation has been facilitated by the interaction of slower wage-price inflation and an appreciating Deutschemark.

5 Ireland

In Ireland, the development of National Pay Agreements (NPAs) during the 1970s was the consequence of the government's threat to legislate a prices and incomes policy. In a sense, the Irish experience might be considered as a possible embryo of centralised bargaining (see Sweden) but in the very early stages of development and without the existence of strong central organisations of the social partners.

Although NPAs stem from free collective bargaining in which only two parties are involved, and have no statutory backing, they none the less possess something of the character of public law since all employers and employees are expected to observe their terms and conditions whether or not they are represented at the negotiations.

The seven NPAs negotiated between 1970 and 1978 have been described in detail elsewhere (Addison, 1979) and only a bare framework will be provided here. Table 8.5 charts their broad terms and conditions. Over the period 1971–3 the government accepted – albeit cautioning against the potential inflationary effects – the 1970 and 1972 agreements. These led to annual increases in industrial earnings well in excess of price increases. At the same time, income tax personal allowances and earned income relief were allowed to fall in real terms by over one half (for married taxpayers) and by over a third (for single taxpayers).

From the table it can be seen that the emphasis turned to percentage increases in 1972. However, even here, minimum payments were guaranteed. Again, a cost-of-living escalator applied during the second phase of the agreement.

The 1974 NPA proved considerably more difficult to negotiate than its predecessors. Given the background of accelerating inflation, the unions proved reluctant to commit themselves to a fixed-term agreement. The government intervened in the negotiations by proposing a 'social contract' with the unions, involving income tax reliefs by way of higher personal allowances in the next budget, a promised review of the entire system of taxation, and improved social welfare benefits and payments. This, coupled with an improved employer offer, ensured agreement.

Demand and activity weakened markedly over 1974, leading to what was at that time the deepest recession experienced in Ireland since the war. The ensuing 1975 NPA marked something of a watershed. Each of the three previous agreements had provided larger increases than its predecessor and each had provided increases greater than the contemporaneous movement in prices. In the discussions for a new agreement the government decided to secure some form of standstill arrangement – the maintenance of living standards through self-discipline in incomes and tax relief and capital expenditure on the part of the government. In the middle of the year the government successfully appealed for a renegotiation of the 1975 agreement in return for substantial indirect tax reductions.

Discussions in 1976 focused around the government's desire to introduce a six-month pay pause, following the termination of the 1975 NPA in mid-1976. In the event a short-term agreement without indexation provisions was concluded. Clause 22 of that agreement stated:

As a preliminary to negotiations in the Employer–Labour Conference, it is agreed that both sides of the Conference will participate ... with members of the Government on economic and social strategy for the next two years. Such discussions which will commence with a Tripartite Conference in

Table 8.5   The National Pay Agreements, Ireland, 1970–8

Year	Phase	Pay Increase
1970 (18)	Phase 1	Men £2·00 a week, women £1·70.
	Phase 2	4% plus cost of living escalator supplement of 15p a week for each 1% increase in the CPI over 4% in the year covered by Phase 1.
1972 (18)	Phase 1	9% on the first £30 of basic pay or, if greater, £2·50 a week for men (increasing to £2·70) and £2·25 a week for women (increasing to £2·45); 7½% on next £10 and 4% on remainder.
	Phase 2	4% plus cost of living escalator supplement of 16p a week for each 1% increase in the CPI in the year covered by Phase 1.
1974 (12)	Phase 1	Either 9% on the first £30 of basic pay, 7% on next £10, 6% on next £10 and 5% on remainder, together with 60p a week *or*, if greater, £2·40 a week.
	Phase 2	4% plus 60p a week. (There was a cost-of-living threshold increase amounting to 1% for each 1% rise in the CPI over the interval November 1973 to November 1974. The threshold increase amounted to 10%.)
1975 (12)	Phase 1	8% (i.e. amount of increase in CPI, November to February 1975). Minimum increase £2.
	Phase 2	Amount of increase in CPI, February to May 1975, subject to a minimum increase of 4% and a maximum of 5%. (The increase payable was 5%, the CPI rising by 6·1% over this period.) Minimum increase £1.
	Phase 3	Amount of increase in CPI, May to August 1975. (No increase was payable; the CPI falling by 0·8% over this period.)
	Phase 4	Amount of increase in CPI, August to November 1975. (The increase payable was 2·8%.)
1976 (7)	—	3% of basic pay plus £2 a week, subject to a maximum of £5 a week *or* £3 a week if greater.
1977 (14)	Phase 1	2½% of basic pay plus £1 a week, subject to a minimum increase of £2 and a maximum increase of £4·13 a week.
	Phase 2	2½% of basic pay plus £1 week, subject to a minimum increase of £2 and a maximum of £4·23 a week.
1978 (15)	Phase 1	8% of basic pay or £3·50 a week.
	Phase 2	2% of basic pay.

Note: Figures in parentheses indicate duration, in months, of the relevant agreement.
Source: Addison, J. T. (1979), *Wage Policies and Collective Bargaining Developments in Finland, Ireland and Norway* (Paris: OECD), Table 2, p. 62.

September will cover the availability of resources, employment welfare, prices, public revenue and expenditure and all forms of income.

Although these discussions proved abortive, the idea of what was described as an 'integrated' pay deal was established.

The eventual 1977 NPA, which contained no cost-of-living escalator, reflected tax cuts and special measures to increase employment opportunities. (Examples of increases in disposable income arising from the contribution of standard increases under the NPA and personal income tax reliefs are given in Addison (1979).)

Given the major changes in taxation introduced under the budget, the 1978 NPA was accepted with more than a degree of reluctance by the government, whose initial proposals had centred on a wage rise of 5 per cent. Government ministers pointed out at the time that the agreement might well cost Ireland some 4,000 jobs. While not including an indexation clause, the 1978 NPA did allow for a margin of flexibility in respect of local bargaining. Employers and unions could negotiate additional wage increases up to a limit of 2 per cent of the weekly/monthly basic pay cost of the group(s) of workers concerned.

The year 1979 witnessed a new initiative in pay policy with the government, employer bodies and the Irish Congress of Trades Unions negotiating a National Understanding for Economic and Social Development which sought to provide an integrated programme of action in the areas of employment, pay, taxation and social expenditure.

It was proposed that pay agreements would be of fifteen months' duration from the termination of the 1978 NPA. Payments were to be in two phases of nine and six months.[11] The provisions for wage increases distinguished between (a) rises to cover cost-of-living increases, and (b) the growth in incomes arising from the expansion in national output. This departure from earlier approaches failed to be ratified by the trade union membership in May 1979.

New pay arrangements were announced by the government in June, involving a guideline of 7 per cent within which pay increases might be negotiated over a period of six months following termination of the 1978 NPA.

A revised National Understanding was agreed upon in July. Under the first phase basic pay was increased by 9 per cent, subject to a minimum of £5·50 per week, to operate for a period of nine months. Under the second phase, of six months' duration, basic pay was to be raised by 2 per cent plus very similar threshold payments and minima as envisaged under the original National Understanding.

The government announced its commitment to full employment, to be achieved within five years. An annual job creation target of 25,000 per year for three years was set and in part underwritten by a special joint public and private sector employment programme. New agencies were to be set up to implement longer-term policies on employment.

The government also announced its commitment to keep the absolute burden of taxation as low as possible and also to ensure that taxation was equitably distributed. Within the PAYE sector the priority was to improve the relative pay position of lower-paid and married persons. For the self-employed, the government determined to continue its policy of ensuring that every income-recipient pay his full share of tax.[12] As a contribution to promoting the National Understanding, the government provided a special allowance for PAYE taxpayers at a cost of approximately £39m. in 1979 subject to a budget position reasonably in line with expectations.

6   The Netherlands

The major postwar era of guided wage policy, or statutory incomes policy, came to an end in 1967. But since that time the Netherlands has experienced a number of mandatory price/wage controls that have alternated with years of free bargaining. The main thrust of policy has been to limit price increases, while imposed wage settlements have tended to set a floor under wage increases.

Price controls of varying stringency were applied in the Netherlands from late 1969 until mid-1971. The legislation remained in force and controls were reinstituted late in November 1972, with the aim of freezing profit per unit of output sold in the domestic market, following a marked rise in the ratio of value added to wages in the private sector. Global productivity norms were laid down for the industrial and service sectors to be used in calculating that part of wage increases which could be taken to represent a cost increase which could then be passed on in price increases. Thus, from November 1972 to mid-1974, one third of wage increases could be passed on in the industrial sector. With slower productivity a rising proportion of wage costs had to be absorbed, although widespread exemptions continued to be granted. Appreciation of the exchange rate was used to curb inflation (September 1973).

After the wage explosion in 1963 and the clear breakdown of the guided wage policy in 1967 the year 1972 appeared to mark a new beginning for wage policy, which is not to argue that the former approach was based on enforcement alone.

The first, and as it was to prove only, central agreement between the central union and employers' organisations to restrain wage settlements with a view to curbing inflationary pressures, and in exchange for a number of social and economic benefits to be provided by the government, was signed in December 1972. The original intention was to come to a tripartite 'social contract' on a completely voluntaristic basis committing:

(i)   the unions: to moderating wage demands;
(ii) the employers: to limiting price increases; and
(iii) the government: to agreeing to a list of demands with regard to taxes, education, employment, spreading of investments and social housing.

No instrumentality was involved other than the promise of the contracting parties to abide by these commitments. Preparatory talks began in May 1972. They were delayed by a government crisis in the second half of the year and, in view of the uncertain political situation, it was decided to conclude the contract on a bipartite basis between the central employers' and workers' organisations. After some controversy between the government and the largest trade union federation, the twelve-month agreement came into force in January 1973.

The contract stipulated that real wages accorded in collective agreements should not rise faster than 3·5 per cent (to include fringes and the overhang of wage increases from 1972). This ceiling was based on a productivity forecast of 4–4·5 per cent provided by the Central Planning Bureau. Full compensation for rises in cost of living was accepted. Special attention was to be given to low-paid workers. The government, though it had not signed the contract, agreed to a package of measures to be implemented in 1973. These related to employment policies and investment policies in a framework of integrated regional policy. The government agreed to renounce certain planned measures such as increases in VAT. The contribution of the government to the contract was mainly conceived as an improvement of public services and not as a reduction in income taxes.

One interesting development during the early 1973 enterprise negotiations was strong union pressure to introduce, within the framework of the central agreement, a redistributive element into wage settlements. This took the form of applying flat-rate across-the-board increases instead of percentage increases for real wages together with higher cost-of-living bonuses for the low-paid. This action encouraged fairly widespread strike activity. And in trying to determine salary increases for professional staff, the unions encountered strong resistance from industry and of course the professional staffs themselves to prevent an erosion of differentials. The membership of newly organised white-collar associations had increased considerably and the traditional unions were forced to accept them as an additional bargaining agent in plant-level negotiations.

In the second half of 1973 negotiations started on a new central agreement for 1974. The package of government measures requested by the unions was even more comprehensive than in the previous year. Progress made in reconciling the different viewpoints was slow. Although an outline agreement providing for a 2·5 per cent increase in basic wage rates and for further redistribution of income among wage and salary earners by differing degrees of indexation was agreed upon at the national level, the details could not be settled. Industry-by-industry negotiations were suspended when the government announced it would seek special powers to deal with the situation caused by the oil crisis. The Special Powers Act reinstalled full government control over wage determination, and in January 1974 the government duly introduced a statutory incomes policy with controls on wages, rents, dividends, and certain professional incomes. The intention was to ensure that much of the burden of deterioration in the terms of trade would be borne by higher income groups and profits.

The wage regulations supported a continued rise in real contractual wage rates over and above full compensation for price increases. All employees received a wage increase of 15 guilders a month in January 1974 and two further increases of the same amount later in the year. An adjustment of 3 per cent to compensate for price increases was granted three months earlier than the normal mid-year timing. A floor for price compensation was introduced so that wages were increased by at least 150 guilders per year for each percentage point rise in the price index. Further redistribution of real disposable income was achieved by the introduction of minimum wages for all young employees (and a 2·5 per cent increase in all minimum wages in April 1974) and by the effects of progressive taxation.

Real disposable income rose by some 3 per cent in 1974. The rise in prices was kept down by the operation of price and rent controls under the Special Powers Act and by the effect of the continuing appreciation of the guilder during 1974. The steep rise in wage costs squeezed profits and led to labour shedding.

In an attempt to reduce wage pressure in 1975 and facilitate a central agreement the government introduced temporary reductions in income tax.[13] In the event, no central agreement was reached. The main trade union federations issued guidelines for revised contracts in major industries, which included provision for a 2 per cent increase in basic rates from January 1975 and for threshold adjustments in March and October. Wages rose by more than 13 per cent and were a major factor in the continued rapid rate of price increase and mounting unemployment.

In October 1975 the Expert Group of the Economic and Social Council[14] recommended *inter alia* that wage indexation be discontinued until mid-1976. Following their advice the government again decided to intervene in the wage settlement process, this time with the aim of limiting the increase in the wage bill per employee to 8·5—9 per cent over 1976. To achieve this goal, a six-month wage freeze was imposed from 1 January 1976, maintaining wages at their November levels plus the 4·5 per cent compensation for price increases over the April-October 1975 period.[15] Price controls were maintained.

By mid-1976 no agreement had been reached between employer and employee representatives and during a one-month prolongation of the freeze the government imposed a flat-rate 30 guilders a month increase, combined with downward adjustment of various social security premiums. The intention was to maintain the real disposable income of workers earning 20,000 guilders a month (somewhat less than the average in industry) with increases/decreases for those earning less/more than this amount. The wage bill per employee rose by 10·5 per cent in 1976, compared with 13·5 per cent in 1975, and price increases decelerated.

Centralised negotiations again broke down in late 1976[16] and on this occasion the government indicated its unwillingness to intervene. Negotiations continued at industry level and after a two-day strike in several sectors employers agreed to pay a 1·5 per cent increase in basic rates plus full indexation on the basis of a new price index excluding indirect taxes and subsidies and giving a lower weight to medical costs. Year-on-year contractual hourly *rates* rose by approximately 6·5 per cent, and prices by 6·75 per cent. As in previous years the existing system of price control was applied during the year.

Although attempts at a central wage agreement failed at the beginning of 1978, and industrial relations deteriorated when automatic price compensation again came under debate, sectoral bargaining led to rather moderate settlements. On average the agreements led to an increase of about 10 per cent. Pay indexation early in the year was linked to the higher price increase in 1977 and so contractual wage rates in the first quarter were more than 7 per cent higher than a year earlier, or 2 per cent higher in real terms. The legal minimum wage was again raised over-proportionately and the subsidisation of minimum wages continued.

At the end of 1977 the authorities had announced the new price rules covering 1978. In industry, prices might be raised by 2 per cent times the wage cost share. This measure was designed to counteract an unintended squeeze on profit margins over 1977.

In June 1978 the government presented its medium-term policy memorandum, known as 'Blueprint 1981', to Parliament. This identified the deterioration in competitiveness and profitability as the main constraint on solving the medium-term problems of employment and inflation. On the basis of unchanged policies, the Central Planning Bureau (a government agency) had computed an unfavourable unemployment and inflation scenario. In order to achieve a higher growth rate and lower unemployment, the government placed a major part of the emphasis on medium-term adjustment on the cost side. Rates of pay increases were to be minimised, subject to maintaining the purchasing power of the typical industrial employee.

Higher-income groups would be expected to suffer a small decrease in real incomes. The details of the cost and price goals and outcomes were as follows (percentages):

Inflation rate	2–3
Pay indexation	2–3
Real contractual pay rates	0
Wage drift	1–1½
Total nominal pay	4
Productivity	3
Unit labour costs	1

7 Norway

Incomes policy has been pursued in Norway in one form or another since 1945. Norwegian wages determination has had two essential characteristics. First, negotiations are carried on regarding the main features of wage settlements through centralised bargaining between on the one side the Norwegian Federation of Trade Unions (LO) and on the other the Norwegian Confederation of Employers (NAF). Both central organisations have wide powers over their constituent members. (Negotiations for wages in agriculture and forestry, state and local government, shipping and certain other occupations take place separately from and after negotiations in industry but are in accordance with the pattern of the industrial settlement.) Secondly, in national wage negotiations a great deal of regard has always been given to the country's overall economic situation. Both LO and NAF have been willing to co-operate with the government of the day in regard to their wage policies although, as intimated above, the form which this co-operation has taken has varied through time. In addition, it has all along been an underlying aim of the trade union movement to secure equivalent returns for corresponding effort and skill in different industries and to raise standards of lower-paid workers. It has also been Norwegian policy to keep the trend of receipts to agricultural producers and fishermen in line with industrial earnings. This has been reflected in the subsidy and price-fixing arrangements for agriculture and the assistance given to the fishing industry.

Since 1962, the main body to serve the dual purpose of being a preparatory forum for discussion on wage and price developments and of maintaining reasonable inter-sectoral incomes parity has been the Contact Committee. This provides the interest groups (the Prime Minister, as chairman, and the relevant Cabinet Ministers, together with representatives of LO, NAF and the organisations for farmers and fishermen) with an opportunity to discuss basic assumptions before the parties fix their strategies for wage and incomes negotiations. The government, for its part, has often sought to inform the parties on the major features of economic policy *inter al*. Economic conditions for wage and price settlements were likely to be discussed in the Contact Committee both before and during the biennial bargaining round. In the autumn of 1965 a new government-appointed expert committee – the Aukrust Committee – was established to facilitate the work of the Contact Committee, and to make its discussions more reliable and credible. Thus, before the negotiations in 1966, the Committee was asked to project the economic consequences of alternative changes in wages and farm prices. In 1967 the Aukrust Committee was reappointed, this time to include representatives of the interest groups. In regular reports this Technical Expert Committee, which became permanent in 1969, has presented alternative estimates of income and price developments, both before and after wage settlements.[17]

A new phase of incomes policy, distinguished by a more active role of government, was initiated in 1973 with the negotiation of a 'combined settlement' or package deal arrived at by the government and the labour market organisations in the spring of that year. The package deal, initiated in the Contact Committee, included increased subsidies on agricultural products, a subsidy on imported flour, and a freeze on prices of certain public services. With these contributions by the government, wage increases were restricted to an amount compensating for 45 per cent of the increase in the cost of living (as compared with 70 per cent compensation under the 1970 agreement) during the year ending March 1973.

In 1975 a further combined index settlement was negotiated between LO, NAF and the government.[18] Here, the wage increase granted amounted to 30 per cent compensation for the rise in the cost of living over the period November 1974–September 1975.[19] In return for this, withholding taxes were reduced and child allowances increased. Additionally, agricultural price rises were to be offset by subsidies until June of the following year and a price freeze was imposed until the end of 1975.

In the budget for 1976, the government declared its wish to expand price and income co-operation the following spring if such co-operation could dampen the cost effects of the new wages and income settlements due in the spring. The effective decision on the form of the income settlement was made in the Contact Committee in January 1976, when NAF and the farmers' and fishermens' organisations gave their support to an LO proposal for co-ordinated and combined procedure.[20]

The 1976 agreement marked a new phase in incomes policy. For the first time in Norway, a truly comprehensive wage and incomes settlement covering most of the incomes and price formation in the economy was concluded with the government as a third party. The agreements were thoroughly co-ordinated with general economic policy and contained a combination of nominal increases, tax reductions and other measures directed to dampening price and cost inflation whilst at the same time securing a 'reasonable' increase in real disposable incomes for households and other economic aggregates.

Unlike the more *ad hoc* 'combined' settlements of 1973 and 1975, or for that matter the decentralised bargaining outcome in 1974 (see Addison, 1979), the agreement of 1976 did not contain any indexation or escalator provisions. Rather, the intention was to secure an average increase in *real disposable incomes* for wage earners of some 3 per cent, coupled with a somewhat larger improvement for pensioners (financed by increases in social security contributions) and, most important, a significantly larger increase in the real disposable income of farmers. A parliamentary decision in the autumn of 1975 decreed that farmers should achieve an income level equivalent to that of the average wage-earner in manufacturing industry. This objective was to be realised within six years and the significant relative improvement recorded by farmers in the 1976 settlement marked the first stage in the up-rating of farm income.

As its contribution to the combined settlement, the government offered a reduction in personal income taxes (covering both tax allowances and tax rates), a lowering of the employers' contribution to social security, a prolongation of the temporary food subsidy scheme, and an increase in family allowances.[21]

During the international recession in 1974/75 and the two subsequent years of weak recovery, the emphasis of economic policy in Norway was upon the maintenance of a high level of activity and employment. There was reason to think that this policy might succeed without entailing undue pressures on prices or the external balance, given that incomes policy, helped by a high degree of national consensus, had during much of the postwar period been operated with a degree of success; and the development of the oil sector with the prospect of considerable future exports of oil and natural gas meant that the balance of payments was not a serious constraint. But international growth remained weak and economic policy became more expansionary than required to achieve stabilisation. Over the four years to 1977 real domestic demand rose at an annual rate of more than 5 per cent, bottlenecks developed with strong pressures on wages and prices, and the external deficit rose sharply to a record 14 per cent of GDP. It therefore became clear that corrective measures were needed. The reorientation of economic policy was initiated in late 1977 and continued into 1978. A relatively modest combined incomes settlement was agreed in 1977,[22] which at least can be said to have prevented a further worsening of the situation. The settlement was facilitated by a devaluation of the krone in April and a reduction in employers' contributions to social security.

As noted above, policy objectives were gradually modified from the autumn of 1977 with a view to curtailing the growth of domestic demand and reducing cost increases while maintaining high employment conditions. In January 1978 the LO again announced its willingness to pursue a combined and co-ordinated approach to wage determination. Centralised negotiations on the economic frame were to be conducted, although individual unions were to be free to distribute the frame in industry-level negotiations. Priority was to be given to low-wage groups via a minimum earnings guarantee, whereas for the majority of wage-earners the real purchasing power of 1977 was to be maintained in 1978.[23]

The Norwegian Confederation of Employers, on the other hand, saw no scope for further wage increases over 1978, pointing to the unfavourable development of Norwegian unit labour costs *vis-à-vis* those of her trading competitors over 1971–6 and especially during 1977. But NAF again favoured a combined incomes settlement and called upon the government to initiate a widely-based co-operation between the political parties and the organisations of the labour market.

For its part, the government expressed the view that there was little scope for advance in real disposable income for most groups over 1978, given the pronounced deterioration in Norway's external position during the course of 1977. There was the need to restrain the growth in domestic demand – particularly private consumption – and hence the government went to the income negotiations with the view that its possibilities to contribute economically were strongly reduced compared to the experience of preceding years.

Although formal agreement on the efficacy of a combined and co-ordinated settlement was reached in the Contact Committee in February, subsequent bilateral negotiations between LO and NAF reached deadlock on the basic issues of minimum earnings guarantees and wage drift. For only the third time since 1950 the government had to resort to compulsory arbitration with respect to these negotiations. The arbitrated settlement was reached in May. It included a relatively modest general wage advance (1·8 per cent)[24] together with a layered low-wage supplement for those groups earning less than 90 per cent of the industry average in 1977.

Extensive price-control measures were introduced in February 1978 and from September of that year a general prices and incomes freeze was instituted which was to continue until the end of 1979.

Thus, an important test of prices and incomes policy will come in 1980 when the wage and incomes settlements lapse. After two years of little, if any, increase in real take-home pay, wage pressures may be relatively strong. Yet this has to be seen as a necessary correction of the large increases that took place over the preceding period.

8 Sweden

Because of the autonomy of the collective bargaining system, wage policy in Sweden is less a domain of the government than of the unions and employers. The most important element is that the framework for bargaining at various levels is firmly set at the centre and enforced by both the employer and union federations. Within this system the negotiations between central organisations of manual workers (LO) and employers (SAF) have primary importance not only for their affiliated members but also for the negotiations in the white-collar union sector and in the public sector. The negotiations at central level were not created and developed since 1956 with a view to arriving at wage restraint. For the LO at least, the goal was to create a mechanism for implementing its strong political objective of arriving at a more egalitarian wage structure (Robinson, 1974). It is rather that, in spite of this particular goal, which is resisted by the employers, the social partners have (until recently) been in broad agreement about the need to reconcile wage policy with the economic and social needs of the country.[25]

There is no formalised 'machinery' for discussions on general economic matters between the government and the labour market parties but frequent contacts on an informal and personal basis take place continuously. Moreover, in recent years the government has sought to influence the outcome of wage bargaining via a trade-off approach.

The first attempt by the government to condition the formulation of wage claims by offering tax concessions occurred during 1973/74. After consultation with the three principal central organisations of the manual and white-collar workers in 1973 the government, as from January 1974, shifted some of the tax incidence from wage earners to employers by abolishing the so-called 'basic pension charge' which stood at a proportional 5 per cent rate to be paid on taxable incomes under Kr30,000 per year. In order to compensate for the corresponding loss of public revenue, a social insurance fee was introduced which had to be paid by the employers. In order to prevent high wage demands in response to a steep rise in profits during 1974, the government also introduced a scheme which sterilised 35 per cent of pre-tax profits in special work environment and investment funds. Finally, a large number of transfer payments (child allowances, housing allowances, and so on) were increased from January 1974.

There was considerable controversy as to whether the numerous fiscal measures introduced by the government marked a new era of government-sponsored wages policy. Whereas the profits sterilisation and the increase in transfer payments had multiple purposes of which the impact on wage negotiations was but one, there was intentionally a direct link between income tax reform and the wage settlements. One of the initiatives for this measure had come from two economists of the Metal Workers' Union who had recommended early in 1973 that direct taxes be reduced in exchange for wage restraint.

Against this background wage negotiations in 1974 were both short and smooth. A moderate settlement for manual workers, incorporating as in previous settlements 'low-wage kitties' and a wage-drift guarantee (Robinson, 1974), was followed by moderate settlements in the public sector and for salaried employees in private industry in February and April respectively. However, the rivalry between the blue-collar and white-collar unions that had marred previous negotiating rounds was distinguished by its absence.

The booming Swedish economy in 1974 put a stress on the settlements made earlier in the year and led to a considerable amount of wage drift. In fact drift narrowly exceeded the contractual provisions of the 1974 agreement.

In order to influence the 1975 bargaining climate the government adopted a new package to increase real after-tax earnings. Employers' payroll taxes and social security contributions were increased, allowing for a further reduction in income taxes for 1975. And to clear the way for a two-year agreement, a decision was taken to lower income taxes again as from January 1976. Since the wage claims tabled by the unions were geared to a 3 per cent increase in real disposable income for 1975, the tax reductions are acknowledged to have had a restraining impact on initial wage claims. Having said this, the final settlement for blue-collar workers was relatively high by past standards. While this development did contribute a sharp acceleration compared with the trend of earlier years it was not out of line with past patterns of wage formation, at least on the basis of the EFO model.

Moderate wage settlements were negotiated during May 1977,[26] helped by direct personal income tax concessions. As a result, 1977 witnessed a clear easing in the growth of wage rates following two years in which Swedish cost levels had outstripped those in most competitor countries by a wide margin. Thus hourly earnings in industry after rising by 18 per cent in 1976 increased by only 6·7 per cent in 1977. Contractual increases fell between the two years from some 8 per cent to 3·5 per cent and, reflecting weakening labour market conditions and profitability, wage drift declined from 5 per cent to 3 per cent. Wage and salary earners in fact suffered some moderate decline in real disposable income, reflecting the improvement in transfers.

In August 1977, the government announced an economic stabilisation programme intended to reduce the deficit on current account, to bring down the rate of inflation, and to safeguard employment. The government intended to maintain the volume of private consumption roughly constant over the two-year life of the programme. To this end, discussions were carried out between the government and the social partners regarding the form of income taxation for 1978, changes in indirect taxes and the general direction and formulation of an economic policy for the country geared to reducing inflation while maintaining employment.

To facilitate acceptance of moderate wage settlements in the spring of 1978, personal income tax rates were reduced and automatic indexation of income tax scales was introduced. The ensuing centralised incomes agreement for the private sector was indeed moderate. Under the agreement reached in March, increases of 1·9 per cent and 3·1 per cent in 1978 and 1979 respectively for blue-collar workers and 1·6 per cent and 2·6 per cent for white-collar workers were agreed. In the agreement it was stipulated that the employee organisations could call for new negotiations should the CPI at any time during 1978 exceed its January 1978 level by more than 7·25 per cent. A similar provision applied should the index rise by more than 5 per cent during the period January–October 1979 above its December 1978 level. The actual rise in the index between January and December 1978 amounted to 5·2 per cent. Despite lower taxes, real after-tax wages per employee fell by 4·5 per cent between 1977 and 1978.

Notes: Appendix 8A

1 On the nature of the unique Austrian 'Chambers', see Suppanz and Robinson (1972).

2 As in other Nordic countries, collective bargaining in Finland is strongly centralised. However, the central organisations, and in particular the predominantly manual-worker central organisation (SAK), are weaker than their counterparts in Norway and Sweden. Thus, SAK cannot bind its member federations to the terms of a centrally negotiated wage contract. Each federation or branch of SAK may renounce within two weeks the terms and conditions of that contract. Another interesting characteristic of the labour movement in Finland is that it is broadly divided into a Social Democratic majority and a strong Communist minority.

3   A special Incomes Policy Official was appointed in 1967. It was his role to co-ordinate, as required, the negotiations between the interest groups on behalf of the government. It came to be his responsibility to pass on information to the negotiating parties and to ensure that they began negotiations. He has in certain critical times been able to assume the role of a mediator by stepping in with a conciliation proposal when talks between the parties have become deadlocked – see below.

4   Resulting in a 16 per cent devaluation of the Markka.

5   These were designed to give additional wage increases to compensate branches for their differential (lesser) wage drift experience. The clause of the proposal reflected strong demands for protection by government and commercial employees.

6   Corresponding to a flat rate 30 pennies per hour.

7   The so-called 'social package' included in the agreement was relatively modest due to the economic situation. But tax concessions amounting to some 2 per cent of household disposable income were implemented.

8   The government announced a form of contractual price freedom to enterprises which were willing to sign long-term planning agreements with the government for the duration of the Fifth Plan. Such contracts included sectoral guidelines for price increases and for the allocation of productivity gains between wages, dividends, investment, and developmental research. The contracts permitted industries freedom in price determination if they agreed to a compulsory review procedure (see OECD Economic Surveys, France (Paris: OECD, May 1967) p. 27).

9   Automatic adjustment of wages other than SMIC for prices is forbidden by law, but an increasing proportion of collective agreements provided for de facto indexation by the inclusion of a clause providing for renegotiation in the event of a marked rise in prices or by guaranteeing an additional increase in wages if the rise in prices exceeded that foreseen at the time of the settlement. The latter arrangement was common in the public sector but infrequent in private industry.

10 However, in the course of presenting alternatives in its annual reports, the Council has implicitly made recommendations and, indeed, has proffered a series of explicit proposals in the incomes policy field.

11 Under the first phase, provision was made for a 7 per cent increase in basic pay to compensate for rising prices, subject to a minimum increase of £4 per week. An additional 2 per cent was proposed for wage-earners' share in real growth. Under the second phase, basic pay was to be increased by 1 per cent for each 1 per cent rise over 7 per cent in the CPI in the year to November 1979, subject to a limit of 4 per cent. In respect of any increase in the CPI above 11 per cent, an amount of £0·50 for each one percentage point was to be paid, subject to a limit of £2 per week. The minimum increase under this phase was to be £2 per week. Over and above these cost-of-living increases the second phase provided for a further rise of 1½ per cent for wage-earners' share in real growth.

12 Increases in personal tax allowances and an adjustment of the lower tax bands at an estimated cost of £30m had been introduced in the February budget. Also, there was a reduction in the threshold for liability to income tax by farmers and an increase in the average tax rate bringing total farm taxation for 1979 to an estimated £52m or 5½ per cent of farm income (compared with £38m or 4½ per cent of farm income in 1978).

13 At the same time a decision was taken not to charge employers and employees with the cost of recession-related increases in social security costs.

14 An institution which had far-reaching control functions under the earlier regime of guided wage policy.

15 The wage freeze did not apply to minimum wages, and enterprises employing large numbers of minimum wage earners were granted subsidies.

16 The proximate cause of breakdown was the refusal of the employers' representatives to continue the practice of automatic compensation for inflation.

17   On the basic model underpinning these calculations, see Aukrust (1970), Bjerkholt and Longva (1974), Ferunes (1975).

18   There was no centrally negotiated agreement in 1974, see Addison (1979).

19   This compensation was in the form of flat rate payments and was thus redistributional.

20   As an adaptation to the new incomes policy approach important changes took place in the work of the Contact Committee, which now was to serve as a body in which decisions of central importance were arrived at; that is, where a co-ordinated approach was agreed upon and the settlements accepted by the parties involved — see Addison (1979).

21   The new incomes policy approach was influenced in no small part by the deliberations of the Skånland Committee — see Appendix 8B — although falling well short of that committee's recommendations.

22   The details of which are reported in Addison (1979).

23   Additional increases in respect of groups earning less than 90 per cent of the national average and compensation for groups experiencing drift were also demanded.

24   The subsequent settlement for central and local government employees gave increases of 6·8 per cent and 7·3 per cent respectively.

25   Since the beginning of the 1970s an economic model developed jointly by the chief economists of LO, SAF and the main white-collar union, the so-called EFO model (Edgren, Faxén and Odhner, 1973), has had a considerable influence on collective bargaining. On the basis of this model the central federations of labour and management in Sweden have tried to make wages respond flexibly to world price movements. If they had succeeded in doing so on a year-to-year basis, the expansionist policies originally pursued by the Swedish authorities would have been justified *on the model* as a response to the world price increases which occurred in the early 1970s; it would have been possible for them to have brought down their rates of domestic cost inflation without suffering increased employment. In practice, the parties were unable to produce the requisite degree of fine-tuning so that when the rate of inflation in world prices declined in 1975/76, the rate of inflation in Swedish labour costs actually decreased and more deflationary policies had to be resorted to.

26   Under the one-year agreement, in which the two main union groupings negotiated jointly for the first time, average rates rose by 3·1 per cent and 3·8 per cent within the blue-collar and white-collar sectors respectively. Taking into account the carry-over effects from the 1975 two-year agreements, average contractual increases in 1977 are estimated to have amounted to 3·4 per cent and 7 per cent respectively.

Appendix 8B   The Skånland Report

In September 1972 a powerful committee, under the chairmanship of Hermod Skånland (Deputy Governor of the Norges Bank), was appointed to provide a detailed assessment of the problems lying at the root of the Norwegian inflationary process.

The report of the committee, which was presented to the government in June 1973, reviewed the past trend in prices in Norway since 1945. It drew attention to the following inflationary elements:

(i)   demand – the general demand situation was held to be intimately related to the pace of inflation, although the degree of association was by no means stable through time;
(ii) world market prices – these had contributed strongly to domestic inflation, especially since 1970;
(iii) income transfers – these had had an independent role in the inflationary process since the end of the 1960s;
(iv) nominal incomes growth – this had exceeded the corresponding rate of growth of productivity.

In its discussion of targets and policy instruments the committee sought as a reasonable first step to moderate the rate of change in prices to levels that had prevailed in the 1950s and 1960s. However, demand management alone was considered insufficient to secure the price target while maintaining employment levels characteristic of the 1950s and 1960s. The committee declared itself strongly in support of incomes policy. But since incomes policy could not ensure a desired trend in prices and incomes if other economic policy measures were directed toward opposite goals that policy too had to be considered as but one component of an overall economic policy.

In the opinion of the committee, then, incomes policy should be formulated with the aim of becoming an integral part of economic policy. In order to ensure a reasonable measure of success, the following basic principles should in general be observed:

(i)   incomes policy must encompass a wide range of incomes;
(ii) although often having a basis in political decisions, incomes policy should rather be based on extensive co-operation between the authorities and the organisations which would have to share in the responsibility for its implementation;
(iii) the targets set must be realistic. Unrealistic targets would only serve to bring incomes policy into disrepute;
(iv) whilst the central aim of incomes policy was the trend in prices, considerable emphasis should be placed on incomes distribution;
(v)   incomes policy must be of a long-term nature, so as to consolidate what had already been achieved and to permit attainment of those targets, for

example income distribution, which had a longer-term horizon;
(vi) other economic policy, and demand policy in particular, must be directed towards the same objectives.

The committee proceeded to draw up a blueprint for a prices and incomes policy tailored specifically to Norwegian requirements. A hallmark of the proposal was the establishment of a Council for Prices and Incomes Policy to replace the Contact Committee. This council was to include all the interest parties.

The committee drew attention to the fact that the Contact Committee and the Technical Expert Committee (see Appendix 8A section 7) had hitherto not aimed at making any decision with regard to the incomes settlements which should be binding or serve as a guideline for the parties in their further negotiations or for the policy pursued by the authorities. It suggested that the traditional view that wage negotiations were a question of distributing real resources between two opposing parties was spurious. Negotiations between the main labour market organisations affected not only the members of those organisations but also all those whose incomes in various ways were affected by wage increases obtained by labour union members, such as enterprises in the 'sheltered sector' and farmers. Furthermore, given the progressiveness of income taxes, public tax revenue would rise relatively more than private income. And, if the public sector used its higher revenue for purchasing more goods and services than previously, it would absorb an increasing share of the greater production. Consequently, there would be less room for an increase in the private sector's purchase of goods and services. Only if the greater revenue was used for increasing transfers and subsidies would private consumption be stimulated.

In this situation, conflicts could easily arise between the targets set by government and those set by labour market organisations. Thus, if the authorities and the organisations favoured mutually incompatible targets with regard to the distribution of the total supplies of goods and services and if the authorities had, in addition, some commitments as to the trend in prices; and if both groups made use of the measures at their disposal for obtaining as much as possible of their own targets, none of the targets would be reached.

This line of argument led to the proposal that the authorities and the principal interest groups dealing with wages and other forms of income should be able to influence each other's policies so as to yield compatible aims. The committee set up a series of guidelines for ensuring that the targets set by the organisations were mutually compatible as well as the institutional procedure best equipped for establishing these guidelines. The guidelines were to be based on certain assumptions regarding the basic economic facts which the authorities could not influence (at any rate in the short run), namely the expected amount of production and the movement of import and export prices. These assumptions set the limits within which the incomes settlement and other decisions affecting the use of resources had to be made. The guidelines would apply to the various factors affecting incomes and prices policy, namely (a) the amount of the public sector's purchases of goods and services, (b) the relationship between wages and profits, (c) the trend in wage-earners' real disposable income, (d) the price trend, and (e) incomes other than wage incomes. The objectives laid down for all of these items had to be kept compatible with each other. Thus the government would have an obligation to keep its use of real resources within specified limits (which would affect expenditure, subsidies, taxes and borrowing), and local authorities would also be affected in so far as they were subject to central government influence. Similarly, employers' and workers' organisations would have to undertake to keep the total amount of wage rises determined by agreements within specified limits, and steps to limit wage drift should be undertaken. Increases in agricultural incomes would continue to be linked to the wage settlement and guidelines for prices and margins might be determined in co-operation with the organisations representing industry and commerce.

As noted above, the committee recommended that co-operation in drawing up guidelines should be carried out by a Council for Prices and Incomes Policies which would replace the existing Contact Committee and have somewhat wider membership. It would deal with all questions affecting incomes, wages, prices, taxes, levies, subventions and subsidies. The guidelines which it would establish would require unanimous approval. The Technical Export Committee was to be retained. As before, forecasts were to be made of the trend in prices and incomes based on various alternatives regarding the income and agricultural settlements.

The main task of the council was to secure harmonisation of the agreements and fiscal policy with the guidelines agreed upon by the parties. But it was likely that the council would also have to function *between* actual settlements. Thus there might be a failure of the assumptions referred to above, or non-adherence to the guidelines in certain quarters.

The basic idea of these proposals is, then, that both the government and the interest groups should give up some of their power of independent action while engaging in wider co-operation. The government (subject to normal parliamentary control by the Storting) would gain greater influence on growth of nominal incomes. The organisations for their part would have to share with the government bodies the authority to stipulate nominal increases in income. Equally, they would have greater opportunity for exerting influence on the real value of the income increases stipulated and thereby on their members' income.

The reaction to the Skånland Committee's proposals can be viewed at two levels. First, the Norwegian Federation of Trade Unions (LO), although expressing support for closer co-operation between the government and the various organisations, was not prepared to accept the proposed Council for Prices and Incomes, preferring the 'less rigid' arrangement of the Contact Committee.

The government, for its part, issued a comprehensive statement on Skånland in April 1975 and in so doing outlined its future policy. The policy document supported the Committee's analysis of the determinants of inflation and accepted the need for closer co-operation and exchange of influence between the authorities and the social partners on questions concerning incomes policy. However, as with the LO, the recommendation of a Council for Prices and Incomes Policies which would establish a binding framework for income distribution was rejected as too inflexible for practical purposes. The decision-making process, the government argued, should not be tied to one specific organisational form but, rather, assume *ad hoc* forms according to the circumstances.

Chapter 9

Incomes Policies, Inflation and Relative Pay: an Overview

R. F. ELLIOTT and J. L. FALLICK

> *Many things difficult to design prove easy to performance.* Samuel Johnson

Perhaps there will come a day when an analysis of incomes policy will be able to conclude by echoing the sentiments of Samuel Johnson, but we are certainly not there yet. In fact when incomes policies were first conceived as an instrument of macroeconomic policy they had the appeal of simplicity, for in contrast to the existing macroeconomic instruments they appeared to be simple to design: in the extreme they simply prohibited all wage rises. With the benefit of hindsight we can now conclude that while they may have possessed this virtue they have, to stand Samuel Johnson on his head, proved difficult, if not impossible, 'to performance'. In consequence effective incomes policies are now proving extremely difficult to design.

It was during the 1960s that incomes policies emerged as an additional instrument of macroeconomic policy in several of the advanced industrialised nations. The traditional tools of fiscal, monetary and exchange rate policy appeared unable to cope with the 'stagflation' that began to emerge in the late 1960s and early 1970s and it was thus to incomes policies that governments increasingly turned. Yet no sooner had the new policy been tried than the orthodox Keynesian policy of demand management was under attack from what has come to be termed the 'new classical macroeconomics'. Indeed of all the instruments of macroeconomic policy that very instrument which was specifically introduced to reduce the rate of change of nominal wages and prices while ensuring an acceptable level of unemployment appeared to be found the most wanting. Incomes policy was designed to deal specifically with events in the labour market, a market which was generally neglected in orthodox Keynesian analysis, and it was this market which, in the end, proved the least amenable to control. Thus the recent criticism of fiscal policy can also be seen as applying with even greater force to incomes policies. Precisely why this should be so and what role incomes policy still has to play is one of the major insights provided by this book.

The principal aim of an incomes policy is to reduce the rate of change of nominal wages. A rapid rise in nominal wages may mean that wages are established and for some period remain above the market clearing level and thus there is cause for concern. One explanation of how this can occur is a central feature of the view of certain prominent Keynesian economists who argue that the determination of money wages is essentially a political question. In the extreme, as Artis (chapter 1) emphasises, this school would view wage determination as 'orthogonal' to the economy and hence for them the Phillips curve is essentially horizontal. This is of course the interpretation of the *General Theory* promoted by Hicks (1937) in the ISLM diagram which now forms the core of most intermediate-level undergraduate textbooks. Thus until recently these books largely neglected discussion of the labour market and as a result failed to incorporate within the main body of their analysis the reality that incomes policy was by now an important addition to the conventional macroeconomic instruments of government policy.

Real wage resistance

An extreme version of the 'real wage resistance hypothesis' can be seen as falling within that part of the Keynesian tradition which argues that the determination of money wages is a political question. Also within this Keynesian tradition is the argument that concern about relative rather than real wages lies at the heart of the wage bargaining process; but we shall come to this later. It can be argued that real wage aspirations determine the rate of change of money wages and that these aspirations are established completely independently of the economic system. Such a view is an essential feature of the arguments of the Cambridge Economic Policy Group (see Cripps and Godley, 1976), who conclude that those incomes policies designed to reduce real wages will have no permanent effect on the rate of inflation since the target real wage is impervious to the effects of incomes policy. As a result any reduction that is achieved is only temporary for this is soon recovered via catch-up increases once the policy is off.

The idea that money wages are determined in a bargaining context which stresses after-tax real wages implies, contrary to conventional wisdom, that tax increases are inflationary while tax cuts may be deflationary. Thus governments concerned about the level of wage settlements could offer tax cuts in exchange for moderation in wage demands (Artis, chapter 1), thereby ensuring that real wage aspirations were satisfied at a lower level of wage settlements than would otherwise have occurred. Of course this is just what happened in the UK during Phase II of the Social Contract in 1976–7 which is widely regarded as one of the more successful examples of incomes policies, although it should be noted that in 1978 the TUC rejected a similar deal. They did so because the earlier phases of the Social Contract had successfully secured the necessary reduction in real wages but in turn this made many unions reluctant to engage in further restraint. This emphasises the point that it may not always be possible to satisfy the real wage aspirations of workers and even when some growth in real incomes is possible there need be no agreement between government and unions as to exactly how great this should be. It should also be remembered that, in the absence of equivalent cuts in government expenditure, tax cuts will increase the budget deficit and therefore can in themselves fuel inflation. All this is not to deny that real wage aspirations exist. It merely serves to emphasise that it is extremely difficult to infuse such notions with operational significance, for the target rate of growth of real disposable income will presumably vary between workers at different stages of their life cycle and may vary according to family circumstances. Thus the target will presumably be higher for younger workers and may be established in terms of the family rather than the individual. This has led one author, Wachter (1979), to suggest that the slowdown in real wage growth in recent years may account for the increase in two-worker families which has also occurred over this period. These points emphasise the inherent difficulties of designing a policy which rests on the notion of some aggregate target rate of growth of real after-tax wages.

Of course as Henry (chapter 2) has emphasised, to subscribe to the 'real wage model' is not to subscribe to the view that the target is immutable and unaffected by cyclical conditions in the economy. Indeed, as Artis (chapter 1) points out, an unfeasible path for aspirations of real wages must produce either continuous inflation or deflation if the actual real wage path falls below or above it. We might argue that under these conditions agents would revise their aspirations of real wages in a downward or upward direction respectively. Of course such revisions might only occur slowly as agents learn the true paths of the relevant variables and thus there is a role for a mild form of incomes policy which aims to educate economic agents about the paths of these variables.

The provision of information is the most basic ingredient of all incomes policies and in most continental European countries there exists a structure to promote a dialogue between unions, employers and governments (see Addison, chapter 8). In some cases the committees were established on the initiative of trade unions and employers' associations while in others the government has played a more active role, but in all cases they appear to have had an important impact on collective bargaining. They provide for an exchange of information and afford the parties the opportunity to discuss their basic assumptions before they finalise their strategies for the coming wage and income negotiations. In some cases the government also provides the parties with its forecasts of the future paths of the key economic variables under alternative wage outcomes, in an attempt to ensure that the parties adopt the more favourable strategy. The policy of 'concerted action' in Germany is perhaps the most familiar example of this, but, as this illustrates, a vital element in the success of such an approach is a degree of consensus among the parties to the discussions. Clearly these policies will be most successful if all parties subscribe to the same underlying economic model and it is therefore an open question just how successful such a policy would be in the UK. None the less if such a forum were established and its deliberations conducted in public it would at a minimum result in a greater public awareness of the underlying economic relationships and to this extent might result in a positive feedback on the bargaining process. It could be argued for example that had the public been informed of the necessity for a fall in real incomes following the oil price rises of 1973 and 1974, they might have elected to take that cut sooner rather than later and they would thus have avoided many of the problems that were eventually experienced during the mid-1970s.

The alternative to these mild forms of incomes policy which attempt to reform behaviour by educating economic agents about the paths of the key economic variables is certainly less palatable. In both the 'old' and the 'new' classical macroeconomics, spells of unemployment serve as the educator if real wage aspirations exceed the feasible level. While on this view wage aspirations would converge on the equilibrium real wage, a sudden shock to the system which necessitated a real wage fall might result in excessive real wage aspirations for a period. Thus if government policy could serve the role of educator it would be a desirable alternative to the spells of unemployment which would otherwise perform this function. Yet neither educator is without problems. 'One man's wage rise' is, given present institutional arrangements, frequently 'another man's unemployment' and this may be of little concern to the former. On the other hand, for the government to prove a more successful educator it must have an information advantage over the private sector. Presumably it has a more accurate model of the economy and thereby can inform the parties to the discussion of the market clearing path for real wages, but the experience with indexation in the UK in 1974 and 1975 alone raises some doubts whether these requirements are always met.

The new classical macroeconomics is, however, not without its critics. The augmented Phillips curve is one of the two pillars of this school (Buiter, 1980), and this attributes the major part of the explanation of wage movements to changes in the excess supply of labour. Parkin (1979) has argued that the real wage model is theoretically indistinguishable from the excess supply model, while Kuh (1967) has argued that the net real wage represents the supply side and a time-trend the average productivity of labour. On this interpretation the real wage model and augmented Phillips curve become one. However, Henry (chapter 2) demonstrates that 'the argument that the real wage effect merely echoes the excess supply mechanism . . . is simply not supported by the evidence', and once he has corrected for the theoretical weaknesses of the excess supply model of Parkin, Sumner and Ward (1976) he can show that there is little empirical support for this hypothesis. In contrast, a real wage model where the target is real net earnings appears particularly robust and in the light of the failure of the excess supply model would seem to point to some form of bargaining behaviour. However, as we have already noted, his model seems to suggest that tax reductions can serve to defuse inflationary wage demands but in fact the response to such 'bribes' in the UK has been mixed. While successful during Stage II of the Social Contract, a similar approach was rejected in 1978 while in 1979 cuts in direct taxation were offset by rises in indirect taxation and thus the net tax reductions were minimal.

In the context of this discussion about real wages it should also be emphasised that while 'Muth-rational expectations', the other pillar of the new classical macroeconomics, implies that incomes policies can have no effect on either the path or level of wage inflation, the assumptions of this model (see Buiter, 1980) limit its plausibility for the labour market. Less restrictively interpreted, 'partially rational expectations' 'might be taken to suggest that a credible incomes policy has a potentially powerful role to play in disciplining expectations' (Artis, chapter 1), although it is clear that this role will soon vanish if the government continually fails to reduce inflation by this method. Indeed it has to be acknowledged that the experience to date suggests that incomes policies provide some support for the prescriptions of the rational expectations model. For when an incomes policy is widely expected, as in the late summer of 1972 in the UK, bargaining groups may attempt to 'beat the gun'. As Artis (chapter 1) emphasises, such actions may force the earlier adoption of the policy than planned or may lead to the introduction of a policy when none was intended. In order to avoid such a contingency, a government which is sceptical of the value of such a policy may be forced to declare its scepticism in stronger terms than its own convictions would otherwise warrant, in order to defuse expectations that it will introduce such a policy. In turn this is likely to weaken the credibility of the policy when it is adopted. Attempts to 'beat the gun' are but one aspect of the growing realisation that incomes policies themselves are endogenous to the economic system. Henry (chapter 2) recognises this problem but argues that the wage equation is probably not subject to simultaneous equation bias from this source. Pencavel (chapter 7) goes further and constructs a simple model aimed at explaining the determinants of incomes policies in the USA. Given that incomes policies are in general popular in the USA (see his Table 7.1) he argues that 'governments have been inclined to turn to an incomes policy when the popularity of the government is low, when the economy is moving from a recession and into an expansion and when the growth of real wages is falling below its trend.' Incomes policies give the impression of 'doing something' and are often erroneously viewed as policies which affect price and wage inflation without affecting output. More importantly, in the US, where fiscal and monetary policies respectively are in large measure effectively under the control of Congress and the Federal Reserve, incomes policy, it could be argued, is the one instrument of demand management more fully under the direction of the executive. This last argument is clearly less relevant to the UK but there is no denying that incomes policies are precipitated by a certain concurrence of events and are therefore in principle at least predictable. In the UK they have often been used to secure a reduction in real wages in contrast to the US, and as a result they perhaps enjoy less widespread public support.

The problem of relative wages

But to return to our original proposition. If the case for an incomes policy rests on the argument that wages may be established and for some period remain above the equilibrium level, we might inquire once again how this set of events can occur. Possibly an exogenous shock requires a downward adjustment in real wages in the absence of an offsetting upward surge in productivity, but why does this fail to occur? Why in terms of the new classical macroeconomics do 'expectations' or, in terms of orthodox Keynesian theory, 'real' or perhaps only 'money wage aspirations' fail to adjust in the required direction? The argument is essentially that relative wages enter the labour supply function, at least in the short run, and thus while each individual bargaining group may wish for a generally lower level of money wage settlements they will not initiate a move in this direction for fear of a deterioration in their relative wages (Tobin, 1972).

Furthermore, if each bargaining group feels that its wage bargain has little effect on the general level of prices it will try to match the level of settlement achieved in other wage bargains and will have no incentive to wage restraint.

Substantial evidence now exists of the considerable inter-dependencies that exist between the wage settlements of different bargaining groups throughout wide areas of the economy (Addison, 1974; Brown and Sisson, 1975; Elliott, 1980b) but these should not be overstated. There is little evidence for the extreme version of this form of interdependency, the 'national wage round' (Elliott, 1976), and plenty of evidence that the relative wages of different bargaining groups change over time. Moreover the mere observation of interdependencies in the wage bargaining process can be interpreted as either a market or a political/institutional phenomenon (Addison and Burton, 1979). None the less the implications of these inter-dependencies seem clear. An exogenous shock to the system, which either raises the relative wages of a single bargaining group or requires a general reduction in real wages, can set in train a wage–wage spiral which may be explosive and certainly establishes wages above the equilibrium level.

What then are the courses of action open to the government under these circumstances? Crucially it matters whether the interdependencies in the wage determination process are market or institutional phenomena. That is whether they reflect workers' judgements about the rate of change of wages in the alternative employments to which they might aspire – a market interpreta-tion – in which case we should not be surprised to find wage changes equalised across what is essentially a common labour market (Oswald, 1979); or whether they reflect some institutional phenomenon and take the form of 'coercive comparisons' (Dunlop, 1957). If the former, these need not pervade the whole of the economy, or if they do should be very short-lived, and thus these need not detain us further. If, however, they are the latter, they may either reflect substantial monopoly power on the part of certain parties to the wage bargaining process, namely the trade unions, or other institutional rigidities in the wage bargaining process. Thus one approach to the problem is the familiar argument that the government should intervene to reduce the welfare losses of monopoly pricing but, as Pencavel (chapter 7) points out, such an argument is relevant in a world of constant prices no less than in a world of inflation. However, it is at least possible that, while a rise in prices is itself a consequence of the exercise of monopoly power, this in turn will encourage increasing militancy on the part of workers which leads them to realise any latent monopoly power that had previously remained unexploited. While it seems unrealistic to attribute all elements of the *exercise* of monopoly power in the labour market to inflation there seems little doubt that inflation can intensify this. Friedman (1951) has, of course, observed that an increase in the monopoly power of a trade union will lead to a once-and-for-all increase in wages, as the monopolistic element is exploited, but that it will not in itself lead to wage inflation – a continuing rise in wages. This is of course true if the whole of the monopoly gain is exploited *at once* and the increases in monopoly power are infrequent. However in a world of imperfect information in which actors may well learn of the true state of the world largely through experience it appears possible that while inflation may not result in increases in monopoly power it may provide the spur to greater militancy; one result of which is that trade unions gradually learn of and exploit their existing but latent monopoly power. Thus the resort to and successful outcome of the first strike might encourage a more militant posture by the trade union and a willingness to engage in further strikes as it gradually realises its true monopoly power. Trade unions are unlikely to know with any precision the elasticity of the demand for labour function that confronts them and inflation could provide the spur for them to attempt to discover this although it is at just such times that this may be most difficult. Inflation means it is difficult to distinguish relative changes in prices from absolute changes in prices and thus the process is subject to great uncertainty. On this view therefore incomes policy would seem desirable, for it could obviate the very circumstances which otherwise might have led to trade unions realising the full potential of their monopoly power. On this view incomes policies 'hold the ring' but presumably should be accompanied by longer-term policies aimed at changing the conditions which give rise to the monopoly position of the trade unions in the first place.

If in contrast the interdependencies in the wage bargaining process result less from the exercise of monopoly power and instead reflect other institutional rigidities in the wage bargaining process such as 'customary relativities', then incomes policy can play a much more positive role. Incomes policies can under these circumstances assume the quality of a public good (see Artis, chapter 1) because now similar wage gains can be secured with less inflation. Statutory incomes policies would of course achieve this result directly, if they were adhered to, but the search for a voluntary policy has led a number of people to advocate the introduction of a policy of 'concerted action' supported by greater synchronisation of wage settlements to secure this goal. Greater synchronisation of wage settlements, a concentration within a few months of the year, would, it is argued, avoid the phenomenon of leap-frogging. The structure of differentials would emerge at an early stage in the discussions and we would not have to wait until the annual cycle of wage settlements was well under way before this became apparent. This would obviate the need for catching up increases and the need for groups to 'hang back' to see what 'going rate' emerges, as presently occurs.

It is of course arguable whether any consensus over differentials would emerge from such a forum or whether any agreements reached would be adhered to. Perhaps the major reason for this latter doubt is that wage bargaining in the private sector of the UK is more decentralised than in many other European countries (see Mayhew, chapter 4) and it is clear the more centralised the structure the simpler the discussions and the implementation of the policy. It might be argued that it is by no means evident that an incomes policy assumes the quality of a public good even under these circumstances, for the proposition that each separate bargaining group feels that its wage bargain has no influence on prices may be incorrect. Where well-established 'customary differentials' exist, bargainers may be well aware of the impact of their wage settlement on the other wage settlements which are traditionally linked to theirs, and of the repercussions of these for the general level of settlements. Thus the well-documented interdependencies within the utilities in the public sector (see Fallick and Elliott, chapter 5) are well understood by the bargainers in this area and the impact of these on the general level of settlements might be suspected, if not known with any precision. If the general repercussions are not known and cannot be predicted with any precision, wage restraint could retain the qualities of a public good and may be the only approach to the problem of relative wages.

The reform of the pay structure

Clearly the problem of relative wages lies at the heart of the arguments for incomes policies for as Tobin (1972, p. 13) has emphasised, the key to a successful incomes policy 'is to find a formula for mutual de-escalation which does not offend conceptions of relative equity'. This has led some observers to propose that we should act directly to reform the structure of relative wages. This is a course of action which is often advocated by those emphasising the political nature of the wage determination process and emphasises that a reform of the wage structure according to some generally agreed principles would remove the focus of the discontent. A national job evaluation scheme has been suggested as one approach (Jones, 1973) while others (Brown, 1973) have emphasised that there exists a broad consensus concerning the relative worth of different occupations, and that this could serve as a basis for realigning wages in different employments. The latter view emphasises the role that considerations of equity or fairness play in establishing relative wages and draws on the results of surveys of relative pay conducted in recent years to support the argument that a broad consensus exists on this issue (see Behrend, 1973). Considerations of fairness or equity have also been stressed as the principal determinant of 'coercive comparisons' although this is by no means the only way to explain these phenomena. In fact it is extremely difficult to infuse notions such as fairness with any objectively determined and therefore predictable content (see Burton, 1977), while the evidence of the surveys is in fact ambiguous on this point. For while it emerges that most individuals interviewed ranked all occupations but their own in roughly the same order, each individual placed his own occupation much higher in the ranking than did the others in the sample, and thus no consistent overall ranking was possible. Nor can the objective exercise of job evaluation provide an answer once we turn away from subjective notions such as fairness. Job evaluation has increased in sophistication in recent years but has experienced considerable difficulty in developing generally accepted criteria for evaluating certain attributes of occupations, such as responsibility and risk. Thus the search for some general principles with which to reform the wage structure is likely to prove fruitless. Indeed in so far as such an exercise tackles symptoms – discontent over relativities – rather than causes, many would argue that it is doomed to failure from the start.

This same lack of consensus or absence of generally agreed criteria for establishing an acceptable structure of relative wages could also frustrate attempts to reform the wage bargaining system by synchronising wage claims and awards. If awards are concentrated within a relatively short period and all parties know at the time they settle what the structure of relative wages will look like over the coming twelve months this will act to defuse a wage–wage spiral – it is argued. Of course it may not: it may at best postpone the struggle for a further twelve months and at worst intensify it by concentrating the struggle within a relatively short period. Indeed if the policy is voluntary, the emergence of unanticipated inflation would ensure that the policy was short-lived, for in the UK wage contracts are not legally binding and the traditional response to unanticipated inflation has been to renegotiate wage contracts.

A move toward concentrating discussions about pay within certain months of the year would, however, afford the government the opportunity of making clear to the parties to the discussion just what the outcome in terms of prices and unemployment would be if they proceeded with their proposed wage increases. Earlier it was emphasised that such a policy might provide a mechanism whereby the inflationary consequences of the struggle over relative wages could at least be minimised and this therefore merits serious consideration.

However, it is open to doubt whether the government would provide such information and more importantly whether the parties would even believe it, let alone draw the same conclusions from it.

The parties to the discussions may certainly come to realise that the level of settlements being proposed might have undesirable consequences but whether they would be prepared or able to turn round and recontract is another matter. Both trade unions and employers' associations may have insufficient power to ensure compliance by their members in a system of wage bargaining which in the private sector is considerably decentralised in some areas. Whether such discussions would promote greater centralisation is an open question and it is certainly not clear that this is always desirable. It is, furthermore, always possible that some negotiators would be sufficiently convinced of the justice of their own claim, and unconvinced about the predicted consequences, that they would go ahead regardless. Other countries which have adopted such policies have done so through the voluntary co-operation of employers and trade unions (see Addison, chapter 8), and this in turn reflects the underlying social and economic cohesion of these societies. It is questionable whether the same conditions exist in the UK.

The problem of the public sector

None the less the search for some generally agreed non-market criteria for establishing wage levels will go on, in one area at least, for some criteria are needed to establish the wages of employees in large parts of the public sector. At present comparability with wage levels in other employments plays the central role in determining the wage levels of a majority of employees in the public sector, but in recent years this purportedly objective method of establishing rates of pay has led to some rather strange results. For the UK, as Dean (chapter 3) points out, wage settlements and earnings in the public sector generally increased at a faster rate than in the private sector in the early and middle 1970s; while as we emerge from the past decade the recommendations of the Clegg commission seem certain to result in a further improvement in the relative pay of large numbers of public sector employees. This higher rate of change of pay and the growing volume of public sector employment (by the mid-1970s almost one third of all employees in employment were to be found in the public sector) have in turn placed an additional burden on public expenditure and over the period labour costs have come to account for an increasing proportion of current government expenditures. How do we account for these events? One possibility is that the formal comparability exercises which establish the pay of civil servants seriously undervalue certain non-pecuniary aspects of public sector employment — most notably the non-contributory pension and, until recently, greater security of employment — but clearly these factors alone cannot account for this change round. Rather it would appear that as Fallick and Elliott (chapter 5) suggest the dispersion of pay levels in the private sector has grown over this period, with the result that changes in the average level of private sector pay are now less representative of the size of settlements enjoyed by the groups with whom the civil service compares — the highest-paying organisations. Inevitably this raises the question whether civil servants should have their pay set with reference only to the best employers in the private sector. This is an issue for public debate.

Recent criticisms of the role of comparability in determining public sector pay (Beenstock and Immanuel, 1979) have focused on the absence of market criteria when wages are established via this process. Thus they argue that the rates of change of pay for each occupation in the public sector should be determined by recruitment needs. Shortages would merit a higher level of settlements than the average while a surplus of applicants would suggest a fall in relative wages. However, while appealing in theory, in practice such a policy would be likely to prove highly unsatisfactory. Existing vacancy figures, which Beenstock and Immanuel employ in support of their argument, are a very imperfect indicator of labour shortages for many reasons but not least because they are in part a product of the existing *negotiated* establishment levels. These establishment levels are frequently the outcomes of a bargaining process and in turn may reflect the monopoly power of trade unions and professional organisations. It is a common if somewhat anecdotal complaint that public sector services are overmanned and this approach would do nothing to remedy this. Rather it might ossify existing manning levels and preclude the more efficient utilisation of labour in this sector.

The presence of almost one third of all employees in the public sector means however that 'incomes policies are with us all the time' (Artis, chapter 1). Attempts to control public expenditure via cash limits involve estimates of, and attempts to enforce a certain level of settlements throughout large areas of public employment. In the past this has resulted in claims of 'unfair treatment' by public employees who believe that while their pay is being constrained the private sector is moving ahead. There is some evidence that this occurred during the breakout from incomes policy during the late 1960s and perhaps again in 1977 and 1978 (see Fallick and Elliott, chapter 5; Dean, chapter 3) but there is little evidence that this is a general feature of pay restraint. Moreover, the procedures of comparability provide inbuilt safeguards against just such an eventuality with provisions to restore the traditional relationships once the pay restraint has ended. Of course this can mean that the public sector becomes an accomplice to earlier breaches of incomes policy when they subsequently restore parity with private sector wage levels which were themselves achieved by breaking the incomes policy. Most importantly the large catching-up increases that may eventually be recommended, as for example under Clegg in 1979 and 1980, place a severe strain on public expenditure in those years and may further fuel inflationary expectations.

One reason why the public sector may do better than the private sector during some periods of incomes policy is that it emerges quite clearly from the studies in this volume that pay norms virtually become entitlements in the public sector. On the other hand it is by no means apparent that the same goes in the private sector (see Mayhew, chapter 4) and thus in those policies in which the norm has also proved an effective ceiling the public sector may do better than elsewhere. Certainly it does better than the wages council sector, which covers a large group of low-paid workers in the private sector, for seldom have norms become general entitlements in this sector. On the contrary, as Steele reveals (chapter 6) wages councils failed to secure even the full benefit of those flat-rate incomes policies which were specifically designed to award the largest increases to the low-paid. Where the public sector loses out is where the incomes policy is effectively policed in the public sector but less widely adhered to in the private sector, as appears to have happened over part of the period 1976 to 1979 (see Dean, chapter 3).

Wage drift

For a long time during the 1960s the composition of the earnings of manual workers was different in the public and private sectors and this served as an additional source of tension. Basic rates of pay accounted for a smaller proportion of the actual earnings of workers in the private sector and substantial wage drift was a marked feature of the middle 1960s. Wage drift is by its nature difficult to control and it has also caused problems for other European countries in which bargaining is more highly centralised than in the UK (see Addison, chapter 8). In the UK the rates of pay of public sector workers were effectively controlled by the incomes policies of the mid-1960s while earnings in the private sector rose rapidly (Elliott, 1977). The attempt by public sector manual workers to restore their position relative to private sector earnings is one of the main explanations of the surge in public sector wage rates in the late 1960s. Inevitably the question arises: could the same happen again and thus jeopardise any future wage restraint? The simple answer seems to be that it is unlikely to occur to the same degree again.

In recent years, wage drift has reduced considerably not simply because labour markets are much slacker than they were in the middle 1960s but largely because pay structures have been brought increasingly under control. Brown and Terry (1978) emphasise that plant and company bargaining has 'bought out' piecework and other forms of payment system that gave rise to much of the drift in the past, while Elliott (1980a) has emphasised that in certain industries national agreements continue to exert a powerful influence over earnings. In consequence, formal procedures at the industry, company and plant level now play a larger role than at any time during the last two decades in determining effective rates of pay and thus the prospects for monitoring pay settlements, should a future incomes policy so require, are enhanced.

Drift has always been far less of a problem when it came to non-manual workers for almost the whole of their pay is accounted for by formally negotiated salary scales. Evasion of incomes policy via drift was therefore of smaller concern in this area. None the less, as Pencavel (chapter 7) reminds us, the wage or salary an employee receives may be only part of his total remuneration. Non-wage (including non-pecuniary) items account for the rest, and these can always be increased to compensate for any constraints on the size of pay settlements. This avenue of evasion is generally believed to be most fully exploited in the case of non-manual workers in the private sector of the economy but just how significant this has been *vis-à-vis* the non-pecuniary benefits accruing to labour in other sectors is difficult to say. Manual workers have enjoyed substantial gains in holiday entitlements in recent years, while the security of employment of non-manual workers in the public sector should be balanced against the increase in company cars and other fringe benefits, confined to non-manual private sector employees, that attract public attention. Perhaps most importantly, the growth of non-wage items in the total job package as a response to incomes policies means that money wage signals now become less accurate indicators of the total benefits to be derived from a particular employment. Thus incomes policies reduce the efficiency of the price mechanism as an information network and this may have serious allocative effects. Of course it has to be recognised, as Mayhew (chapter 4) points out, that employers have always viewed pay as only one of a range of alternative adjustment mechanisms to balance their demand for labour with its supply, but there can be no doubting it is the most important. Thus the proliferation of non-wage elements in the total job package can only be achieved at a much higher cost than could an equivalent increase in money incomes.

Non-wage elements both constrain worker choice, in that they determine the commodities he will receive in exchange for his labour, and hinder labour market clearing by reducing the information conveyed by the wage system.

The impact of incomes policies on differentials

Not surprisingly the impact of incomes policy on rates of pay as between occupations with different levels of skill appears to be limited. Certainly the flat-rate policies of the mid-1970s played their part in narrowing differentials at this time but they were by no means the only forces at work. There is evidence that the narrowing of differentials was well under way before the inception of the incomes policies of the mid-1970s (Elliott and Fallick, 1979; Dean, 1978; and Brown, 1976) and thus the skill shortages that characterised the economy throughout the 1970s, despite the existence of high levels of unemployment, cannot be attributed solely to incomes policies. Perhaps even more interesting is the suggestion of the aggregate data on the dispersion of pay in the private sector (Mayhew, Tables 4.5 and 6 above) that the narrowing of the mid-1970s was compensated by widening for all but the highest-paid during the last half of the decade. Thus the impact of incomes policies on the distribution of earned income is both uncertain and any discernible effect is short-lived.

It follows from this that the lower-paid have not enjoyed any permanent improvement in their position over the period. The incomes policies of the mid-1970s were sold on the basis of improving the lot of the low-paid and while they resulted in a temporary improvement this was not sustained once the policy was removed. Indeed the evidence of Steele (chapter 6) suggests that incomes policy has not redistributed income toward the lowest-paid. Where they have done so, the effects have been short-lived as differentials are restored once the policy is off, while those earlier policies which provided clauses for exceptional treatment for low-paid industries failed to implement these clauses. The lessons of incomes policy seem to be that the problem of low incomes cannot be tackled by the wage system and the sooner this is recognised and appropriate fiscal measures devised to deal with it, the better.

Final thoughts

Thus the conclusions of this volume are essentially negative. The studies reveal that incomes policies can reduce the rate of wage inflation in the short run but no more. Once the policy is off, catch-up increases occur with the result that incomes policies affect the *path* but not the level of wage inflation over time. Catch-up increases presumably aim to restore real disposable income but the specification of these real-wage targets is still a subject of dispute, and until such time as it is resolved we cannot conclude that attempting to trade off tax cuts against wage restraint will prove successful.

Of course short-term gains are all that might concern politicians. The life of Parliament is short and U-turns in mid-term are not unknown. Thus a policy which reduces the rate of wage inflation over the short run in the run-up to the next general election is appealing, for the costs of this will only be revealed later. Such policies, however, increase the instability of the inflation rate and thus increase uncertainty which will further undermine our economic performance. It seems reasonable to conclude therefore that incomes policies have in the past done more harm than good.

In contrast some success on the incomes policy front has been achieved in continental Europe. Perhaps the most successful policies have been those in which the action of the government is largely confined to influencing the climate within which the negotiations between employers and trade unions have taken place. They are therefore, in general, far from the direct government intervention in pay bargaining which has been a feature of British incomes policies and their success is arguably less the result of income policy *per se* than of the size of the countries and the underlying degree of social and political cohesion. The practical results achieved would also appear to have depended on the appropriateness and consistency of the mix of monetary and fiscal policies and the exchange rate regime rather than the efficacy of incomes policies measures alone. Generalisations are therefore hazardous, although this is not to deny that some of the instruments which have been employed are worth while. This is perhaps most obvious in the context of information exchange.

In the UK in contrast, it could be argued, society is far less homogeneous; there is less consensus and therefore greater room for dispute about the causes and consequences of any economic event. Thus only under extreme circumstances are groups willing to forgo opportunities to improve their position in the short term even if they realise that this may result in a worse outcome in the long term. In a society such as ours incomes policies have an appeal because they hold the ring in the short term, but if they are not to lead to a recurrence of the events of the 1970s they must be accompanied by the appropriate institutional reforms.

Yet this damning indictment cannot stand as the last word on incomes policies for at least two reasons. First, despite the poor general performance of incomes policies in the UK it is not immediately apparent that there is a superior method of reducing the rate of wage change, given the present structure of labour markets;

while secondly, as we have already noted, in one sense incomes policies are always with us – the case of the public sector. The struggle over relative wages lies at the heart of the arguments for incomes policy and the market appears to provide an unacceptably slow de-escalation of this struggle. Moreover, it seems unlikely that the institutional reforms which would be necessary to increase market disciplines, and thus speed this process, will be introduced by any British government in the near future. Thus some form of incomes policy seems the most likely outcome and the experience of the recent past would seem to suggest that such a policy will be of a voluntary nature. Moves to synchronise the wage-bargaining process and towards tripartite discussions between the government, employers, and trade unions seem the most likely first step; but if these fail, as seems highly probable, we should expect the imposition of a wage freeze. A wage freeze 'buys time' and it is therefore crucial how the time thus bought is employed. It should not be squandered as in the past.

References: Chapter 9

Addison, J. T. (1974), 'Productivity Bargaining: The Externalities Question', *Scottish Journal of Political Economy*, vol. 20

Addison, J. T., and Burton, J. (1979), 'The Identification of Market and Spillover Forces in Wage Inflation: A Cautionary Note', *Applied Economics*, vol. 11

Beenstock, M., and Immanuel, H. (1979), 'The Market Approach to Pay Comparability', *National Westminster Bank Review*, November

Behrend, H. (1973), *Incomes Policy, Equity and Pay Increase Differentials*, Scottish Academic Press

Brown, W., and Sisson, K. (1975) 'The Use of Comparisons in Workplace Wage Determination', *British Journal of Industrial Relations*, vol. XIII

Brown, W. (1976), 'Incomes Policy and Pay Differentials', *Oxford Bulletin of Economics and Statistics*, vol. 38

Brown, W., and Terry, M. (1978), 'The Changing Nature of National Wage Agreements', *British Journal of Industrial Relations*, vol. XIV

Brown, W. (1973), *The Earnings Conflict* (Harmondsworth: Penguin)

Buiter, W. H. (1980), 'The Macroeconomics of Dr. Pangloss: A Critical Survey of the New Classical Macroeconomics', *Economic Journal*, vol. 90

Burton, J. (1977), 'A Critique of the Relative Deprivation Hypothesis of Wage Inflation', *Scottish Journal of Political Economy*, vol. 24

Cripps, T. F., and Godley, W. A. H. (1976), 'A Formal Analysis of the Cambridge Economic Policy Group Model', *Economica*, No. 43

Dean, A. J. H. (1978), 'Incomes Policy and Differentials', *National Institute Economic Review*, no. 85

Dunlop, J. T. (1957), 'The Task of Contemporary Wage Theory', in J. T. Dunlop (ed.), *The Theory of Wage Determination* (Macmillan)

Elliott, R. F. (1976), 'The National Wage Round in the UK: A Sceptical View', *Oxford Bulletin of Economics and Statistics*, vol. 38

Elliott, R. F., and Fallick, J. L. (1979), 'Pay Differentials in Perspective: A Note on Manual and Non-Manual Pay over the period 1951–1975', *Economic Journal*

Elliott, R. F. (1980a), 'Are National Agreements Dead?', paper read at the British Universities Industrial Relations Association Conference

Elliott, R. F. (1980b), 'Wage Rounds and Wage Contours: Evidence of Interdependencies in the Wage Determination Process in the U.K. over the Period 1950 to 1975', Aberdeen University Occasional Paper, 80

Friedman, M. (1951), 'Some Comments on the Significance of Labor Unions for Economic Policy', in Wright, D. M. (ed.), *The Impact of the Union* (Harcourt-Brace)

Hicks, J. R. (1937), 'Mr. Keynes and the Classics: A Suggested Interpretation', *Econometrica*, vol. 5

Jones, A. (1973), *The New Inflation* (Penguin)

Kuh, E. (1967), 'A Productivity Theory of Wage Levels – An Alternative to the Phillips curve', *Review of Economic Studies*, vol. 34

Oswald, A. J. (1979), 'Wage Determination in an Economy with Many Trade Unions', *Oxford Economic Papers*

Parkin, M., Sumner, M. T., and Ward, R. (1976), 'The Effects of Excess Demand, Generalised Expectations and Wage Price Controls on Wage Inflation in the U.K.' in Brunner, K., and Meltzer, A. (eds), *The Economics of Wage and Price Controls* (New York: Brookings Institution)

Parkin, M. (1978), 'Alternative explanations of U.K. Inflation: A Survey', in Parkin, M., and Sumner, M. T. (eds), *Inflation in the U.K.* (Manchester University Press)

Tobin, J. (1972), 'Inflation and Unemployment', *American Economic Review*, vol. 62

Wachter, M. L. (1979), 'Comment on Schelde-Andersen's paper' in *Collective Bargaining and Government Policies* (Paris: OECD)

Appendix

Incomes Policies:
a Short History*

The aim of this Appendix is to detail the progression of prices and incomes policy, as it has directly been applied to the labour market in the UK, in the post-war period. The major emphasis is placed on providing details of the specific provisions of the successive policies, which are dealt with in chronological order and summarised in the table at the end.

The earliest postwar incomes policy was adopted in the setting of widespread controls and restrictions. The Labour government appealed to both sides of industry for higher productivity (Cmd 7018, January 1947, *Statement on the Economic Considerations Affecting Relations Between Employers and Workers*), in an attempt to invoke social improvement whilst making good wartime damage. In *1948* the Government White Paper *Statement on Personal Incomes, Costs and Prices* (Cmd 7321, February 1948) declared that 'until more goods and services are available for the home market, there is no justification for any general increase of individual money incomes' and ushered in the first incomes policy of the postwar period. It was not made clear in the statement whether the policy was to apply to wage and salary rates or to earnings, the complexity of wage and salary make-up never being alluded to or discussed.

The only exceptions to this were to be where there was a need to redirect labour between industries and wage increases were considered the only way to achieve this. Furthei, the document stated that each individual claim had to be considered on its *national* merits, and a reconsideration of the directive would only be undertaken when the general rise in prices had rendered personal incomes 'inadequate'. This policy nationally ran until the summer of *1951*, although it is generally agreed that its effectiveness had ceased by October 1950.

From July 1951 onwards free collective bargaining was allowed but this, combined with a relaxation of wartime price controls and subsidies, meant that wage inflation again came to be regarded as a threat. This led, in *March 1956*, to the Macmillan 'price and wage plateau' which was instigated as the

---

* This appendix was prepared by Mr M. Ingham of Manchester University. Thanks are due to Mr C. J. Simson of the Department of Employment and Mr J. Gilbert of Aberdeen University for help with the data. The Editors and Mr A. J. H. Dean made substantial comments on an earlier draft, and the final version has benefited from these and the comments of the other contributors to this volume.

result of a series of discussions with both sides of industry, and which lasted until December 1956. Voluntary undertakings not to increase prices were secured by the government from the boards of all nationalised industries and from certain private employers and employers' federations. The policy did not, however, attempt to deal directly with public or private sector pay – the reasoning being that adherence to the policy as it stood would, hopefully, in turn influence the rate of increase of pay, both by making employers less able to pay and employees less militant. January 1957 however saw the official return of market bargaining. Macmillan's successor at the Exchequer, Peter Thorneycroft, nevertheless did attempt to affect both the public and the private sectors of the economy. At that time there was no liaison between the Conservative government and the trade unions, as there had been with the previous Labour administration in the late 1940s. As a result of his efforts, an external body independent of the government, known as the Council on Prices, Productivity and Income (CPPI, or, more picturesquely, 'The Three Wise Men') was set up in *August 1957*. Its terms of reference were extremely general, as outlined by Thorneycroft in the House of Commons on 25 July 1957, when he stated that the Council

> is not concerned with specific wage claims or disputes. . . . Our hope is that it will create a fuller appreciation of the facts, both in the public at large and amongst those more immediately concerned with cost and price matters. (*Hansard*, vol. 574, cols. 650–1)

The Council could have regarded this statement as an invitation to comment on economic policy in general, and in fact, this is what it did. Thus, in its first report published in *February 1958*, the Council saw the cause of the rise in prices and incomes as an abnormal level of demand consistently maintained over a lengthy period. By the time of its fourth and final report (1961), however, the Council's view had changed substantially.

In *July 1961* the CPPI observed that

> experience had shown that removing excess demand was not of itself enough. . . . inflation has another cause, an upward push as rates of pay are raised and profit margins are maintained by rising prices. (A. Jones, *The New Inflation*, 1973, p. 50)

It recommended some form of incomes policy. This, its final report, was accompanied by the announcement from the then Chancellor, Mr Selwyn Lloyd, on *25 July 1961* of a 'wage pause' (House of Commons debate, 25 July 1961 – *Hansard*, vol. 645, cols. 222–3) for government employees accompanied by a request that the same should apply in other areas, public and private. The main points of his speech were:

(a) The government saw a need for the 'pay pause' until such time as productivity had risen 'sufficiently'.
(b) However, where commitments had already been entered into, these should be met.

(c)   A pledge that during the pause the government would 'work out a sensible long-term relationship between increases in incomes of all sorts and increases in productivity'.

Whether the pause was to apply to pay rates or to earnings in general was once again left unspecified in the statement.

In *February 1962* the government published the White Paper *Incomes Policy: The Next Step* (Cmnd 1626, February 1962) in which they indicated that increases in wages and salaries were to be kept in line with the rate of increase of national output. This 'guiding light' was seen to be in the 2–2½ per cent region for 1962, and the following paragraph from the White Paper lucidly demonstrates the government's concern to control the rate of increase of earnings.

In considering increases in wages and salaries what matters for costs and prices is not simply the change in rates but the amount actually paid. It will therefore be necessary to have regard to the likelihood, judged from past experience, that basic rates will in practice be supplemented in certain employments by local or special payments. Changes in pay made under particular agreements (e.g. related to the cost of living) and reductions in hours or similar improvements will also have to be included in the reckoning. (Cmnd 1626, February 1962)

However, this was *not* to be regarded as *a norm* to which all were automatically entitled; rather, the following criteria were laid down for the guidance of negotiators:

(1)   Claims based on cost-of-living, productivity or profit trends did not in themselves provide a sound basis for an increase.
(2)   Increases might be justified as part of an agreement which led to increased productivity or a reduction in costs.
(3)   Much less weight was to be given to comparability claims than in the past.
(4)   Where the building up of manpower in one industry relative to others or the prevention of a relative decline was plainly necessary, an increase would be justified. This did not mean that labour shortages within particular firms or industries of themselves warranted an increase.

To assist in the implementation of its policy the government created two new bodies to replace the CPPI. Thus the *National Economic Development Council* ('Neddy') was charged with the broad function of surveying the general economic climate. Chaired by the Chancellor of the Exchequer with the attendance of other ministers, the Council consisted of representatives of both trade unions and management and it was to be served by a body semi-independent of government known as the National Economic Development Office (NEDO). The participation of trade union leaders was one of the most interesting features of the new Council.

Secondly, the *National Incomes Commission* (operational from *November 1962*) was created to deal with specific cases referred to it by the government. However, it was to be independent of government, employers and trade unions and had no direct liaison with the latter two bodies. The NIC was concerned exclusively with incomes, this emphasis being due, in part, to a belief in productivity agreements as an effective instrument for reactivating the international competitiveness of the UK as well as for stimulating competition within the sheltered sector of the economy. Furthermore, prices were relatively stable and there was a belief that this stability could be maintained by aggregate demand policies if unit labour costs could be prevented from rising. This notwithstanding, prices were felt difficult to control because of the great number of decisions involved, whilst on the other hand collective bargaining was seen as the predominant factor in wage determination; hence the movement of wages and salaries was effectively controlled by a manageable number of bargaining units, with the changes occurring relatively infrequently. From this reasoning it was deduced that no great administrative machinery for price control was required.

Acting upon evidence produced by the National Institute of Economic and Social Research, the NIC substituted what it regarded as the more realistic norm range of 3–3½ per cent for the initially announced figures, and subsequently the Chancellor of the Exchequer, in his budget speech of *3 April 1963*, officially recognised this revision.

Following the election of the Labour government in *October 1964*, the NIC was abolished in *November 1964*. However, a voluntary incomes policy was maintained with the same norm as previously. This was launched in *December 1964* by the *Joint Statement of Intent on Productivity, Prices and Incomes*. In return for a government commitment to a plan for the renewal of the British economy with both economic and social objectives the General Council of the TUC accepted that in conditions of full employment it is possible for incomes to get out of line with output, with the result that costs and prices go up. Whilst rejecting solutions based on deflation and the creation of unemployment, it recognised that continued failure to keep costs down would itself inevitably result in unemployment. Therefore, in view of the Government's declared economic and social objectives, it would be in keeping with the aims of the trade union movement to underpin the programme by working out a policy for prices and incomes. The statement was ratified at the *1965 TUC Congress*.

In *February 1965* the *National Board for Prices and Incomes* (NBPI) was established under the chairmanship of Mr Aubrey Jones. There were nine other members of the board including a businessman and a trade unionist, with the others having expertise in such fields as law, accountancy, economics and industrial relations.

Conceived as a voluntary undertaking, with cases being referred to it by the government, the NBPI's role was to examine these in order to advise whether the implied movement of prices, or of wages, or other money incomes, was in the national interest, after having consulted the management and unions concerned.

In *April 1965* the government published the details of a more rigorous policy in *Prices and Incomes Policy* (Cmnd 2639, 8 April 1965), the main points of which were:

(a) Increases in money incomes were to be kept in line with increases in real national output; the 'norm' was therefore to be 3–3½ per cent. In applying the 'norm' to wages and salaries it would be necessary to take into account not only increases in wage and salary rates but also increases in costs resulting from reductions in working hours, without loss of pay; from higher rates of pay for shift and overtime working and from improvements in fringe benefits. Clearly, therefore, this was a policy explicitly relating to earnings.

(b)   Exceptions to the norm were to be confined to the following circumstances:

(1)   Where the employees concerned made a direct contribution towards increasing productivity;
(2)   where it was essential in the national interest to secure a change in the distribution of manpower, and a pay increase would be necessary for this purpose;
(3)   where there was a general recognition that existing wage and salary levels were too low to maintain a reasonable standard of living;
(4)   where there was widespread recognition that certain groups had fallen seriously out of line with the level of remuneration for similar work and in the national interest required improvement.

Just over one month after the NBPI's first report, in *June 1965*, there was a balance of payments crisis. The new machinery for regulating prices and incomes had been allowed, by the time of the crisis, little time to exert any influence on the economy. Even so, in the wake of the *July 1965* crisis, the government produced, in *November 1965*, a White Paper entitled *Prices and Incomes: an Early Warning System* (Cmnd 2808, 11 November 1965) in which it proposed to tighten its control over prices and incomes even further. This it would do through the establishment of an 'early warning system' for proposed increases in prices, or of claims relating to pay. The system for pay claims was that 'affiliated' unions had previously agreed to notify the General Council of the Trades Union Congress of any impending claims. The TUC, after examination and discussion with the appropriate unions, would keep the government informed of developments, with the object of meeting the government's 'early warning' requirements. Non-affiliated unions or associations were required to notify all claims direct to the then Ministry of Labour.

A further balance of payments crisis in *July 1966* saw the policy take a statutory form, as outlined in *Prices and Incomes Standstill* (Cmnd 3073). A six-month standstill was to apply to all increases in pay and reductions in working hours, but not to other conditions of service, except in so far as these were likely to add significantly to labour costs. However, the term 'increases in pay' was rigorously defined, to include, in addition to basic pay, rates of pay for overtime, piece rates and the like and the policy should therefore be seen as an attempt to control earnings. It was not intended to apply to:

(a)   Increases in payments made in specific compensation for expenditure increases;
(b)   increases in pay resulting directly from increased output;
(c)   increases in pay genuinely resulting from promotion with the same, or a new, employer;

(d)   normal arrangements for increases in pay either for age or by means of regular increments of specified amounts within a predetermined range.

A new departure in this policy was that it was to apply to commitments entered into, but not implemented, before the commencement of the policy, whether in the form of a wage council proposal, under a long-term agreement or part of a cost-of-living sliding-scale arrangement.

In *November 1966* the government published a further White Paper *Prices and Incomes Standstill: Period of Severe Restraint* (Cmnd 3150) to cover the period *January 1967* to *June 1967*. This policy continued with the zero norm, and as pay was defined as in Cmnd 3073 it must again be considered to have been explicitly concerned with increases in earnings. Under its provisions, the 'early warning system' was to assume even greater importance. Furthermore, previously negotiated agreements were again to be affected by its provisions, although those already deferred under the previous policy could now be honoured. Once again, however, exceptions to the norm were to be allowed – provided they could meet one of the following criteria:

(a)   Agreements designed to enhance efficiency and productivity, although the increases should not be paid 'on account', but some benefit was also intended to accrue to the community as a whole in the form of lower prices, or improvements in quality.
(b)   After taking account of both earnings and hours worked, pay increases might be justified to improve the standard of living of the worst-off members of the community.
(c)   Some exceptional cases, on the grounds of manpower distribution, might be acceptable, but only after the closest scrutiny.
(d)   Comparability claims were not normally acceptable and exceptional cases, 'in which some immediate improvement in pay is imperative to correct some gross anomaly', would be strictly examined.

For the period from *July 1967* to *March 1968* the government's policy on prices and incomes was set out in the White Paper *Prices and Incomes Policy after 30 June 1967* (Cmnd 3235). This declared a retreat from the limited criteria for incomes increases set out in Cmnd 3150 to the broader considerations of Cmnd 2639 (1965). However, whilst the 'severe restraint' was to be relaxed, the government saw no justification for a return to the 3–3½ per cent 'norm' of the earlier policy. Furthermore, in line with the TUC's stated objectives of encouraging settlements which promoted productivity and improved the relative position of the low-paid, the following additional conditions were to be applied:

(1)   A minimum period of twelve months should, in future, separate settlements.
(2)   It may be appropriate for substantial improvements satisfying the criteria to be met in stages.
(3)   '...the parties concerned should not seek to make good increases forgone as a result of the standstill and severe restraint.' (Cmnd 3235, 1 July 1967)

Whilst the number of exceptions had been increased, the policy was still concerned with the growth of earnings, pointing out that 'the country cannot at present afford any further general reduction in the standard working week or general movement towards longer holidays' and that

proposed improvements in hours and holidays and other conditions of service likely to add significantly to labour costs, as well as proposed pay increases of all types, would need to be justified in relation to the criteria.

The TUC was to retain its role of examining claims and of providing the government with advance notification of these.

The White Paper *Productivity, Prices and Incomes Policy in 1968 and 1969* (Cmnd 3590, 20 March 1968) outlined the government's strategy for the period *20 March 1968* to *December 1969*. In it, a statutory limit of 3½ per cent on wage, salary and dividend increases was imposed, subject to the first three exceptions noted above for Cmnd 3150 (1966).

The ceiling was to apply not only to basic rates, but also to any other elements of remuneration having an impact on earnings, including fringe benefits, hours and holiday entitlements. Guidance on the application of the policy to payment-by-results systems was expected from a forthcoming NBPI report, but in any case increases in earnings under such systems could only be justified on the grounds of increased effort or other direct contributions towards increased productivity from the workers concerned. It was made explicit in the policy that, where more than one group of workers was covered by a single settlement, the 3½ per cent ceiling was to apply to the agreement as a whole, thereby permitting some intra-group flexibility. The policy retained the twelve-month rule, and the requirements for staging and prior notification of settlements. Cost-of-living increases beyond the ceiling were expressly considered unjustified.

In *December 1969* the government published details of the policy that was to succeed the above in the White Paper *Productivity, Prices and Incomes Policy after 1969* (Cmnd 4237, December 1969). The obvious change was a reversion to the idea of a range of acceptable wage increases – in this case 2½–4½ per cent – in place of the previous policy's ceiling limitation, although the focus was again on earnings. Several features of the previous policy were, however, retained. Thus, to guard against the increasingly recognised phenomenon of 'primary wage drift' – where supplementary local bargains are struck in addition to those made at national level – it was suggested that the nationally negotiated increase be somewhat less than the maximum allowable under the policy. This recommendation merely reflected the growing concern that, under conditions of full employment, changes in pay were no longer so strongly determined by formal collective bargaining – see, for example, the Donovan Commission Report of 1968 (Cmnd 3623) – and that wage bargaining no longer appeared easier to control than pricing decisions. Indeed, this marked the beginning of an era in which the institutional assumptions upon which incomes policy was based were increasingly called into question.

The level of settlements within the recommended range were to depend upon a variety of factors affecting the firm or industry; these being the rate of increase of labour productivity, the extent to which low-paid (as defined by the NBPI) or women workers were involved, and the labour market situation. It was further allowed that opportunity be given for changes in the relative pay of different groups of workers. Exceptions to the policy were to depend on the same factors. The twelve-month rule, and the early warning system, were to remain in operation.

In *June 1970* a Conservative government, under the leadership of Mr Edward Heath, replaced Mr Wilson's Labour administration and substituted for the latter's statutory policy on wages and incomes a system of voluntary guidelines, with consequent fuzziness as to whether the policy was meant to apply to wage and salary rates or to earnings. The policy became known as the 'N−1' policy for its declared hope that each new proposal for wage increases in the public sector should be based upon the relevant group's previous settlement, *less* 1 per cent; and although the vagueness of this policy makes its precise starting date difficult to assess, a general consensus suggests that it effectively began around August 1971. It was, however, often seen to be a policy that attempted to influence private sector settlements by more forcefully controlling increases in the public sector, both on the grounds that the public sector accounted for a large proportion of the national wage bill and because it was felt that private sector restraint could only be achieved if the government was seen to be 'putting its own house in order'. However, the following Written Answer (*Hansard*, 11 March 1971, col. 154) from the Secretary of State for Employment to a question in the House of Commons as to what principles governed public sector settlements does not strongly support an interpretation that there was a difference in treatment between the two sectors of the economy.

> The Government has impressed on employers and unions, in both public and private sectors, the need to secure a progressive and substantial reduction in the general level of pay settlements. There are no special principles applying only to the public sector and it is not the Government's intention to specify detailed criteria to be taken into account in negotiations.

A more definite feature of the period, however, was a voluntary undertaking by the CBI to restrain price increases to 5 per cent per annum, made in July 1971.

It was during the discussions leading up to this voluntary approach to incomes policy that the Prices and Incomes Board was disbanded (on *31 March 1971*), after the production of 170 reports on prices and incomes during its lifetime.

By autumn 1972, however, after the failure of prolonged discussions with the TUC and CBI, the government felt the prevailing rate of inflation necessitated a statutory policy. The details of this were published on *6 November 1972* in Cmnd 5125, *A Programme for Controlling Inflation: the First Stage*. In it, a statutory freeze on prices, rents, dividends and earnings was introduced, initially for a period of ninety days, but with provision for a further sixty-day extension, which in the event was deemed to be unnecessary. The freeze on pay was to apply to all increases, except those resulting from extra effort or genuine promotion, and previously negotiated agreements with an implementation date of 6 November or later were encompassed, save for certain special cases in the wages council industries.

Stage Two of the policy was to run from *1 April 1973* until *6 November 1973* and was based on the White Papers, Cmnd 5205, 5206 and 5267. Pay increases previously held back could now be paid, but no group would be allowed an increase in pay within twelve months of its last principal increase. The pay limit for any group of workers represented the maximum amount by which *average* pay per head could increase. This was set at 4 per cent of the average pay bill per head (for the group) for the preceding twelve-month period plus £1 per week per head, subject to a maximum of £250 for any one individual (£1 + 4 per cent so called), and was therefore a policy applied to earnings.

However, in accordance with the Equal Pay Act of 1970, allowance was made for the reduction of male–female pay differentials by one third by the end of 1973. Further exceptions would be made for certain improvements in basic hours, holiday and pension provisions and redundancy pay.

A new *Pay Board*, with the power to fine offenders, was introduced to monitor and enforce the policy and it had to be notified of all settlements affecting more than 100 employees, with prior approval being required for those affecting more than 1,000 workers. The government also introduced the *Price Commission* with the role of monitoring price increases throughout the economy. Both bodies were created under Cmnd 5205 (*The Programme for Controlling Inflation – The Second Stage*), with the Pay Board being formally established on 30 November 1973 and the Prices Commission four weeks later.

White Papers Cmnd 5444 and 5446 outlined *Stage Three* of the Conservative government's statutory policy, which was due to run from *7 November 1973* until *6 November 1974*. It had the same format as Stage Two but with the limit for earnings increases now being £2.25 per head per week or 7 per cent of the average wage bill per head over the preceding twelve months (*whichever was the larger*) up to a limit of £350 for any one individual. Stress was put upon the fact that these were to be regarded as limits and not to be taken as an entitlement.

However, detailed exceptions to the limit were set out as follows:

(1)   An upward flexibility *margin* of 1 per cent of the pay bill was allowed for those groups involved in settlements which included changes in pay structures or systems designed to remedy anomalies or to improve their efficiency.

(2)   Where the Pay Board had approved certain pay schemes designed to improve efficiency which, due to the time necessary for their development might not become operative before 1 January 1974.

(3)   In order to bring premium payments for those who work 'unsocial hours' up to a minimum standard.

(4)   Increases in certain types of London allowance above the prescribed limit would be allowed.

It was estimated that the choice of pay limit, plus the margin for flexibility, would allow an increase in the pay bill of 8–9 per cent on average, within which increases via negotiation would permit increases at higher rates for the lower paid.

The most radical feature of the policy, however, was its introduction of an '*escalator*' clause, linked to the *Retail Price Index*, which allowed '*threshold payments*' of 40p per week if that index exceeded its October 1973 level by 7 per cent, and for every 1 per cent rise thereafter a further similar increment would accrue.

In *February 1974*, however, Mr Heath felt compelled to appeal to the nation for a vote of confidence in his policy following his clash with the mineworkers over his pay strategy. This was lost and Mr Wilson returned at the head of another Labour administration.

No immediate change in policy ensued, except that certain groups, such as the miners and nurses, were designated '*special cases*' and allowed to exceed the official limits.

However, talks had taken place between the TUC and the then Labour Opposition prior to the general election and a document drawn up by the TUC–Labour Party Liaison Committee in February 1973, entitled 'Economic Policy and the Cost of Living', formed the basis of what was to become known as the *Social Contract*. Within this they set out measures considered necessary to control inflation and achieve sustained growth in the standard of living, and these were subsequently incorporated in the Labour Party election manifesto of February 1974.

Reaffirmation of Labour's pledge for an eventual return to free collective bargaining, coupled with an assurance from the TUC of responsible action within such a system, during talks following the election, led, in the first instance, to the disbanding of the Pay Board on *26 July 1974*. However, the Price Commission was retained and, until *August 1975*, statutory price controls ran parallel with voluntary pay restraint.

Even before this, in *June 1974*, concern on both sides about the rate of inflation had led the TUC to issue a policy statement, *Collective Bargaining and the Social Contract*, in which it recommended to its members that wage increases should only cover increases in the cost of living and that major settlements should not be made more than once in a twelve-month period. In return, the government had pledged itself to policies designed to help low-income groups whilst maintaining full employment, with the added assurances that they would repeal the 1971 Industrial Relations Act and abolish the National Industrial Relations Court established therein.

In July 1975 the TUC produced its report, *The Development of the Social Contract*, containing guidelines for the conduct of collective bargaining for the ensuing twelve months. These guidelines formed the basis of the government's attempt to control the rise in incomes over the year following the publication of the White Paper *The Attack on Inflation* (Cmnd 6151) on *11 July 1975* and were, in fact, annexed to that document. Thus, no employee was to have an increase of more than *£6 per week* for the year to *August 1976* and those earning more than *£8,500 per year* were to be allowed no increase at all. Notwithstanding this apparent governmental success in gaining the support of the organised labour movement for its policies, it still found it necessary to declare that the voluntary nature of the policy would have to be reviewed if the rate of inflation continued unabated.

In *May 1976* the TUC produced a report entitled *The Social Contract 1976–77* outlining the General Council's views as to how the co-operative policy with the government should develop over the coming year. The pay guidelines it contained, which had previously been agreed with the government, were again annexed to the next White Paper on the future development of pay policy for the period *1 August 1976 – 31 July 1977* (*The Attack on Inflation – the Second Year*, Cmnd 6507, 30 June 1976). Permitted increases were again based on individual earnings, with those earning £50 per week or less receiving £2.50; those earning £50–80 being allowed 5 per cent and a maximum of £4 being permitted for those with earnings of more than £80 per week. A minimum period of twelve months was once again to separate the allowable increases of any one group.

Following a renegotiation of the terms of the Social Contract by the TUC–Labour Party Liaison Committee (*The Next Three Years and the Problem of Priorities*, October 1976) the emphasis for 1977–8 was switched from individual to group earnings. The White Paper *The Attack on Inflation after 31st July 1977* (Cmnd 6882) recognised the demands for a loosening of controls, whilst at the same time urging that there be no 'free-for-all' wage explosion but an orderly phased return to free collective bargaining. Thus, there was an appeal for the level of pay settlements to be no greater than would allow for a maximum increase in national earnings of 10 per cent and for settlements to last for at least twelve months, in return for which the government would offer tax concessions. The only exceptions should be self-financing productivity schemes and certain agreements regarding occupational pensions. However, the twelve-month rule, which the government regarded as the last remaining element of the original 'Social Contract', was duly endorsed at the TUC Conference after much internal wrangling. Furthermore, many claims, and some settlements, were made in breach of the spirit, if not the letter, of the policy; the major ploy being the forgoing of any Stage Two increases in the hope of a much larger settlement in the freer Stage Three environment.

In an attempt to ensure that settlements were made within the 10 per cent guidelines, the government, in the White Paper, issued warnings of sanctions against firms paying over-inflated awards. These ranged from the loss of Export Credit Guarantees to the removal of government contracts and the imposition of rigid cash limits in the public sector. The rationale for this action was:

(1)   to set, at an early stage, a 'going rate' for settlements of around 10 per cent.
(2)   If very high private sector claims were seen as being met, then there was little hope of moderation in public sector pay claims.

The run-up to the presentation of *Stage Four* was not an easy time for the government. Whilst it had talks with both the TUC and the CBI about the state of the economy in general, neither body was willing to actively support a further period of formal pay restraint.

In the declared hope of keeping inflation in single figures, and with much talk of a forthcoming election, the Labour leader, Mr Callaghan, unilaterally introduced *Stage Four* in *July 1978*. The details were outlined in *Winning the Battle against Inflation* (White Paper, Cmnd 7293), the core of which was that the total increase for any group's earnings compared with the previous year should be no more than 5 per cent. The only exceptions to be permitted were self-financing productivity schemes and rigidly defined special cases – the major one of which was for those earning less than £44·50 for a normal full-time week. Strict application of the policy in the public sector was announced, whilst sanctions were threatened against any private sector companies breaching the limits.

After the announcement of the policy the government continued trying to enlist the support of the TUC, culminating in the narrow failure, in *November 1978*, of the two groups to sign an agreed statement over the conduct of incomes policy throughout the coming winter.

Parliamentary refusal to endorse a proposed package of sanctions against the Ford Motor Company for violation of the 5 per cent settlement ceiling, in December 1978, led to the government withdrawing its policy of sanctions against recalcitrant private companies.

With these setbacks to an agreed approach, in *January 1979* Mr Callaghan, facing a worsening situation on the pay front, amended Stage Four slightly. Thus, he met TUC demands for greater flexibility, especially for the lower-paid, by sanctioning increases of up to £3·50 per week for those earning £70, or less, for a full week's work. Furthermore, he offered more comparability with the private sector in public sector wage bargaining, and a tougher Price Commission in future pay rounds, if the current policy was adhered to for its duration.

A new pact was struck, however, between the government and the TUC and this was published as a joint statement on 14 February 1979 under the title, *The Economy, the Government and Trade Union Responsibility*, which became known popularly as the 'concordat'. This did little more than tacitly recognise that the Stage Four 5 per cent policy had not been a success. Thus, the agreement set a target of less than 5 per cent inflation by 1982 and elicited promises of fewer strikes, less picketing and looser closed shops from the union side.

However, after the so-called 'Winter of Discontent' the minority Labour government was forced into a general election on 3 May 1979 after suffering a defeat in the House of Commons at the hands of a coalition of opposition parties. This was lost and a Conservative administration under the leadership of Mrs Margaret Thatcher was returned.

The newly elected government rejected the idea of pay norms and guidelines in the private sector, believing that wage agreements were best arrived at between the employers and workers concerned, armed with a knowledge of the underlying market forces. In the public sector, settlements should only be reached that taxpayers and ratepayers could afford and government was to ensure compliance with this aim through strict control of the 'cash limits' allowed to public bodies.

Appendix Table: Incomes policies: a chronological summary of the principal regulations and exceptions

Date	Policy	Target	Major exceptions/settlements	Guides to labour	Comments
Feb 1948 – June 1951	Wage freeze	Zero		Redirection of labour	Voluntary undertakings from public sector and certain elements of private sector not to increase prices. Declared hope that this would consequently affect wage-setting.
Mar 1956 – Dec 1956	Wage and price plateau				
July 1961 – Mar 1962	Wage pause	Zero	Existing commitments		Enforced on government and wages council employees, voluntary in private sector.
Apr 1962 – Mar 1963	Guiding light (a)	2 – 2½%	(1) Productivity bargains (2) Manpower needs		Aimed to keep wage increases in line with increases in national output. NEDC and NIC created to aid policy.
Apr 1963 – Apr 1965	Guiding light (b)	3 – 3½%	(as above)		(as above)
Apr 1965 – July 1966	Statement of Intent	3 – 3½%	(as above) Plus: (3) Low pay (4) Comparability		Official TUC support for government policy in return for declaration of agreed economic and social objectives. Early warning system instituted in November 1965.

Date	Policy	Target	Major exceptions/ Guides to settlements	Comments
July 1966–Dec 1966	Standstill	Zero	Productivity deals	Statutory policy intended to apply even to increases negotiated but not yet implemented.
Jan 1967–June 1967	Severe restraint	Zero	(1) Productivity deals (2) Low pay (3) Manpower needs (4) Gross comparability anomalies	(as above)
July 1967–Mar 1968	Relaxed severe restraint	Low	Productivity deals	Twelve-month rule and staging introduced. Catch-up increases after freeze expressly disallowed.
Mar 1968–Dec 1969	Group ceiling	3½%	(1) Productivity deals (2) Low pay (3) Manpower needs	Limit to apply to groups rather than individuals, permitting some intra-group flexibility. Cost-of-living increases expressly forbidden.
Jan 1970–June 1970	Range policy	2½–4½%	(1) Productivity (2) Low pay (3) Equal pay for women (4) Pay relativities	Wage drift expressly recognised and suggested that national deals be rather less than 4½% to allow for it.
Aug 1971–Sep 1972	N–1	1% less than previous settlement		Control centred on public sector with exhortations to private sector. CBI 5 per cent price increase commitment.

Date	Policy	Target	Major exceptions/Guides to settlements	Comments
Nov 1972 – Mar 1973	Stage I (freeze)	Zero	Productivity	Statutory policy applied to virtually all increases including those previously negotiated but not yet implemented.
Apr 1973 – Nov 1973	Stage II (£1 + 4%)	£1 + 4%	(1) Equal pay for women (2) Certain hours, holiday, pension, and redundancy provision improvements	Policy applied to groups with a maximum increase for any one individual of £250 p.a. Pay Board established with power to fine and statutory duty to be notified of settlements. Twelve-month rule introduced.
Nov 1973 – Feb 1974	Stage III	Larger of 7% or £2.25	(1) Flexibility margin of 1% of total wage bill for anomalies, etc. (2) Productivity agreements (3) Unsocial hours (4) Threshold payments	A group policy with a limit of £350 p.a. for any one individual. Stress that figure was a limit, not an entitlement, and that low-paid should do relatively better than other groups. Threshold payments of 40p per week for every 1% increase of RPI once it had risen 7% above its October 1973 level. Twelve-month rule retained.
Feb 1974 – July 1974	Early Labour government (special cases)			Policy continued save for recognition of certain 'special cases', e.g. miners and nurses.

Date	Policy	Target	Major exceptions/Guides to settlements	Comments
July 1974 – July 1975	Social Contract	Informal cost of living agreement	(1) Low-paid (2) Equal pay for women	Policy of 'responsible' collective bargaining. Statutory price control accompanied voluntary pay restraint. Pay Board abolished on 26 July 1974.
July 1975 – July 1976	Social Contract (Phase I)	£6 per week Zero for those earning £8,500+ p.a.		'Agreed' policy between government and TUC for controlling individual earnings. Twelve-month rule.
Aug 1976 – July 1977	Social Contract (Phase II)	5% with Min. = £2·50 Max. = £4·00		(as above)
Aug 1977 – July 1978	Social Contract (Phase III)	10%	(1) Productivity deals (2) Certain pension provisions	Target figure was for rate of increase of national earnings. Sanctions threatened against companies allowing target-breaking increases.
Aug 1978 – Feb 1979	Social Contract (Phase IV)	5%	(1) Productivity deals (2) 'Special Cases' – particularly those earning less than £44·50 p.w.	Amended January 1979 following TUC pressure to allow greater flexibility. Main changes were increases up to £3·50 for those earning £70 or less and greater weight to be given to comparability for public sector.

Date	Policy	Target	Major exceptions/settlements	Guides to Comments
Feb 1979 – May 1979	'Concordat'			Agreement with TUC to reduce inflation to 5% by 1982 and for latter to strike less and loosen closed shop agreements.
May 1979 –	'Policy off'	Reduced rate of inflation		Free collective bargaining.

Index